KARMA *and* REINCARNATION

KARMA *and*
REINCARNATION

Unlocking Your 800 Lives to Enlightenment

BARBARA Y. MARTIN
and DIMITRI MORAITIS

JEREMY P. TARCHER/PENGUIN
a member of Penguin Group (USA) Inc.
New York

JEREMY P. TARCHER/PENGUIN
Published by the Penguin Group
Penguin Group (USA) Inc., 375 Hudson Street, New York, New York 10014,
USA • Penguin Group (Canada), 90 Eglinton Avenue East, Suite 700, Toronto, Ontario
M4P 2Y3, Canada (a division of Pearson Penguin Canada Inc.) • Penguin Books Ltd,
80 Strand, London WC2R 0RL, England • Penguin Ireland, 25 St Stephen's Green,
Dublin 2, Ireland (a division of Penguin Books Ltd) • Penguin Group (Australia),
250 Camberwell Road, Camberwell, Victoria 3124, Australia (a division of Pearson
Australia Group Pty Ltd) • Penguin Books India Pvt Ltd, 11 Community Centre,
Panchsheel Park, New Delhi–110 017, India • Penguin Group (NZ), 67 Apollo Drive,
Rosedale, North Shore 0632, New Zealand (a division of Pearson New Zealand Ltd) •
Penguin Books (South Africa) (Pty) Ltd, 24 Sturdee Avenue,
Rosebank, Johannesburg 2196, South Africa

Penguin Books Ltd, Registered Offices: 80 Strand, London WC2R 0RL, England

Most Tarcher/Penguin books are available at special quantity discounts for bulk purchase for sales
promotions, premiums, fund-raising, and educational needs. Special books or book excerpts also
can be created to fit specific needs. For details, write Penguin Group (USA) Inc. Special Markets, 375
Hudson Street, New York, NY 10014.

Library of Congress Cataloging-in-Publication Data

Martin, Barbara Y.
Karma and reincarnation : unlocking your 800 lives to enlightenment /
Barbara Y. Martin and Dimitri Moraitis
p.   cm.
ISBN 978-1-58542-816-8
1. Karma—Miscellanea.   2. Reincarnation—Miscellanea.   I. Moraitis, Dimitri.   II. Title.
BF1045.K37M37   2010   2010024096
202'.2—dc22

Printed in the United States of America
3 5 7 9 10 8 6 4

BOOK DESIGN BY NICOLE LAROCHE

While the authors have made every effort to provide accurate telephone numbers and Internet addresses
at the time of publication, neither the publisher nor the authors assume any responsibility for errors,
or for changes that occur after publication. Further, the publisher does not have any control over and
does not assume any responsibility for author or third-party websites or their content.

Dedicated to the Holy Ones of Divine Light,

who work so diligently to uplift humanity

Contents

Preface   *xiii*

Introduction   *xv*

Part One
How It All Works

Chapter 1. Your Coin of Wisdom   3
Free Choice and Willpower • The Eternal Law of Karma • The Principles
of Reincarnation • Remembering Past Lives

Chapter 2. The Process of Reincarnation   15
Where Is the Other Side? • What Happens When You Die • Your
Tapestry of Life & Returning to Earth • Summing Up

Chapter 3. Your 800 Lives to Enlightenment   30
Getting Off the Wheel • Fulfilling Your Life's Purpose • Your Spiritual
Evolution • The Stages of Soul Development

Part Two
THE DYNAMICS OF KARMA AND FREE WILL

Chapter 4. THE KARMA OF MONEY   45

The Karma of Wealth • The Karma of Poverty • The Prosperity Prayer

Chapter 5. THE KARMA OF RELATIONSHIPS   60

Guidelines for Relationship Karma • The Karma of Family •
Husband/Wife Karma • Professional Karma • The Karma of Friends •
Adversarial Karma • The Karma of Romance

Chapter 6. THE KARMA OF CAREER   82

The Spiritual Purpose of a Career • Understanding Your Career
Path • Talent—Accumulating Good Career Karma • Abusing Career
Privileges • Love the Work You Do

Chapter 7. THE KARMA OF THE SOUL   99

Qualities of the Soul • How Soul Karma Works • Will the Real Me Please
Stand Up

Chapter 8. THE KARMA OF THE PHYSICAL BODY   109

Earning Good Physical Karma • Genetics and Karma • The Karma of
Illness and Death • The Karma of Murder • The Karma of Sex • Karma
and World Population

Chapter 9. THE KARMA OF NATURE   124

Earning Good Nature Karma • Paying Back Karma to Nature • Nature
Giving Back • Honoring Nature • Blessing Your Food

Chapter 10. SPIRITUAL KARMA   133

Heeding the Spiritual Call • Our Arc of Development • The Karma of
Spiritual Offenses • Your Responsibility on the Spiritual Path

Part Three
OUR COLLECTIVE KARMA

Chapter 11. THE KARMA OF NATIONS, RACES,
AND RELIGIONS   147
National Karma • Karma of Leaders • Collective Relationship
Karma • The Karma of War and Conquest • Race Karma • Religious
Karma • Setting a Good Example

Chapter 12. THE COLLECTIVE KARMA OF THE WORLD   173
A Spiritual History of Civilization • World Karma Related to World
War II • World Karma Related to Africa • World Karma Related to the
Middle East • The Future of Civilization

Part Four
RESOLVING YOUR KARMA

Chapter 13. FACING YOUR KARMA   199
Identifying Free Will • Recognizing Your Purpose • How Do You
Recognize Karma? • You Are Always Given the Power to Face Your
Karma • How Do You Know When Your Karma Is Finished? • Karmic
Guidelines

Chapter 14. FOUR KEYS TO EFFECTIVELY DEAL
WITH KARMA   214
Take Inventory • Meditate and Pray • Ask, "What Is My
Lesson?" • Initiate Right Action

Chapter 15. THE AURA AND KARMA   225
Soul Images • Karmic Soul Energy • Karma and the Fabric
of Life • Subconscious Images

Chapter 16. AURIC KARMA MEDITATIONS   242
12 Transformative Meditations

Chapter 17. THE HEALING POWER OF FORGIVENESS,
COMPASSION, AND GRACE   266
Compassion as a Call to Action • God's Grace Is with You Through
Every Karmic Trial

Chapter 18. THE ROAD AHEAD   276

Appendix: Auric Karma Meditations   279
Acknowledgments   281
Index   283

PREFACE

It is with great joy that I express my gratitude to Barbara and the Higher for being a part of this extraordinary work. I am continually amazed at the depth of Barbara's understanding and awareness as well as the incredible support system of Holy Ones who work through her. The benefits of participating in the spiritual work go beyond words. Every part of my life has been touched for the better and I live in a way more beautiful than I could possibly have imagined.

This book marks a turning point in my life for which I am eternally grateful. After working with Barbara for many years, one cannot help but reach that place where these principles become living truths, and the veil that separates the world of matter and the world of spirit begins to drop away.

The study of reincarnation and karma offers important keys to understanding the mystery of life. Throughout the writing of this book, I was constantly reminded just how much our lives are in God's hands. We go about the affairs of our daily lives, yet in the midst of this activity is an incredible spiritual support system. We are all part of an intricate divine design. Work with this design, and we fulfill our very reason for being on Earth. Work against this plan, and God will stay with us until we get back on track.

If I have one message to share regarding reincarnation and karma, it is to make *every effort to work out your karma*. Reincarnation is real, and no matter how crazy, irrational, or unpleasant a situation may appear in your life, bless it when you recognize karma at work. Facing your karma head-on is the quickest way to accelerate your spiritual growth. In the same manner, resisting or avoiding karmic challenges can hold back your growth, no matter how hard you try in other ways. What's more, if you are blessed with good karma, build on that goodness as it will take you to greater spiritual heights than you can possibly imagine.

The following pages are packed with information. Take time to digest the precious pearls of wisdom and insight. I hope as you read these pages, you tap into the story that is your own soul experience and realize the great destiny that you are a part of.

—DIMITRI MORAITIS

INTRODUCTION

As a spiritual teacher, I am intimately acquainted with the laws of karma and reincarnation. They are necessary tools in helping to guide students in their spiritual journey. Each soul that comes to Earth is bound by karmic law. Clearly understanding how reincarnation and karma work is key to your spiritual unfoldment and evolution.

There are many books on reincarnation and karma, but after teaching these topics for many years, I felt that there were definite gaps and misinformation in understanding these vital topics and that important points were not emphasized enough. My aim is to give you a vivid picture of the process of reincarnation and karma and to show you the central part they play in your life and spiritual development.

The goal of this book is to help you make better choices that are in alignment with your spiritual purpose. I hope to help you better understand the reason you may be facing certain conditions, tests, and trials; the incredible divine plan you are a part of; why certain people are in your life; and the importance of facing and resolving your karma.

Professionally, I am primarily known for my work with the aura. From the age of three, I could see the energy field and have spent my life studying and teaching this fascinating topic. The aura plays an important role in working out your karma as karmic energy shows up very clearly in the auric field.

As a developed clairvoyant, I am open to other experiences in addition to seeing auras. In understanding the inner workings of reincarnation and karma, I have had to call on these other spiritual gifts. One of these gifts is the ability to communicate with celestial beings from the other side.

As we will explore in the following pages, the process of reincarnation and the laws of karma do not work by themselves. They are carefully administered by an incredibly well-organized network of celestial beings under the direction of God. No true esoteric understanding of reincarnation and karma is complete without the connection and cooperation of these Holy Ones. Much of the knowledge shared in this book comes from my direct inner training by these Radiant Ones. I refer to them by various terms such as Holy Ones, celestial beings, the Higher, spiritual teachers; regardless of the term, they are the administrators of God's divine plan.

I became aware of these wonderful beings at a very young age. They would present themselves to me so I could become familiar with them. As time went on, I started having more and more experiences with the Holy Ones. I learned there are many types of celestial beings as they all have their own special gifts and talents.

One of my early experiences with a celestial being was when I was eight years old. My family was living in Martins Ferry, Ohio, and I was participating in a centennial celebration organized through my school. I was dressed as a Dutch girl and had joined in a parade. My family could not attend as there was a religious event my father was participating in in the next town over, Zanesville. As I was expected to finish before they returned, they had left a key under the front doormat so I could get in the house. The parade was very close to my home and my schoolteacher was with us, so I felt safe.

The parade finished, and it was starting to get dark by the time I had changed back into my street clothes and walked home. When I got to the front door, I looked under the mat but no key! The door was locked and I had no way of getting in the house. So I sat on the front porch to wait for my family to return.

Night was approaching, and I was getting worried. Around the corner, I could hear a drunken man walking down the street toward me singing to himself. This frightened me so I ran next door to the church and hid in some bushes. I watched him pass by, and then it occurred to me that the kitchen window might be open and I could get in the house that way. I walked around to the back of the house and saw that the window was open. I quickly climbed a wall in front of the window and crawled in.

As soon as I got in, I sat on a chair next to the kitchen table. I was trembling with fear. I don't know why I was so afraid. In truth, the man was not dangerous; he hadn't even seen me. But in my imagination, I had made him bigger than life.

As I was sitting there trying to calm down, I suddenly saw white light fill the kitchen, and I felt very uplifted. Then in the middle of the room right next to me appeared a beautiful angelic being. I could see a form but it was hard to make out features as it radiated so much light. It didn't have any wings or anything like that, but I was absolutely thrilled to be in the presence of this being. I didn't know what it was but assumed it must be an angel. Later I was to find out it was my guardian angel.

The beautiful being blessed me with light and I quickly calmed down. It mentally sent me the message, "Don't be afraid. You are safe." I felt elated that such a presence would come to help. It made me realize that I had to trust in God and not have fear.

When I got a little older, I began training with these wonderful beings to better understand my own gifts. As part of my spiritual training, I started to be systematically schooled in the principles of reincarnation and karma. This training began in my late teens and was in full swing by the time I was in my twenties.

They clairvoyantly showed me images of some of my past lives. I saw myself as an orphan in England, a soldier in China, an initiate of the mysteries in ancient Greece. It was an amazing experience. They also showed my karmic relationships to my family, how I had known my father, mother, and siblings in other lives. They helped me to work out any unresolved issues. I was taken to magnificent places on the other side where I was shown first-hand how the incredible process of reincarnation works. This training went on for several years.

These experiences carried over into my everyday life. One time, I was attending an Edgar Cayce weekend workshop in the Los Angeles area taught by his son, Hugh Lynn Cayce. During one of the breaks, I went back to my room to rest. For no reason, I was feeling extremely drowsy and lay down. In a half-awake, half-asleep state, I had a wonderful vision in which I saw myself in the royal courts of France. I was in a ballroom in the regalia of the times, the high wigs and full dresses. I was in a beautiful palace and could hear music playing. It was a very happy event and I was really enjoying myself. I felt very comfortable there and was socializing with others as the hall was filled with people. After a few minutes of this, the vision faded and I found myself in my room in Sylmar.

A second phase of my education began in my late twenties when I was specially trained by the Higher in reincarnation and karma to prepare myself as a teacher. There's a tremendous duty as a spiritual teacher not to mislead any student, as you are karmically responsible if you mislead anyone intentionally or unintentionally. I took this responsibility very seriously—to the point I wasn't sure at first that I wanted to be a spiritual teacher. However, the Holy Ones guided me every step of the way. When I took on a student, the Higher would show me the necessary aspects of their karmic chart I needed to know, so I would understand better what their lessons were and how to help them resolve their karma without getting personally involved.

As I was working on this book, I felt the inspiration of my good friend and spiritual teacher Inez Hurd. I have included some of her stories in this book as Inez always encouraged me to share her knowledge with others. It was Inez who told me that I would one day teach the aura, which at the time seemed a near impossible thing to do. She instilled in me tremendous confidence in my own abilities and a confidence in expressing my talents to others. Without question, I would not be where I am as a teacher today without her guidance.

It is an honor and a privilege to be a teacher of metaphysics. It's an amazing process, and I'm still learning. I have been teaching for many years, yet I'm constantly surprised and delighted by new inspiration and knowledge that comes through.

As with all aspects of my teachings, the material shared is based on direct clairvoyant observations and experiences. Of course, these teachings and experiences are filtered through my own consciousness, so inevitably there is an element of interpretation, as no two people will explain a shared experience in exactly the same way. Because of this, I urge you to take what is presented and put the information to your own test and highest standard of what is right and true. The laws of karma are intricate and there is no single book that can begin to cover it all. This is a starting point for further study and exploration.

I wish to offer my profound gratitude to my coauthor, Dimitri Moraitis, for his marvelous collaboration. This was a particularly intricate book to put together and Dimitri has, once again, done an extraordinary job of assimilating and organizing the material in a clear and cohesive way. He made many contributions and suggestions that added immensely to the value of the work. This is as much his book as it is mine.

In my own life, I have done my best to live in harmony with the laws of karma and reincarnation. It was not always an easy choice, but it has been rewarding beyond measure.

In Divine Love and Light,
BARBARA Y. MARTIN

THE LADDER

Unto each mortal who comes to Earth
A ladder is given by God at birth,
And up this ladder a soul must go
Step by step from the valley below.
Step by step to the center of space
On this ladder of Life to the starting place.

In time departed which Time endures
I shape my ladder and you shape yours.
Whatever they are, they are what we made
A ladder of Light or a ladder of shade.
A ladder of Love or a hateful thing,
A ladder of Strength or a wavering string.
A ladder of Gold or a ladder of straw,
Each is a ladder of Righteous Law.

We flung them away at the call of death,
We took them again at the next life's breath,
For the keeper stands by the great birth gates,
As each soul passes this ladder waits.
Though mine be narrow and yours be broad
On my ladder alone can I climb to God.
On your ladder alone can your feet ascend
For none can borrow and none can lend.

If toil and trouble and pain are found,
Twisted and corded to form each round,
If rusted iron or moldering wood
Is the fragile frame you must make good,
You must build it over and fasten it strong,
Though the task be as hard as your life is long,
For up this ladder the pathway leads
To Heavenly pleasures and spirit's needs,
And all that comes in another way,
Shall be but illusion and will not stay.

So, in useless effort then waste no time,
Rebuild your ladder and climb and climb.

—REVEREND VIOLET BROOSTOM

Part One

How It All Works

Chapter 1

YOUR COIN OF WISDOM

Each of us possesses a precious coin of wisdom. This coin is not currency you use to buy goods and services. You do not barter or exchange this coin with others, yet you spend it every day of your life. This coin is unique. It is part of your spiritual inheritance as a child of the divine. On one side of this coin is the right of free choice, and on the other side is the will to act out that choice. How you spend this coin determines if you live in harmony with the divine laws of life or not.

This coin of wisdom is God's gift to your soul. It's what allows you to be an individual and express your divinity. It gives you opportunity to learn and grow, to serve God and the creative process of life. As a spiritual teacher and clairvoyant, I see auras brighten and evolve as souls learn how to effectively spend this spiritual coin. And I see storms and darkness when souls squander the precious opportunities this coin offers.

As you express free choice, you generate karma—the great law of cause and effect. Every day, you spend your coin of wisdom either to pay the price for any misdeed or to reap the rewards of the fruits of spirit. Intimately linked to the law of karma is the process of reincarnation. Reincarnation offers you, through successive embodiments in physical form, the time to work out your karma and fully express the gift of free choice and will.

Much has been written about karma and reincarnation, yet, in my many years of teaching these subjects, I have found that many people still do not have a clear, practical picture of how these principles really work. Whether or not you believe in reincarnation and karma, they are essential and active parts of your life. You cannot outrun or escape their influence. The sooner you work in harmony with these natural laws, the smoother your life will go and the more you will accomplish.

FREE CHOICE AND WILLPOWER

One of God's first gifts to us as human souls is our spiritual freedom. Without free choice and the will to act out that choice, we would be mere automatons unable to express the creative nature of life. Although there is a destiny for each of us and we have to live within spiritual and physical laws, there is still freedom in how we fulfill the great creative plan of life.

Choice is the privilege of selecting. It is your choice to work hard or to be lazy, to be honest or dishonest, to be happy or sad, to be loving or cruel, to aspire to greater things or wallow in miseries of the past, and so on. No one can take that right away unless you permit it. Regardless of the condition or situation you find yourself in, it's always up to you how you choose to act.

With choice comes consequence. As you make choices, you face the fruits of those choices—good or bad. This is how you build character, and learn right from wrong. Making right choices is not so easy to do. You won't always recognize the best course of action and sometimes make choices that are to your detriment. Yet gradually through experiences, through trial and error, you mature and learn to make the distinction.

In understanding your coin of wisdom, keep in mind the difference between choice as a tool for personal growth and choice as license for self-gratification. There is a vast difference between desire—true desire for something—and appetite for something. Metaphysics defines *desire* as the expanding activity of God through which manifestation is constantly sustained, perfected, and enlarged. Please take time to reflect on this definition as it expresses a basic operating principle of life. Desire is an activity, the motor that drives the creative process of life into expression.

Appetite is but a habit established by continued gratification of the feeling nature and is energy focused and qualified by suggestions from the outer activity of life. Clearly, God did not give us our spiritual coin to squander in an endless cycle of self-gratification and self-aggrandizement. Although we have all walked this path at one point or another, there is always an inevitable day of reckoning.

This brings us to a central point of this book. We all make choices, but the gift of free will was not given as an end unto itself. The ultimate purpose of our right of free choice is to choose God—to choose to act in complete harmony with the eternal laws of life.

The coin of wisdom means expressing your free will to serve God. Once you learn to walk the path of God of your own choosing, to choose God out of your own soul desire, your life takes on new meaning. You live the life of grace and walk the path of spiritual enlightenment. It does not mean your life automatically becomes easy, but you express your creative nature in greater ways than you could have imagined. Your life truly becomes a blessing to yourself and to those around you.

The right of free choice symbolizes the word of truth in action. It means choosing to stand up for your spiritual rights, proclaiming your divinity, and confidently expressing that divinity in all parts of your life. You have been given this gift of choice for that very purpose, but you must exercise this right through the other side of your spiritual coin—willpower.

Many people misunderstand what willpower is. They think in terms of force or imposing one's intention upon another.

Will is the stabilizer of thought.

Will holds your thoughts steady until complete materialization, much as the power lathe holds wood in place while it is being fashioned. *Will is not thought*. They are not the same thing. Yet thought without will is powerless.

In expressing free choice, it is your willpower that allows you to realize your choice. What good is free choice if you don't have the power to act out that choice? Yet this is exactly what happens. We've all had goals we wished to accomplish, only to meet with obstacles or detours that stopped us from accomplishing them. Why didn't we accomplish what we were meant to? Our thoughts and desire were there but our wills were weak. We were not able to sustain the goal in our minds until it became a reality.

There will be times in working out your karma that you will make the right choice but somehow you will not fully follow through on that choice because of a weak will. You will allow other things to interfere with that choice. This is normal and part of the growing process, because although willpower is part of your spiritual birthright, it is something you have to cultivate. It is something that builds with use.

As you express free choice, you will need to develop a strong dynamic will. True dynamic will is your expression of God's divine will. What is divine will? Divine will is God's way of sustaining the divine thought patterns projected to creation. Without divine will, God's ideas would not take form. True will has nothing at all to do with imposing ideas or intentions on someone. When you are working with dynamic will, you will never be overbearing or imposing, but you will stay true to your own heart and desire.

Expressing divine will means joining with the power that is sustaining creation itself. It means looking for the best and noblest course of action in any situation, regardless of your personal feelings. To succeed in any karmic challenge, you have to take a magnanimous view of life or you will be endlessly caught in the karmic cycle, coming back again and again, repeating the same mistakes.

It takes courage to place the greater whole of life before your own human wants. Every day, you see so many things your own human will draws you to like a magnet—diverting you from your spiritual path. These are the temptations you must refuse if you wish to reach the spiritual pinnacle.

So here are the two sides of your coin of wisdom. On the one side is your right to choose God and walk the path of light, and on the other side is divine will, giving you the power to act out that choice. Once you have aligned yourself with these two spiritual powers, you are truly ready to go out into the world and spend your coin.

THE ETERNAL LAW OF KARMA

The word *karma* has become so commonplace one runs the risk of trivializing one of the most sacred and essential laws of life. It's amazing to think that not that long ago the word was virtually unknown in the West and now there are coffee shops that bear its name!

The word *karma* is derived from the Sanskrit root *kr*, meaning "to do, to make." It has also been defined as "deed or act" or "volition." So karma is related to action in any form: physical, mental, or emotional. Karma is always followed by its fruit Vipaka, or phalam (result of past deeds). As the term has become more popularized, the entire principle of action and its effect all fall under the single term karma.

The law of cause and effect simply states that for every action we take, there is an eventual and inescapable effect to that action. In the Bible, this law is stated as "what you sow, you reap." In other words, if you plant onions, you are not going to grow tomatoes; you're going to grow onions. In physics there is a parallel in Newton's Third Law of Motion: For every action there is an equal and opposite reaction.

Karma is the balancer of life—the harmonizer. The natural condition of life is harmony. God *is* harmony. When you act in a destructive manner, you unbalance that natural state. This negative expression will reverberate through the very fabric of life, where it will make an impression and then rebound back to the sender. The analogy of a stone being thrown into a pond is a very good one. When you throw a stone into a still, small pond, the water ripples to the edge of the pond and then bounces back. The same happens with your actions. Your actions create a ripple effect against the fabric of life, bouncing back as you put them out. Once this discordant energy has been set into motion, the painful tuning process then begins until harmony is restored.

When you initiate a creative, constructive act, the same law of karma applies but the results are completely different. When you do something that is in harmony with the natural laws of life, this action also reverberates through the fabric of life but instead of throwing off the natural harmony, this "good" energy expands and enhances the ever-expanding, creative cosmic process. You are adding to the divine life, and this blessing will reverberate back to you multiplied!

Looking at life in this way, what is justice but realignment to the natural laws of life? These are the true scales of justice. It's not about punishment or reward. It's about discord or harmony. This is why we need not worry about apparent injustices of life. Life *demands* the inevitable realignment back to a natural state. The trick is we do not know when that alignment will take place.

Karma is generated with your every thought, word, emotion, act, and deed. It can reach into any aspect of your life. You can have karma related to family, money, health, relationships. And there are many different types of karma. There is personal karma, soul karma, mental karma, emotional karma, national karma, race karma, and world karma. That's a lot of cause and effect going on! Fortunately, you have an unfailing helping hand in working out your karma. Although no one can resolve your karma for you, there is tremendous spiritual support in navigating through this intricate part of life.

Karma is essential to your well-being. When you break a spiritual law, knowingly or unknowingly, you face natural consequences. By repeatedly breaking these laws, you slowly begin to understand how they work from firsthand experience. The law of karma is designed in *love* to make you a greater being and realize the great goal you have. Karma is designed always to help build you up, not tear down or punish you. Without the laws of karma you could not grow and reach the heaven worlds you desire.

THE PRINCIPLES OF REINCARNATION

When I was in my twenties, I went through an extraordinary period of spiritual unfoldment and maturity. Although I had been gifted with a highly developed clairvoyant sight from a very young age, it was in my twenties that these gifts fully bloomed for my own spiritual development and to prepare me for the rigors of becoming a spiritual teacher. It was during this time that I discovered the full impact of how reincarnation works. I remember one of my first experiences vividly.

I was visiting a friend, John, in Carmel, California, a beautiful town by the Pacific Ocean. John worked as a hairstylist in town and had moved to Carmel because of his health.

One day, John was working late and told me to walk around until he finished and we would go out to dinner together. It was turning dusk and most of the shops had closed, so there were not many people walking around. I was feeling very happy and relaxed as I loved being in Carmel.

I came across a store that sold Chinese things. There were statues, furniture, and a beautiful jade-green dress in the window. I noticed a woman in the store and thought the store might still be open. I went to the door but it was locked. I knocked but no one came. I then went back to the window and again I saw the woman, and she was looking right at me! I wondered, "Why isn't she opening the door?"

I went back to the door again and knocked harder in case she couldn't hear me. I asked her to please open the door and still got no response. I was perplexed. This seemed odd. I went back to the window, and there she was again looking right at me but doing nothing! I thought to myself, "I guess she's not going to let me in," so I began to leave.

Suddenly, I could see her much more clearly than before. Around my age, she was attractively dressed with jet-black hair. As I looked more carefully at her features, she became more and more familiar-looking. I started to realize she looked like me if I were Chinese. At that moment, I realized I was having a spiritual vision. This young Chinese woman was not real. It was a vision given by the Higher of me in a past incarnation! The Higher flashed in the pictures of my incarnation as a Chinese princess with power and wealth, and, ultimately, my death at a young age.

The image of the woman faded. It was getting dark now. I went to meet my friend for dinner and told him of the extraordinary experience I had just had. This vision made a deep impression on me and confirmed beyond any question the reality of previous incarnations.

It is not my place to try to prove that reincarnation exists. We each have to discover that for ourselves, but I can say from my personal experiences, many of which I relate in this book, that reincarnation is very real and valid. The answer to Job's question in the Old Testament "If a man die, shall he live again?" is emphatically Yes! We have all lived an extraordinary series of lives that has led up to our present experience. And the life we are living now will prepare us for lives yet to be lived.

Reincarnation is the cycle of necessity, also known as the wheel of birth and rebirth. The word comes from the Latin for *incarnate*, which means "to make flesh." Reincarnation is the metaphysical principle that the human soul goes through many incarnations in flesh to gradually perfect itself. The Sanskrit word *samsara* has been translated as reincarnation, or rebirth. Transmigration, reemergence, regeneration, renewal are all words used in relation to reincarnation.

In looking at reincarnation in relation to our coin of wisdom, we find that it is through the process of rebirth that we are given the time to fully express our free will and work out our karma. It would be pointless of God to give us such a precious gift and give so little time to use it. Reincarnation affords us that time. We must put out of our minds that we are here for only a few fleeting years, never to be heard from again. As Henry Ford put it:

I adopted the theory of reincarnation when I was twenty-six. When I discovered reincarnation, it was as if I had discovered a universal plan. There was enough time for me to plan and create. If you preserve a record of this conversation, write it so that it puts men's minds at ease. I would like to communicate to others the calmness that the long view of life gives to each of us.

The concept of reincarnation is a tradition that goes back to time immemorial. Many cultures throughout the world have believed in reincarnation in one form or another. It has been at the foundation of Far Eastern beliefs and religious thought. The mystery schools and ancient mystical learning centers all taught the essential doctrine of reincarnation. Today, reincarnation has crossed cultural borders and belief systems and grown in greater world prominence than ever before. Yet this is only the beginning of a much greater understanding of this essential principle.

Why do we reincarnate? In a word—evolution. We come to this life to learn and grow. Without the process of reincarnation, our souls would not have time to fully develop all the spiritual powers latent within them. It is the obligatory pilgrimage each soul must go through to win the crown of life.

The goal of reincarnation is nothing short of spiritual perfection. By learning all our lessons here on Earth and by resolving all our karmic debts, we earn the right to eventually get *off* the wheel of necessity and become masters of Earth life. We can then go on to the greater divine life. Some reach this goal of spiritual mastery sooner than others. However, it doesn't really matter who gets there first, as it is the plan for every single soul to reach perfection.

I know it can be difficult for us to realize that our experiences on Earth are so much more comprehensive than can be conscribed to a single life. Yet as the philosopher Manly P. Hall stated:

Each of us bears the witness to his or her own character by the thoughts, feelings and actions of lives long past. Each of us is the architect of our own tomorrow.

Our past lives have a very strong impact on our present experiences because we bring our unfinished business from the past into this life to resolve. If we were too passive in a past life, we will have to develop a dynamic will in this life. If we were cruel in a past marriage, we will have to show kindness now. If we were impatient before, we will have to learn patience now, and so on. You will find the character traits you express now are a result of your accumulated past lifetimes of experience.

The beauty of reincarnation is that what you learn is not just for a single life but for eternity. Each skill or art that you master, each character trait you rarefy becomes part of your immortal self. And here is the secret of greatness. Genius and extraordinary human accomplishments are not the result of some biological fluke. Great souls through the ages have brought in those gifts from prior incarnations, slowly building those abilities and powers to the present expression.

Once we see our existence as something more encompassing than a single life, then we can break the hypnotism of physical life and learn to identify with our eternal self. We see that this incarnation is but one chapter in our Book of Life, and we begin to outgrow the attachments to this material life on which we have so willfully placed our attention.

Reincarnation gives us insight to the riddle of suffering—why, for example, there are apparent injustices under an all-powerful and loving God. As we know, the misuse of our free will in this life can create misery for ourselves and others, and there are the natural physical experiences of life we all are inescapably a part of. Yet no matter how you look at it, no doctrine based upon the theory of a *single* lifetime can possibly fully satisfy the riddle of suffering and meaning. Why should some come into this world at a disadvantage and others be born into more of an advantage? Many times, these sufferings are the growing pains of an evolving soul. There's a bigger picture going on if we are to find any moral meaning to the vicissitudes of life. As the Buddha said, "If God permits such misery to exist, He cannot be Good, and if He is powerless to prevent it, He cannot be God."

Reincarnation teaches us that life is not to be evaded but to be lived. As we get more into the knowing how to live that life, our lives become exciting and fulfilling, because we see life from the whole and not the part. Reincarnation is the bigger story of who and what we are. It teaches that we always have a second chance at life. No soul is ever totally lost. We are always given as many chances as we need to succeed in our goal of spiritual mastery.

REMEMBERING PAST LIVES

Without question, the single greatest doubt raised in the minds of skeptics and nonbelievers is the question of memory. If we go through all these lives, why don't we remember them?

May I answer this question by first saying that we all have memory of past lives locked in our subconscious mind. The subconscious mind is the seat of memory and is one of the most intricate aspects of our consciousness. As with all parts of our spiritual nature, the subconscious is not confined to our body. It travels with us in our pilgrimage throughout creation. Its job is to record all the experiences of the soul verbatim, which include past incarnations. So the real question is not whether such memories exist in our consciousness, but why can't we readily recall those experiences?

Gandhi put it best when he said that it is "nature's kindness" that we do not have memory of past incarnations. Quite simply, it would be too cumbersome to bring back memory of all that has transpired in our evolution. We have enough on our plate dealing with the issues that are present in this life. It would be too much for us to carry more. So it is God's design not to bring in such memory at this time in our evolution. You could say that experiences of past lives are partitioned off in the subconscious for our own protection. At a certain point in our growth, when we are reaching the spiritual pinnacle, we do go through a process of retracing our footsteps on Earth. At this point, we rekindle the incarnations we have gone through, but this is strongly directed by the Higher and it begins only when we are well prepared mentally and emotionally for such a journey.

Nonetheless, many people do have some recollection of the past. In my years of teaching reincarnation, many people have shared with me the sense or experience of having lived before. There have been countless testimonials and case histories in which people have related their experiences, some with uncanny clarity and insight.

Memory of past life experiences surfaces in other ways. Most important, there is a rekindling when dealing with karmic situations. For example, when we meet someone we have known before, the subconscious will prompt us to react to that person based on our past life experience, even though we will not bring back actual memory of what transpired. We've all had the experience of meeting someone and taking an immediate like or dislike to that person for no rational reason or having déjà vu when visiting a place for the first time. Often, the reason we have these experiences is we are connecting with the energy of our past, even though the conscious memory of those experiences does not actually surface.

The bottom line is, if you wish to understand the lives you have lived, all you have to do is look at the life and character you are expressing right now. Your talents and strengths, your weaknesses and faults, the key people and events in your life are all part of your karmic path. You have created all that you are through your many experiences.

Chapter 2

THE PROCESS OF REINCARNATION

If there is such a thing as reincarnation, how does it work? How do we actually reincarnate, leading to birth in another body? There's such a mystique surrounding this topic. In understanding the scope of our coin of wisdom, we see that our choices not only affect the life we're living now, but also help shape future incarnations yet to be lived. And the life we're now living has been, to a great extent, shaped by choices we made in lives gone by. The ability to return to Earth in a new physical form can seem incredible. Yet I hope by the end of this chapter you'll come to feel that as amazing as reincarnation is, it's actually a natural process of life.

The first step in understanding reincarnation is to ask the question: Does reincarnation and the balancing of our karmic slate happen by itself or is there a greater intelligence guiding and administering this process? The resounding answer is that reincarnation and karma are not blind forces of nature. They are part of a conscious, intelligent, and intricate activity of the spiritual life.

And this brings us to the question of the other side, or the Hereafter. We cannot look at the process of reincarnation and its connection with karma without looking at the spirit world and how we relate to that world.

Every faith has its concept of the Hereafter. Many depict it as a type of reward or punishment for the way we live our life on Earth. Others believe that the other side is more of a subjective experience and becomes what we make of it, a sort of self-made world. Still others say that we simply return to the universal consciousness or energy from which we came. Of course, there are those who do not believe life goes on at all. For these people, the idea of a life beyond is impossible, which would mean the idea of reincarnating is impossible, too. In this chapter, I will not try to convince you of the reality of the other side or try to color it along lines of any particular faith. I relate my own clairvoyant experiences and leave it to you to come to your own conclusions.

The truth is, there is an existence beyond this Earth. When we die, we don't go into oblivion. Our soul goes to the next plane of existence. What is considered death here is really a birth on the other side. Volumes have been written about the spirit world. It's a magnificent place. It's far more encompassing than Earth could ever be.

The irony is that while the Hereafter may feel like a mystery, in actuality we are all very familiar with the other side. The other side is our real home. It is the place we all came from before incarnating, and it's the place we are going to return to when we finish our time on Earth.

Perhaps one of the greatest comforts in our study of reincarnation is the reassurance that not only does life go on, it goes on in form very familiar to us. We look like ourselves. Our surroundings are familiar. Much of what we know as life continues in a way similar to how it is here. This is no accident. As the spirit world is the originating world, all we see here in physical life was created in the spirit world first. So it should not seem so strange to say the other side has vistas, lakes, trees, flowers, homes, etc., for it has all these things and much more. A familiar afterlife is essential so our soul is comfortable moving from one plane of existence to another.

My first experience of being taken consciously to the other side was a very simple one. I was around ten years old and I was living in New Castle, Pennsylvania. I was living in a large three-story house with my parents and five brothers and sisters. It was a happier time, as we had just moved to this town and were coming out of a difficult Depression-era lifestyle. I was in the fourth grade and going to a Greek school. By this time, I had learned to keep quiet about my spiritual experiences, because I was always getting into trouble. My family and friends could not understand what I was going through.

It was afternoon and I was in the living room dozing off. Everyone was home but in different parts of the house. Without my doing anything, I found myself in another home lying on a bed. It was a simple, pretty house that seemed to be made of wood. There was a feeling of warmth, and although I knew right away I wasn't in my own home, I wasn't afraid.

I didn't know where I was. At first I thought this was a dream, but as I rose up out of the bed, it was very clear that this was no dream, it was very real. I asked myself, "Where am I? What am I doing here?" There was a window to the side of the bed and as I looked outside, I saw a beautiful country setting with flowers and trees.

I started wandering around the home, but saw no one. I wondered where my parents were but again I felt no sense of danger. Just the opposite, it felt very comfortable here. I walked outside to the garden and again had this feeling of well-being. And then, as quickly as I had found myself in this strange place, I suddenly found myself back home in my living room in New Castle. And now it was even clearer that I had not been dreaming but had been taken to some other place.

From that point on, I began a process of traveling to the other side on a regular basis. I was to have far more spectacular experiences, but it all began with this simple experience to communicate to me the normalcy and naturalness of the Hereafter.

WHERE IS THE OTHER SIDE?

The Hereafter is not one place; it's many places. There are many realms and dimensions that are all part of God's creation. As Christ said, "In my Father's house are many mansions." These *many* mansions or spiritual realms are real locations. Some are high up the spiritual ladder and more rarified while others are not. Yet all are part of God's creation, rungs on Jacob's ladder. Each has a part to play in our evolution.

Here on Earth there's a melting pot of consciousness, but this is not true on the other side. You will go to the place and level of consciousness where you have earned the right to be by the spiritual light you have accumulated. You will not take your money, your fame, your earthly possessions to the other side, but you will take the spiritual light you have earned through every good thought, word, act, and deed. This is why it's imperative to earn as much Divine Light as you can: it is your passport to eternity.

The spiritual realm we will primarily put our attention on is what's called the astral world. The astral world is the next plane of existence from the physical, and it is the place every soul must pass through when making the transition to the other side. There are seven realms in the astral world, and depending on the light we have earned while on Earth, we will find ourselves in one of these seven realms when we cross over.

What Happens When You Die

Let's follow the reincarnation process starting with the experience we call physical death. We have made the experience of death or "making the transition" a thing to dread. In truth, it is a graduation to a more beautiful life. In my experience, we all make the same basic journey regardless of our understanding. At a certain point, the experiences of each soul diverge according to our divine purpose and karma, but the basic process of reincarnation is the same for everyone.

The journey I'm going to relate to you is a combination of my own personal experiences and observations over many years. I know this is a bold statement to make. Is not the Hereafter as Hamlet declares "the undiscovered country, from whose bourn no traveler returns"? With all respect to Hamlet, not only do we return from the Hereafter through the process of reincarnation, we are part of that great beyond here and now. We receive constant support from the other side. There are times we are actually taken to the inner worlds during our sleep as part of our spiritual evolution. Most of the time, we do not recollect such experiences but we still reap the benefits.

At the moment of physical death, the soul withdraws from the physical form and moves into the astral body. Our astral body is the surviving body and the body we inhabit when we leave the physical plane. It looks just like us and is the body we will operate in when we are on the other side. At death, the silver cord snaps, separating the physical and astral bodies. This is the true mark of death and separates the near-death experience from the final exit from this life. Wonderful angelic beings assist in the process. One can feel peace and stillness when they are present. Many times, loved ones who have already crossed over lend their help as well.

Once you have made your crossing, you stay on the Earth plane for approximately a week. The first seventy-two hours after death are especially critical as there is still a spiritual disengaging from the physical going on. Although the soul is gone, there are many spiritual support systems to the body that need to be disengaged. This is why I recommend one should not cremate or bury the body until seventy-two hours have passed, to make sure all the spiritual connections with the physical body are completely released.*

What are you feeling and thinking when you first cross over? It depends on the person and how you crossed over. Most people are in a limbo state—half awake, half asleep. They are not really aware of what has happened. Some are quite alert and immediately know they have died and may even feel a sense of relief, especially if they have been suffering through an illness.

The truth is, you are not really that different a person when you cross over. It's better to think of the entire process of making the transition and reincarnation as one continuous life—different places, same soul. Crossing over is like going from one country to another. If you move from Chicago to Paris, you're still the same person even though you're in a different location.

What's most important to remember is that you don't become a saint and your sins don't simply wash away by making the transition. If you had

---

*For this reason, I strongly recommend cremation over burial. With burial, there is the possibility that the energies can linger, which can cause the soul to want to stay close to the physical form. I have seen disembodied souls wandering cemeteries because they do not understand they are no longer part of that body.

difficulty forgiving people in physical life, it doesn't automatically become easier on the other side. Of course, the other side is an extraordinary place, but it's where you are in your consciousness that matters most. This is why it's so important to build your spiritual power and awareness here in physical life. You carry the enlightened consciousness you build in physical life to the greater life.

During the first seven days after making the transition, you generally stay close to loved ones and the places you are most familiar with. You will do things like attend your own funeral! I have seen the departed soul at almost every funeral I have attended. I usually find myself communicating with these souls, encouraging them not to linger on the physical plane and to follow the angels home. I say this because once the week is up, you have to willingly want to go to the other side. Most go, but some refuse, and these are what we call earthbound souls—not a good situation.

When you leave the Earth plane, you are taken to a special meeting place in the astral world. I have seen this place as a beautiful sanctuary. You wake up in this exquisite environment and there are beautiful light rays streaming in. You are greeted by several angelic beings with shimmering auras.

They explain that you have passed on and what is coming up for you. This is usually a shocking experience, because many people don't fully realize they've died. It's a surprise to find out how alive they really are. Sometimes there is unhappiness as they don't want to think of themselves as physically dead. Yet for others, the news is joyful.

At this point, most people have little memory of their life on Earth. This is actually a blessing as it makes the transition easier. Slowly things come to memory, but the truth is, just as we forget our experiences on the other side when we come to Earth, we forget many of our earthly experiences when we go to the other side. As time goes on, certain memories are rekindled, but it remains selective. There really is no need for detailed memory as you are finished with that incarnation.

Once it's clear what's going on, the interaction with the other side really begins. Other types of spiritual beings come around you. These are the teachers—enlightened human souls who have evolved enormously and graduated to the heaven worlds.

You are taken to a wonderful place called the rose room. The rose room is in a spiritual realm the East Indians call devachan, a sort of heaven world. The rose room is in a beautiful storied building that looks a little like a hospital. They call it the rose room because there are rose vines climbing the walls in beautiful designs. There are no windows but a gentle, soft light fills the room and there are ministering angelic beings.

The rose room is a very special place where you go to rest—and I mean a deep, spiritual rest. You may sleep for weeks as your soul relaxes and disconnects from Earth life. Most people are confused when they come over, and it takes time to adjust. Remember, you are steeped in physical matter here, so no matter how spiritually developed you are, an adjustment time is essential.

Once you come out of the rose room, you feel refreshed. You are then given the choice to visit Earth for a period of forty-four days. Most people take the forty-four days although it's not absolutely necessary. This is the time to see how loved ones are doing and to say good-bye to Earth life. This is when you begin to rekindle a clearer memory of your last incarnation on Earth.

There is usually sadness during this time, because you cannot communicate with your loved ones. If there's unfinished business, you feel regrets. The teachers guide you and are with you the whole time. You visit your home, the place you worked, friends and people you knew. Naturally, this stirs up a lot of emotions. You regret mistakes made and things left undone, as well as feel happy for good things you did. It bothers you greatly to see loved ones in grief. You try to tell them you're okay, but they can't hear you as you can no longer communicate with those on the physical plane.

I remember my mother visiting me during her forty-four days. She had died of pancreatic cancer when she was eighty-six. She looked the same age but much healthier and brighter. I was very fortunate to be able to communicate with her clairvoyantly. She told me she missed me and was looking forward to seeing me when it was my time to go over to the other side. She seemed happy and the teachers were around her. She had suffered a lot before she died, and I felt relief that she was okay.

After the forty-four days, you have no choice but to return to the astral planes. (This is not to say you can't come back to help loved ones, which happens often; it simply means the formal period of saying good-bye has come to an end.) You are then taken to a magnificent place of healing. This place looks like a temple from ancient Greece. It's huge with a magnificent domed center. The building is radiant with white and blue light. There are beautiful gardens in front of the building. You enter the building with your teachers and immediately feel blessed by a Divine Light. There's an extraordinary perfume fragrance that fills the air. There are many other people here, but everything feels very organized. There's no sense of commotion.

You come here to receive a deep spiritual healing in all levels of your consciousness. Generally, you stay here for about two weeks as the Holy Beings of this temple continuously work with you. If you were sick on Earth, the astral body was affected and here is where all those energies are dropped away. Your time in here will vary depending on the condition you were in when you made your transition.

When you leave the healing temple, you feel rejuvenated. You have been released from much of the Earth dross, and that has an elevating quality. You adjust to your new environment, and you realize what a magnificent place you are in. At this point, you're ready for the next step—having your life reviewed.

This is where you see for yourself what you did and did not do in your last life. Let me tell you, this is quite an experience. What happens is you are taken into another magnificent temple on a very high plane of consciousness and seated in a special room. There are huge candles lit. Standing in front of the candles are divine beings of light whose job it is to review your life with you. These tremendous beings are called the *Lords of Karma*.

The Lords of Karma are the administrators of the divine law of cause and effect. The Sanskrit term *lipikas*, which means celestial recorders or scribes, has been used in reference to the Lords of Karma as it is they who are the agents of karma and are responsible for recording and managing the Book of Life for humanity.

As one might expect, these celestial beings are extraordinarily developed with shimmering, magnificent auras. There are usually six to ten of them. They stand to greet you, yet the interesting thing is you can't see their faces! They look like silhouettes with incredible light rays coming out of them. The fact that you can't see their faces actually has a calming effect and puts your mind more at ease. Of course, you hear them loud and clear.

In front of them is a very ornate table. On that table is a huge book. This is the Book of Life and it's open to your page. The Book of Life is the record of the things you have done, said, thought, felt in the life you just finished and in other lives as well. It records everything verbatim, so there is no confusion.

The Lords of Karma greet you and explain that you are here to review your life. They begin telling you about the various things you did on Earth. Then you start watching your life as if you were watching a movie. On one of the walls is a screen and the movie unfolds. The key moments in the life you just lived are shown in crystal clarity. You see your accomplishments and your failings. You see the *real* motives behind your actions, what you were thinking and feeling. They show the effects your life had on others, positive and negative. You see everything for what it truly is. It's quite an experience to watch your life like this.

As you can imagine, people react differently to watching their life played back. Some look at the whole process in awe. Others find it difficult to watch or may even try to resist what they are seeing or feel they have to defend their actions.

Afterward the Lords of Karma tell you what you have finished and what you have left undone in terms of your purpose and task on Earth. They pay particular attention to what you have left undone. They're adamant about what still needs to be finished. Their purpose is to help you resolve your karma and fulfill your destiny. It is then decided what the next step is for you. They begin to show you the elements of your next life. They show you why you have to go back and what you will achieve by resolving such karma.

Once your time with the Lords of Karma is done, you are taken out of the temple. Usually, there is more healing work done because many people come out of the experience devastated. It's not easy to see your life in so clear and objective a light, but the experience is necessary for your spiritual growth.

At this point, you are given an experience that is beyond description. It is an experience that is incomparable to any other whether on Earth or in the Hereafter. This is the time when you are given a glimpse of your divine source. I will not attempt to put this experience into words as it is too sacred a moment to belittle with human description. What can be said is that we all have this experience. The purpose is to drink from the well of eternal life, to remind us of what life is all about and to rekindle our divine purpose. It gives us encouragement and love, and refreshes us for the journey that lies ahead.

After such a vision, much of our concerns and apprehensions about our transition have dropped away. Then comes fun time. You have a reunion with family members, friends, even pets who are on the other side! This is wonderful because you discover that no love is ever lost. You are taken to a special place, and you are in this area for a few days. You're very happy to be there, and never thought you'd see some of these people again. You remember people you have known not just from your last life but from other incarnations as well. You feel a great deal of love. You start to remember places you have known in the astral worlds and things become even more familiar.

At this point, the formal transition process is finished. You are now acclimated to the other side. Each person's experience will vary. Depending on your chart, you may spend time in the astral planes or begin the process of reincarnation very soon. It is at this point you will find that you gravitate to the astral plane you have earned the right to be at. You will also find yourself in an environment you are most comfortable with. For example, if you lived your life as a Hindu and you enjoyed the Hindu experience, you can find yourself in similar surroundings.

During this period, you assimilate and build on knowledge gained on Earth so that when you come back, you return with more knowledge than before. While in the astral planes, you may find yourself doing things you were good at on Earth or had a strong desire to do. For example, great artists such as Beethoven and Mozart continue to write exquisite music on the other side.

I had a wonderful experience with my father after he had made his transition. On Earth, my father was an excellent Greek Orthodox priest. He died suddenly, and I missed him a great deal. In one of my travels to the other side, I was taken to a church where I saw him conducting a service in Greek to a full congregation! I was amazed to discover he was continuing the work he had done while in physical life. He was very happy and robust. After the service, he took me aside and pointed out two of my aunts who had also made the transition. They were holding hands and very happy. My father was trying to show me that they were doing very well.

YOUR TAPESTRY OF LIFE & RETURNING TO EARTH

How long do you stay on the other side? That entirely depends on your karmic chart and what you are meant to accomplish. If your time on Earth was cut short, you may reincarnate quickly. Generally, you will stay awhile, but not too long, as there are more experiences to gather back on Earth.

Once your designated time on the other side is nearing an end, your teachers prepare you for your return to Earth. You say your good-byes to the other side and to people you are with. There can be a bit of sadness as you do not want to go, but you understand that you have no choice. And, of course, you know it's only for a time, and that you will return to the astral planes.

You are taken to a wonderful place known as the Temple of Instruction. This temple has a golden hue to it and resembles a building you would find on an idyllic college campus. The building is huge and is usually packed with people. Here, your teachers prepare you for the life that is to come. They explain the reincarnation process and what you need to do in your next life. Your instruction here is done privately, and with other souls in a huge auditorium where you are taught by great ethereal beings. This training goes on for days.

Then comes an extraordinary moment. You are taken to a special room and shown your *Tapestry of Life*. The Tapestry of Life shows images of your upcoming incarnation. On this tapestry you see pictures of some of the major events and the main goals you are meant to accomplish in your next incarnation. The images are shown in sort of panels; usually about ten images are shown with your teachers explaining what they mean. Your tapestry shows key people who will be in your life and the karmic ties. So before you incarnate, you know what's going on. I have remembered this experience, and it is amazing. I saw my future children, what they would look and be like, as well as other people and events.

You are shown key elements of the life you are to live *before* you live it. Please impress this on your mind. When you come to Earth, this experience is submerged, but the memory is placed within your subconscious to prompt you. Slowly, you are meant to rekindle that memory. For some, this happens almost immediately once the next incarnation begins. For others, it can take time.

The wonderful thing is when the right people, opportunities, and desires come up in the new incarnation, memory of what the tapestry showed you is rekindled, helping to steer you along the right path. This means if you're feeling lost or unsure of what you're meant to do in life, know that the knowledge of your purpose is already locked within you. It's a matter of realigning yourself with that knowledge, and things will again start clicking for you.

Where does free will fit into your Tapestry of Life? Do you have a say in the life you are about to lead? This brings us to one of the most important points about reincarnation and our relationship to the divine. If your future life is shown to you beforehand, what happens to free will? Do you not choose things like your livelihood, the person you will marry, important people in your life?

Of course, free will operates at every level of existence. Yet there is a big difference between the inevitable karmic destiny we weave through the expression of free will and the actual form that destiny takes. From our perspective, we cannot possibly understand all the intricacies of our karmic credits and debts we have generated, as well as what is needed for our spiritual growth. This must be done by a loving hand far more developed than we are. It is better to think of our incarnations on Earth as assignments—missions uniquely designed to develop our highest and most noble desires and qualities.

In truth, there is little negotiating with the Higher when it comes to future incarnations. But please understand this does not mean that there is no free choice on your part. Although the key elements of your life may be predetermined as part of your cosmic plan, it's your job to *make* that destiny happen. It's not going to happen just by itself. The elements shown in your tapestry must be woven together by you in physical life. You must search out and find that dream career, those people who are meant to be part of your life—as you are meant to be part of their lives. The things you are meant to accomplish may be shown to you beforehand, but it's going to take all your skill, desire, ingenuity, and talent to make them real.

Having said this, the Tapestry of Life is not set in stone. Life is fluid, and there is always room for modification and adjustments as the need arises. In addition, only select moments of what you are meant to accomplish are shown. Some karmas and experiences are not revealed, so there is plenty of room for free expression. Many details are left entirely up to you. You can make a request to change something in your tapestry. If the request is in line with your spiritual purpose, it will be granted, otherwise it won't.

Of course, you can reject the opportunity presented to you altogether, which some people do. Unfortunately, this sets you back spiritually. The divine designs another incarnation based on other karma, but sooner or later you have to face all your karma. And the longer you wait, the harder it gets. The majority of people accept the incarnation presented because they know how much it will help them and they are eager to progress spiritually.

Once you agree to the new incarnation, you are taken to the spiritual realm where the actual embodiment process begins. It is here you are shown who your next parents will be, and the karmic links with these souls are clearly shown. You then meet your new parents astrally. Even though they are on Earth, they are taken up into the astral world where you must all agree to the union. Soon after that, physical conception takes place, and you will end up as a little baby to begin another lap on Earth!

SUMMING UP

Naturally, this overview cannot cover all the details and intricacies of the reincarnation process. Also, there are variations, but the key points are pretty much the same for everyone.

What about the transitions of extraordinary souls such as Mother Teresa or Mahatma Gandhi? They go through the same process as we do. In the case of highly evolved souls, their transition is glorious. They're shown the extraordinary things they did on Earth and the great service they performed, and they meet some of the people they were so helpful to. Naturally, they find themselves in the high spiritual spheres, and in communion with great spiritual beings.

In the case of tyrants and souls who committed great atrocities, they, too, go through the same transition process as we do, but their transition is much more difficult. They're shown the evil they committed and meet some of those they abused. They will inevitably find themselves in the lower nether-worlds, where they will be surrounded by those of like mind and vibration. Their spiritual climb is difficult as they feel the extreme effects of their misdeeds. Yet from the metaphysical perspective, no soul is past redemption. Even in these situations, the divine tries to help lift these souls. They cannot reincarnate to start paying back their karmic debts until they are out of those hellish regions.

Where is God in this journey of reincarnation? Of course, God is the guiding force in all we do, whether on this or the other side. In the higher astral world and beyond, God's presence is felt everywhere. The question of God does not come into the picture as it does here in physical life. The advantage of the other side is you know your life is guided by a loving presence greater than yourself.

It's the goal of every soul to return home to God. It was God who created each of us and to God we shall return. God is guiding all parts of our spiritual growth. As mentioned, we are given a vision of the divine as part of our experience in the Hereafter, but to reach into the realm where we join God in Eternity, we have to pass through many spiritual planes and reach into the highest levels of the heaven worlds. We are simply not ready for this in our present state of growth. As metaphysics teaches, "We do not go to heaven, we *grow* to heaven." When we reach the pinnacle of our spiritual evolution, we will evolve into that heavenly state and join with God once again, the culmination of our spiritual pilgrimage. What a glorious day that will be.

Chapter 3

YOUR 800 LIVES TO

ENLIGHTENMENT

Whenever I lecture on reincarnation and karma, someone invariably makes a comment such as, "I don't want to come back! I want this to be my last life on Earth!" Such a comment is often made with a sense of frustration with the challenges that life presents, or perhaps a feeling that they have not accomplished all they wanted to or that things did not work out as they wished.

I hope I'm not bursting anyone's bubble when I say it's one of the greatest challenges to get off the wheel of necessity. The lessons of physical life are not mastered overnight or even in a single lifetime. The truth is, there's nothing wrong with returning to Earth. It's nothing to fear. It's part of life to participate in the cycle of earthly incarnations. The key is to do your best to complete what you're meant to in this life so your next life is not a repeat of what was not learned before.

How many lives do we go through on this Earth? Let me say that there is a plan. The number of lives on Earth is not arbitrary or endless. Just as there are grades in school, there is an overall arc to the reincarnation process. If we are diligent in our spiritual development, we can accelerate this process to a certain degree, and if we are negligent, we can retard the process. Yet the basic plan is the same for everyone.

Metaphysics teaches us that there are approximately 60 billion souls currently going through the human experience. This number includes souls at various levels of spiritual advancement. Out of this number, only a certain percentage of souls are going through the process of reincarnation. And of that number, only a small percentage is immersed in physical life. These numbers clearly tell us that the vast majority of souls are in the spiritual realms and only a small number of souls are on the Earth plane at any one time.

Our soul going through the human experience will incarnate in physical form approximately *800* times in its quest for spiritual mastery. This is not a fixed number as some souls advance a little faster and others a little slower, but this is an average. The ancient philosophers used a mystical calculation of 777 lives constituting the complete incarnation of the human soul. Of these 800 lifetimes, the soul goes through three distinct phases. It spends approximately 200 lifetimes in the instinctual phase, 500 lifetimes in its intellectual phase, and 100 lifetimes in its enlightened phase.

In our soul's first phase of human development on Earth, the first 200 lifetimes or so, it is introduced to physical life in all its vicissitudes—pain, pleasure, birth, death, sex. Life in this stage is more or less survival of the fittest. The key component of humanity at this phase is *instinct*. Although it has human mental faculties, it's primitive and does not yet have the spiritual gift of an awakened mind. So life in this phase is an immersion in material consciousness. Some spiritual schools have associated this immersion with the fall from grace, for at this juncture the soul has forgotten its awareness of God and identifies only with the physical surroundings it perceives. This time has also been called a period of *in*volution as the soul descends into matter before it begins its upward journey to its spiritual home.

Life in this period of growth was similar to our idea of the caveman existence. We did not live very long, and things moved slowly. When we crossed over to the other side, we assimilated our experiences before returning, but again the process was very gradual. Yet even though life was difficult at this early stage, there still was wonder, joy, and love.

When the human soul finished this cycle, it began the next phase of growth—the intellectual phase. One of the great moments of our evolution occurred at this time. We received the precious gift of mind. At this turn, a whole new world opened up to us. The process was gradual, but we now became *self*-aware. Thus the intellectual levels of our consciousness were born and with them the potential for a maturing emotional nature. We lost some of our primal innocence, but it was a thrilling experience to receive the fuller power of mind, like waking up from a dream.

Along with this gift of intellect came a price—accountability. Free choice and willpower now came into the picture. We now received our precious coin of wisdom. In the beginning of this new cycle of incarnations, we more or less continued along the spiritual path. Yet as time went on, we realized the power this gift of intellect gave us. All of us, at one point or another, began to digress and divert from the spiritual path laid out for us. And this was the beginning of creating karmic conditions. It was inevitable that this would happen so we could learn right from wrong by firsthand experience. We learned what it meant to reap the benefits of good karma and pay the price for misdeeds. The pace of our advancement started to differ. Until now, we all grew more or less at the same pace, but with free will in motion, we could do as we wished.

During this second phase of incarnations, we began participating in and building cultures and civilizations. Although the process of building a society is guided by those of a higher enlightened consciousness, the ability to manifest the arts, sciences, and religions as we know them could not have happened until souls reached this intellectual level of consciousness. The average length of time spent in this second phase is 500 incarnations. These 500 lifetimes take into consideration lifetimes of mistakes and misdeeds all souls make as part of the learning process.

As we mature intellectually, the soul starts to reach a critical stage where it asks, "Is this all there is? Is there more to life than what can be seen with human eyes?" The soul ponders the meaning of life and yearns for a greater existence. Now the soul starts to feel the glimmer of its divine origin. It starts to search for God, not just because it was born of God but because it desires God of its own free will. This spiritual awakening is the culminating moment in 500 lives of intellectual development. Now the soul is ready to begin its *conscious* ascent on the spiritual path.

Through effort and training, the evolving soul prepares itself for its final phase of incarnations—the enlightened levels. The soul spends the last 100 incarnations learning how to consciously harness the spiritual powers it has been immersed in for so long. It is in this third phase of life that the soul really begins to enjoy the fruits of spirit it has been searching for. Through these lives, the soul is building tremendous spiritual power and climbing the spiritual ladder very quickly.

Here is where you find geniuses and great achievements in all phases of human endeavors. Souls progressing through the enlightened phase may hold high public office and guide many or work quietly behind the scenes. Either way, the soul is making tremendous advances as well as being of great service to humanity. Pain and suffering are not absent in this phase of life by any means, but the soul has a very different perspective at this point. It is in the final phase of these enlightened lives that the soul learns to pierce the veil of matter and operate from the mystical levels of consciousness.

In looking at the arc of the 800 lives, we must bear in mind that not all people are at the same place in their spiritual development. This is due partly to the fact that some souls have been more diligent in following their spiritual path than others. The other reason is that there have been many life waves of souls that have come to Earth and many more to come. God did not create one set of souls and that's it. This doesn't mean one person is better than another, but it does mean that some are further along in their cycle of incarnations.

Humanity is at a crossroads. A great number of souls are getting ready to make the leap into the enlightened cycle of incarnations. Some have already made the jump. The spiritual renaissance that is blossoming is no accident. Humanity is preparing for a glorious new day in evolution where it will work in closer connection with the divine than ever before.

GETTING OFF THE WHEEL

What happens when you are finished with the 800 lifetimes? When you've paid back your karmic debts, learned your lessons, and mastered your spiritual skills, you win the crown of life; you're freed from the wheel of necessity. It's something we're all aiming to reach. Once you're off the wheel, you become part of the greater life known in the Western esoteric tradition as *Spiritual Etheria*.

In the heaven worlds of Spiritual Etheria, you have reached the next plateau in your spiritual development. The most important thing you can do, the goal to always keep in mind in your spiritual quest, is to do everything in your power to get into Spiritual Etheria. Once in Spiritual Etheria, you continue your spiritual ascent and continue to serve God in more beautiful and sublime ways. And it is this steady service and spiritual growth that eventually leads you Home to your Divine Creator.

How do you know where in the 800 lives you're at? How close are you to the blessed day of liberation? If there's one thing I hope you've been getting from this chapter, it's that life evolves *SLOWLY*. I can't emphasize this enough. There is a glorious, *gradual* unfoldment of life, spiritual and physical, that we cannot shortcut nor should we want to. There is beauty, drama, and excitement in every phase of life. Each moment counts and each step on the spiritual path is challenging yet fulfilling in its own way. To truly reach the spiritual maturity and enlightenment you seek, you need to adopt the long view of life, to embrace the idea that while life itself is eternal, your soul develops over great stretches of time.

The best advice is to be patient. It's not easy to know where you are in this great process. Clearly, if you are feeling the spiritual quickening, you have already reached a turning point in your evolution. Just as the divine has guided you to where you are now in your consciousness, at the right time, the fuller understanding of your evolution will be revealed to you. Pay attention to the task at hand and do not force anything. You have evolved from an amazing process of life and there's an even more amazing journey ahead of you. Be persistent and stay close to the path, but let life unfold naturally. Each step in your unfoldment is necessary and beautiful.

FULFILLING YOUR LIFE'S PURPOSE

Reincarnation and karma are, in part, tracing our origin as a humanity—where we came from, why we're here, and where we're going. Before looking at the dynamics of free will in the many activities of life in Part Two, I would like to look at the big picture of how karma and reincarnation are part of our spiritual growth and the divine plan of life.

Metaphysics teaches unequivocally that there is a glorious plan of life for each of us. Life is not happenstance. There is a stupendous design that exists on all levels of creation. This design has been implemented for the purpose of expanding the expression of life. By fulfillment of the divine plan, something new is created. The creative power of life is constantly manifesting new forms of expression. One could say that this divine plan is life itself in all its potential and expression.

Everything in life is a participant in this great design, from the simplest atom to grand planets, stars, and galaxies; from the simplest microbial life forms to the most radiant archangel. We participate in this plan according to the degree of our own awareness, yet every aspect of life is an *essential* part of the totality of life. While an amoeba cannot participate as self-consciously as an archangel in the divine plan, both are equally essential.

As children of God, humanity plays a central part in this divine plan. We can fight or resist for a time, but eventually each soul surrenders to the natural flow of life as this brings out our highest and most noble qualities. We are like cells in the body of God. As each cell in our physical body must do its part to effectively maintain health and well-being, we must do our part to maintain the health of the divine plan.

The key to fulfilling our purpose is our active participation. Our purpose does not manifest by itself. We have to make that destiny happen through our own efforts. When we look at our own life and the conditions of the world around us, what we see is not so much the expression of the divine plan, but how effectively *we* are expressing that plan. It's too easy to blame God for our own mistakes as it's too easy to forget that there is a greater intelligence that is lovingly guiding our life.

Dharma is a wonderful Sanskrit word that essentially means "destiny." We each have our own dharma. It is our job to fulfill this dharma. In taking the steps to fulfill our dharma, we initiate karma. Our karma brings us closer to or delays fulfilling our dharma.

What if you do not wish to be part of the divine plan? What if you want to do something else with your life? Certainly it is your free will to do so. Yet remember this: What you are destined for ultimately *is* your desire. It may be camouflaged for a time, but it is there.

If you feel the desire to fulfill your purpose is not strong, all this means is you have to develop this part of you through willpower. Sometimes your desire has to be fanned. Through effort, your spiritual desire inevitably grows and blossoms. It has always been there, but perhaps at times needs your loving encouragement.

It is a sad fact that too often we do not fulfill the destiny that has been laid out for us. Many times we finish our incarnated life without completing the goals that were fully within our ability to attain. Nothing is more satisfying than living and fulfilling our purpose. And nothing can create a greater sense of longing, disappointment, and emptiness than missing out on what we could have achieved.

YOUR SPIRITUAL EVOLUTION

To fulfill your purpose, you must evolve. How can you become part of the greater unfoldment of life if you yourself are not unfolding?

The word *evolution* comes from the Latin word for "to unfold" or "to unroll." We see the process of unfoldment in every aspect of life. A seed unfolds and becomes a plant or a tree, a child becomes an adolescent, then an adult. An idea germinates and unfolds to become a beautiful work of art or an invention. Nothing in life is static. Some things develop quickly, while others take great stretches of time to develop.

It's ironic that despite the constant development of life around us, the idea of evolution is a relatively new one to the Western mind. In Eastern beliefs, evolution has been a part of religious and philosophic thought for ages. Yet for centuries the West has followed a belief that God created the world and everything in it, including humans, whole and complete, in one great creative outburst of activity. As Huston Smith puts it:

> While the West was still thinking, perhaps, of [a 6,000-year-old] universe— India was already envisioning ages and eons and galaxies as numerous as the sands of the Ganges.

Many brilliant people through the ages supported the traditional Western interpretation of creation, from Saint Augustine to the German mathematician Johannes Kepler, and even Isaac Newton. They used biblical genealogy in an attempt to estimate the actual moment of creation. In the mid–seventeenth century, the Irish bishop James Ussher wrote a highly influential work in which he tried to put the issue to rest, concluding: "The beginning of time . . . fell on the beginning of the night which preceded the 23rd day of October, in the year 4004 BC." This date was generally accepted for the next two hundred years!

Questions regarding the accepted belief of creation began in the 1800s when scientists realized that the natural geological processes of the Earth were incredibly slow and took much longer than the 6,000 years allotted for the creation of the Earth. At the same time, there was a revolution in understanding the origin of life as fossil evidence pointed to life beginning much earlier than previously believed. Then when the English naturalist Charles Darwin put forth his ideas of organisms developing over long periods of time, the awareness of evolution was born.

Today we understand that our Earth and solar system is close to 4.5 billion years old. The universe itself is many more billions of years old. Where we thought life was created about 6,000 years ago as well, we now know that there was life on Earth as far back as 3.5 billion years.

In the same way, we now understand that not only does the Earth revolve around the sun, but our solar system is one of many solar systems, all of which are part of an entire galaxy of solar systems, and that our galaxy is one of billions of galaxies in the universal plan. This stupendous vastness of life in terms of time and space has caused us to look at life here on Earth from a very different perspective than before. And this includes a more mature understanding of the nature of our spiritual self and God.

Some have become bewildered and even disillusioned by this greater scope of life. How do we count and how can God be an intimate part of us in the vastness of the universe? First let us recognize that each soul is precious. Creation would not be complete without each of our souls. All of us play an essential part in the grand scheme of life, no matter how grand that scheme is. Our awakened awareness to the vastness of life is God's way of opening the door to a new chapter in understanding the beauty and grandeur of ourselves and God.

THE STAGES OF SOUL DEVELOPMENT

In many ways, the metaphysical perspective embraces both scientific and religious ideas of human development. It recognizes the divine origin of humanity, yet also recognizes that life is undergoing an evolutionary process. As with all spiritual philosophies, metaphysics recognizes that God is at the center of all understanding. God is the creator of all that has been, is, and shall ever be. We are a product of God's design. What's more, God is guiding and maintaining every aspect of creation, which means God is guiding us as well. God is the source and sustainer of life.

To understand our spiritual evolution, we must make a distinction between the evolution of the soul and the evolution of the physical form the soul inhabits. The two are related but distinctly different processes. We are a soul inhabiting a body. Let's be very clear about that. We are not our body. If we were, there could be no such thing as reincarnation because there would be nothing to reincarnate. Consciousness and life would be extinguished with physical death and that would be the end of it.

This brings us to a central point about evolution. While modern science teaches that life comes from a concurrence of matter, metaphysics teaches it the other way around: matter is born out of life. It is the job of form to give expression to life. As life evolves, it molds matter in new and more eloquent forms of expression to reflect its greater experience and awareness. Stars and planets are born not out of blind forces of nature but by the stupendous motivation of life seeking greater expression. In the same way, we evolve because life within us is seeking greater expression.

This spark of life within us is what we call our soul. Our soul is a spark of God. Our soul is endowed with all the divine attributes of its Creator— immortal and everlasting, unbounded by form, space, and time. This is our true nature. It is our soul that gives us our life and our consciousness. However, some of the divine attributes of the soul are *latent* until developed through experience. To experience life and grow, the soul has embarked on a magnificent journey through creation, where it develops all the potential powers within it.

The process of spiritual maturation can be likened to a seed planted in the ground. All the potential for the seed to become a mighty oak or radiant rose is already held within. What are needed are the right elements in which to grow; if nourished and undisturbed, the seed cannot help but become that great flower or tree. Our soul is like a seed that God plants in the garden of creation. All that is needed for the soul to grow is already contained in the core of the soul.

In this cosmic picture, life on Earth is a schoolhouse and all our experiences are part of our spiritual growth. Because the soul cannot possibly learn all the lessons of life in a single lifetime, it must come to Earth many times to forge its spiritual mettle. Lifetime after lifetime, the soul comes to experience physical existence in all of its wonders, vicissitudes, and contrasts. Yet behind all of our experiences lies our greater spiritual purpose. Whether pleasant or painful, the things we go through in life are learning experiences.

Love is always the bond that unites us to the divine. No one is past forgiveness, redemption, and enlightenment. Since we are endowed with the gift of free choice, and the will to carry out that choice, we are accountable for our actions and deeds. Yet regardless of what we have done and gone through, we are always given a second chance in life. Mistakes and missteps are part of the growth process. We are always given the opportunity to turn our feet back on the path to God.

In this glorious pilgrimage, our soul experiences life in all its phases. The soul matures from simpler to more elevated levels of consciousness. As the Kabbalistic axiom states: "A stone becomes a plant; a plant a beast; a beast a man; a man a God." Or as Rumi so beautifully expressed it:

I died as a mineral and became a plant,
I died as plant and rose to animal,
I died as animal and I was Man.
Why should I fear? When was I less by dying?

I see this process of evolution in the study of the aura. When I clairvoyantly look at the mineral kingdom, I most definitely see life. What we consider inorganic material, in truth, is rich with life! There is a whole life stream of primitive mineral souls that have been embedded within the rocks, crystals, and metals of the Earth. At this point, there is no individualized form for these souls to inhabit, yet they experience life through the very process of being immersed in physical material. They even go through a primitive form of reincarnation as these nascent souls are periodically withdrawn back to the spiritual realms to assimilate their experience and then reimmersed in physical form.

Once the cycle of life is finished in the mineral kingdom, the soul ascends to the plant kingdom. Here the plant soul has the chance to express its inherent intelligence through the form it inhabits. It learns to adapt to its environment and express the beauty of its form and function. We have seen countless examples of how ingenious nature is in its adaptability. A plant will push its way through a crack in the sidewalk in order to thrive. Life will regenerate in a forest that has been ravaged by fire.

Plant souls most definitely express desire and can even feel a rudimentary sense of joy or sadness. The leaves of a plant turn to the sun not only because of a biological impulse, but also because the soul of the plant *desires* the nourishment of the sun. The roots of a plant search for water not only by biological impulse but also because the soul of the plant yearns for the nourishment of water. In the same way, the soul of a tree enjoys offering shade to people and animals. A fruit tree wishes to share its fruit with others. The rose—one of the most ethereal plants on Earth—enjoys the beauty and inspiration it radiates. When the plant dies, the plant soul is withdrawn but will reincarnate in another plant form.

From the plant kingdom, the soul moves up to the animal kingdom. In this kingdom, there is greater freedom of expression as the soul now inhabits a much more sophisticated form in which to operate. Much could be said about this wonderful and diverse kingdom. Animals most definitely have intelligence, and they have a soul. They have wonderful auras that show the inherent consciousness they possess. Their intelligence operates on an instinctual level as they are not yet capable of reasoning the way humans are.

When the cycle of life is finished in the animal kingdom, the animal soul graduates to the human kingdom. The human kingdom is the highest expression of physical life on Earth. Those who say we are nothing more than smart animals clearly cannot perceive the spiritual dimension of life. We may share a similar basic physiology with other forms of organic life, but spiritually we are in a completely different class of evolution. The human consciousness is far more developed than the animal, as now we are dealing with a self-aware being. Because of this greater development and intelligence, souls in the human kingdom have far more responsibility for their actions.

From the human kingdom, our evolution continues. There is no such thing as spiritual growth stopping. We eventually evolve to the spiritual kingdoms, which reach beyond the material world. In these higher kingdoms, we participate in the creative process of life in even more glorious and splendid ways. Our evolution continues as our soul eventually ascends back to its celestial origins where we become a co-creative being with God.

Part Two

THE DYNAMICS
OF KARMA AND
FREE WILL

Chapter 4

THE KARMA OF MONEY

When we look at the distribution of wealth in the world, we find ourselves asking, "What's wrong with this picture?" If there are plenty of natural resources for all to live well, how is it that some people have so much while others have so little? Why are some people born into wealth and others into poverty? In our own circle of family and friends, we see the same apparent disparity of wealth. We are not supposed to covet our neighbor's belongings, yet we constantly compare what we have with others.

In this section, we explore how karmic law works in the various areas of our lives. We begin with that ever important topic—finances. Understanding money and how it works is one of the most basic and essential lessons we can learn. The mismanagement or mishandling of money is behind so much of the world's woes and our own personal challenges.

All money, all resources of abundance and supply, comes from one source and one source alone—God. Regardless of the avenue of expression of that wealth—stocks, bonds, paycheck, investments, gifts, etc.—the ultimate source still goes back to God. God is infinite wealth, and as children of the divine, it is our right to partake of that divine inheritance. When we see the bounty of nature, we catch a glimpse of the tremendous abundance that is available to us. God is not frugal. Although there is economy in nature and life, the divine does not share in the immortal bounty sparingly. God is generous and we are all meant to be a part of God's riches.

As a clairvoyant, I see the spiritual power of abundance as a brilliant turquoise light. This spiritual energy brings in the consciousness of God's divine abundance. When I see this light to a marked degree in a person's aura, I know that person is in the awareness of prosperity and using that awareness in a productive way. When a person is in a true wealth consciousness, that person will have turquoise in their aura even if that prosperity may not at the moment be showing itself. On the other hand, when people gain wealth through greed, deceit, theft, etc., there will be a dark, dirty avocado green and other very unpleasant energies. It is a completely different aura from that of the person who is working in harmony with God and wealth.

So why does inequality of money exist if we are all meant to partake of God's riches? Free will is always the number-one reason. It must be said that while we are all equal in the eyes of God, we are not all equal as far as where we are in our spiritual unfolding. When it comes to money, there are some people who have simply done a better job of expressing the principles of prosperity than others. In this way, it's not so much a matter of equality or inequality. Rather, it's more a matter of effort, intelligence, and skill. If you apply yourself in matters of finance, you progress. The other great problem, of course, is greed. The single greatest sin in the world today is greed. We are well aware of greed that exists on a large scale with corporations, financial institutions, and governments. Yet the sad fact is that too much greed exists on a personal level. If we could wake up and truly see what we are doing to ourselves and to one another, the world would change very quickly.

To compound the problem, there is a tremendous amount of money karma that has accrued on a personal and collective level. The majority of financial conditions we find ourselves in, especially the financial climate we were born into, are the result of good or bad money karma we have generated. Please, in using such terms as good or bad karma, I want to avoid the idea of crime and punishment. *Karmic conditions are lessons.* They are designed to teach us to be better people, to help us in our spiritual growth. So we will find ourselves in situations that will best help us learn our spiritual lesson.

The karmic lesson of money is to learn its value and how to manage it!

You have to earn your prosperity through your own efforts and right actions. It sounds simple, but learning how to properly handle money can be challenging. There are lessons for those who do not have it, and lessons for those who do. The attainment of money is a necessary element in pursuing your life's purpose. Yet you may pursue money for different reasons. There is the basic need for money to live and care for one's self and/or to care for one's family. There is the attainment of money for power or luxury. Some obtain wealth to reach a certain goal, as in producing a work of art or developing a new invention. All these reasons will generate a karmic condition accordingly.

THE KARMA OF WEALTH

Many people complain and endlessly commiserate with themselves because someone they know has not had to work for his or her living and has plenty of money. There is often a sense of envy with such people. There can also be suspicion of those with great wealth that somehow this money came at the cost of others. As the humorous axiom states, "Behind every great fortune is a great theft!"

Why is someone born into royalty or a family of millionaires or billionaires? Quite simply, that soul has karmically earned the right to such a privileged birth. Think of attaining great wealth as having a talent; it builds from lifetime to lifetime. If someone is born into extreme wealth, in most cases this soul has proven its ability to handle wealth through *several* lifetimes of good work.

Great wealth is the accumulation of many lifetimes of hard work. And these are not lifetimes of merely accumulating wealth, but using money in a healthy and productive way. In past lives, such souls showed generosity and kindness when it came to money matters as well as showing great acumen when it came to the handling of finances. They come into their present life of wealth and abundance to build on past merits and climb to greater heights.

Such souls are meant to take the great wealth they were born into and put it to even greater good use. This becomes their act of service as well as their greatest test: to prove by deeds done in this present life that they have truly overcome the lower self and learned the true brotherhood of man. When such a soul passes the test of wealth, good karma will continue to accumulate. They have learned how to remain of service to God no matter how much is put in their hands. These souls realize it is not really their money to begin with. They are the custodians of those funds and the money they have obtained is meant to be shared with others.

As we know, not everyone who was born into great wealth uses it wisely. It is unfortunate that many who have reached this pinnacle fail in their test of wealth. Wealth ends up getting the better of them. Many become spoiled, selfish, snobbish, greedy, or outright evil in handling the wealth given to them. These souls become so hypnotized by the wealth they were born into that they forgot how hard they worked in past lives to earn such a privileged life.

What happens to souls who spend their spiritual savings account and make no more good karma? Unfortunately, in their next life they will have to start all over again. Depending on the degree of their misuse, they may have to experience poverty, ill health, even starvation to wake the soul up again before they can earn enough credits to reclaim what they once had. Having money means being responsible for that money. The more you have, the more good is required of you.

There are many variations on the theme of wealth. There are those who were born into a comfortable financial situation but at some point accumulated great wealth. Often these souls were at the tipping point. They proved in other lives that they were able to manage money well, and this was the life when those efforts came to fruition. So it was no accident or stroke of luck that these souls attained the wealth they did; again, they earned it.

How about the rags-to-riches scenario? What is the karma of someone who was born poor but through hard work became wealthy? What often happens in these cases is the soul had wealth in a previous life, but misused it and was born into poverty to rekindle the soul to the value of money. Each case is unique, but perhaps in a previous life such a soul was spoiled and pampered and now has to learn to do without and to struggle. If such a soul passes its test in the poverty stage, it can sometimes rekindle its former wealth because such knowledge is still very much in the consciousness of the struggling soul.

What about those who are completely corrupted by wealth—those who have earned great wealth through many lifetimes of good work, but then become seduced by the power that money brings and become callous and cruel? Such souls have a long trip back home. It will take several lifetimes to pay back the karma they have accumulated and be entrusted again with such wealth. And this is on top of paying back other karmas they will have inevitably accrued.

It comes back to the motives that generated a particular action. The key with good money karma is to refuse to take money for granted and continue to handle it well. Learn how to take care of your needs and those who are entrusted in your care or those who cross your path who are in need. If you misuse it, you lose it. Be a good steward of your money and watch how it multiplies!

If you see someone well-off, you can bet that this person has, in past lives, known starvation and poor circumstances and worked hard for his or her daily bread. This person has experienced the vicissitudes of life and is being given the chance to reap the benefits of lessons learned from those experiences. Such a soul is an example of what you are capable of achieving.

It has been often asked, "If you wish to live spiritually, should you enjoy that wealth or should you use it in service to others?" There is nothing wrong with enjoying your wealth as long as you are not overdoing it and as long as you are sharing it with others. You are meant to enjoy the fruits of your labor. That's part of the divine plan. Just keep money in its proper perspective.

There have been people who renounced wealth in service to God. Perhaps the most famous of all is Siddhartha, who renounced all his worldly fortune to eventually become the Buddha. There are times when God asks you to walk away from fortune or a comfortable lifestyle to follow a particular mission. We all go through such sacrifice in the process of our evolution, but this kind of sacrifice is not meant to be used as an excuse to avoid the lessons that money presents. These moments are specifically designed to help us develop a certain side to our spiritual nature. Such sacrifice does not go against the laws of prosperity. In truth, good money karma continues to accrue because such souls are not idle. They are very much in the throes of service and eventually it will come back to them.

This is why you should not worry too much if you are not always properly compensated for the work you do. Of course, do all you can to be treated fairly. As the Bible says, "The laborer is worthy of his hire." Yet always remember, if you have earned it, the money will come back to you in some way. That's the divine law. Unfortunately, there have been situations where people have done terrible things because they felt they were cheated of money that was rightfully theirs. Instead of letting life balance things out, they compounded the situation by taking matters into their own hands and generated new karma.

Regardless of what life is now giving back to you, the key is for you to continue to be of service. Some people say, "God, make me rich and I will use that money to help others." Why wait? Help now and let goodwill accrue. It doesn't matter if you have a dollar in your pocket. If your brother or sister is in need, give fifty cents. It will come back to you. This is not about being generous to a fault, where you give so much you do not care for your own needs. It's about not waiting until you feel comfortable in the giving. As the adage tells us, "Give till it hurts."

I learned an important lesson early in life regarding generating money.

When I was in my teens, I lived in New York City for a time. I had gone there to enroll at Columbia University to study journalism. In those days, college tuition was not nearly as expensive as it is today. I brought with me in cash the money I had saved up to attend school.

I sublet an apartment and took in a roommate, a girl I had only briefly met, to help with the rent. We had been living together for just a few days when I got a big surprise. In my naïveté, I went out to run some errands and left all my tuition money in a drawer in my room. When I returned, my roommate and the money were gone!

So there I was, in New York, with only the money in my pocket. There were no credit cards in those days, and I had not yet opened a bank account, so I was stuck. What was I to do? I could have wired home for some money or turned to relatives, but I asked myself, "What if I didn't have anyone to turn to? What would I do?" I took the whole experience as a challenge and decided to resolve it on my own if I could.

I went looking for a job. All day I tried to find some kind of job but found nothing. After a full day of looking, I got tired and stopped to rest in front of a movie theater. I happened to overhear the manager arguing with the cashier. He was accusing her of taking money. The girl became indignant and quit right there. I had done some cashier work, so here was my opportunity. I went up to the manager and said, "I think you need a new cashier." I told him my experience and he hired me on the spot. He even gave me an advance, so I had some money to live on. The interesting thing is, though my going to college was delayed, I wound up getting a job working for the Hellenic Press in New York as a journalist, which gave me some practical writing experience.

The Reincarnation of Donald

I would like to share a reincarnation story of Donald. This true story is told by the Higher as an example of how good money karma will eventually come no matter what the obstacles.

Donald was born in England to a very modest family in the 1700s. Donald's father worked in government, but was having a difficult time being able to provide for his family. As Donald grew up, he showed a strong talent for medicine and wanted to become a doctor. Unfortunately, his parents could not afford to send him to medical school. Donald got a job as a carpenter. He liked the work and was able to make his own living. Slowly he was able to save some money. Some years later, an opportunity opened up for him to attend law school. Although it was not medicine, he grabbed the chance and quickly became a top student.

Upon graduation, he joined a law firm and became a successful trial law-yer handling criminal cases. He became rich as a lawyer, married and had two children. Fortunately, he handled his wealth well. He was generous with others and always ready to lend a helping hand. Yet despite his success, in the back of his mind he still had the desire to practice medicine. However, he was so established that he felt it was too late to change careers. He remained a lawyer to the end of his days and died at fifty-seven, when he was hit by a stagecoach in the streets of London.

In this life, Donald was able to overcome financial struggle and become successful in his own right. He also showed that once he accumulated wealth, he used it for the betterment of himself and others. Yet despite his successful life, he did not actually complete the task he came to Earth to fulfill—which was to become a doctor. So even though he accomplished so much, this part of his life remained unresolved.

In Donald's next life, he was given the chance to fulfill that destiny. This time he was born in Sweden in the late 1800s. He had loving parents who were financially well-off. From a very early age, Donald once again showed a strong desire to be a doctor. This time, he did go to medical school and graduated with honors. He became a successful surgeon and developed inno-vative surgical techniques that helped many people and earned him much esteem. He again married and had a family of his own.

In this incarnation, Donald built on the good karma accrued in his past life in England and fulfilled the purpose he was originally destined to reach.

THE KARMA OF POVERTY

There is no clearer picture of man's inhumanity to man than in the living conditions of many people in the world. All too often, those who have the financial resources simply do not do enough for those who don't have those resources. The hoarding of wealth without regard for the people who are paying the price for that greed is generating the majority of the world's finan-cial problems. There are millions of people in the world who have earned the karmic right to decent living conditions and opportunity yet are being denied that right by those in power and influence.

What will happen to people in this situation? Eventually, the karmic slate will balance out. If you have been denied the good fortune that you have earned because of the actions of others, your good fortune will come back to you sooner or later. In addition, you continue to accrue good money karma as long as you do not fall prey to the challenges impoverished conditions present. Many a good person has turned to lying, cheating, and stealing, etc., to get through difficult times, and this naturally creates new karma.

Having said this, a good number of people who are facing financial difficulties are facing money karma. This means that somewhere in a past incarnation, there was a misuse of money and now the karma has come full circle. In understanding the karma of poverty, it is important to remember that God brought you to Earth to succeed. If Earth is a spiritual schoolhouse, no one enters a place of education with the intention of failing. The lessons may be hard but the goal is always to learn and be the better for it. No one is worthless or unimportant. It doesn't matter if you haven't a penny in your pocket; you remain precious in God's eyes.

God does not bring poverty into the world; we have brought that on ourselves. God permits this to happen because of the gift of free choice. If God interferes, then how will we learn? God is keenly aware of the poverty that exists. Don't think the divine is unaffected or unmoved. The divine works ceaselessly to help better our conditions and sheds tears of compassion over how we treat one another. Yet as desperate as many of our situations can appear, there is, at some point, opportunity to overcome the privation. I know overcoming poverty is one of the most difficult lessons we can face. When we look at the millions upon millions of people who live in poverty, we catch a glimpse of the scope of the challenge.

So what is the karmic reason some are born into poverty? Such a person may have had wealth in a past life and misused it. Maybe that person was stingy or miserly with their money. Or that person may have simply mishandled money in a past life by spending it frivolously and ended up broke. In more serious cases, the soul might have been ruthless with money, using it for personal gain without thought of the distress or harm it caused others. We see corporate greed running rampant today and you can bet that those who are in decision-making positions will be held accountable for their actions.

There are, of course, many variations on the theme of poverty. There are those who are not impoverished but face chronic financial problems. This again can be a karmic situation. I had a student once who faced unusual chronic money issues. In her situation, I had clairvoyantly picked up that the karma stemmed from a past life where she was meant to pay back money karma to others and refused to. So instead of finally resolving that karma, she compounded the situation, resulting in the difficult financial condition she faced in this life.

There are situations where the loss of money comes later in life: reversal of fortune. This can also be karmic where in the past you robbed or cheated someone who had a very stable, happy lifestyle. In this incarnation, you are now the one feeling sudden loss. As with all types of karma, financial karma tends to come back to you in the same way you put it out.

There are those who look down on or avoid those who do not have money. There are many in India who mistakenly believe that those who were born as untouchables should be left in that condition because they are paying back bad karma from a past life. Nothing could be further from the truth. If you see a man drowning, do you say to that person who is crying to you for help, "Go ahead and drown. That must be your karma"? Of course not. You help that person the best you can. You're not thinking, "Now why is that person drowning? Has that person done something bad and deserves to drown?"

Yet when it comes to helping others, we all too often judge the situation or person and refuse to help. A big part of our job on Earth is to help one another. If you are in the privileged situation of being able to help another soul, help that person. If you don't, you may find yourself in that very situation at some point down the line!

Regardless of the financial situation you may find yourself in, you can overcome present financial hardships. There is an inspiring story of a man who was homeless and decided he'd had enough of living on the street. He managed to scrape up enough money to enroll in a correspondence course in accounting. He had to do his studies on park benches or wherever he could, but he kept at it. Eventually, he passed his exams and found an accounting job. He found an apartment in which to live and reunited with family members who had given up on him or thought he was dead. He completely turned his life around, and he was not a young man when he did this. When asked what the most challenging part of rebuilding his life was, he said not listening to others around him who kept telling him he would never succeed.

Take charge of your financial life. If you find yourself financially challenged, recognize that you have the opportunity to reclaim your divine inheritance. You may have to work hard, very hard, but things will turn around. You cannot be idle or lackluster in generating wealth. There's an old saying, "Laziness travels so slowly that poverty soon overtakes him." Once things turn around, that good fortune will stay with you. If you already have earned good financial karma, then it becomes your job to build on that goodness and become an even greater example of God's bounty.

The Reincarnation of George

In this story, shared by the Higher, we explore what can cause someone to be born poor. Again, in looking at this story, please do not assume that every person born into a difficult financial situation is paying back money karma. The purpose here is to look at how the mishandling of money can create challenges in an incarnation further down the line.

George was born in New York City in the early part of the twentieth century. He was an only child, and both his parents loved him. Unfortunately, they were struggling financially and living in poverty. George's father owned a small candy store by the harbor, but it was not doing well. They had barely enough to eat and to take care of basic needs. George was a good soul but felt his plight keenly. He was very frustrated and even as a child was ambitious to do better for himself.

His parents saw that he had an aptitude for science. They saved what little money they could and put him through school, which he excelled at. As he grew, he met a benefactor who saw his talent and the difficult situation he was in and offered to put him through medical school. George worked very hard and once again excelled.

His parents were very proud of what George was doing, but, unfortunately, while he was in school his father passed away, and his mother struggled even harder to keep the candy store open on her own. He contemplated leaving medical school to help her, but decided that the best course of action was to continue his studies; once he finished, he would be in a better position to help his mother. Yet once again tragedy struck. As he was finishing his studies, his mother contracted influenza and died. So it was that as he graduated and began his life as a doctor, his parents were not there to see his success. Yet he took solace in the fact that they knew he was going to be a success. Even though there was nothing he could do, he regretted that he wasn't able to help them somehow.

George became a successful neurologist. He met a good woman of modest background who understood the kind of life he came from. They married and had two children together. He built a successful practice in New York City and became wealthy. He enjoyed the life he made for himself, but in the back of his mind he was still haunted by some of his childhood experiences as well as the thought of his parents, who were not able to enjoy the better times with him.

In this incarnation, George did a beautiful job of working through his money karma and succeeded in making a better life for himself. He ended up overcoming adversity and fulfilling his life's purpose. Yet the question to ask is: What was the karma that caused him to be born into deprivation in the first place?

While money was the single greatest challenge of his life, in other ways he had good karma. He had good karma with his parents, good career karma, and good romantic karma. Had he failed to work through his money karma, these other dynamics might never have had the chance to express themselves. This tells us several things: You need to face the challenges at hand. Whatever dreams you have, no matter how close or far they may seem, by successfully facing what is right in front of you, you set up the conditions for other aspects of your life to fall into place. Another thing this shows is that God always gives you the strengths you need to meet and master your karma.

To find the cause of George's money karma, we need to open the Book of Life to his preceding incarnation in Germany. This is now the early 1800s in Frankfurt. George (we'll maintain the same name for clarity) was once again male, but this time born into a family of wealth. There was a similar pattern in that his parents were again store owners, but this time the business was a thriving hardware store.

He was again an only child and had a very good relationship with his parents. He was a jovial, nice-looking man, and slightly spoiled by his parents. As he grew up, he was expected to take over the business, but he was not interested in doing so. He traveled for some time, and eventually decided he wanted to become a professor of mathematics. His parents agreed and he became successful as a professor, and he liked what he was doing. He had a love affair that went sour when the woman left him at the altar. He became so disappointed that, bitter on the subject of love, he thought he would never marry.

Despite some bumps on the road, life was moving in the right direction for him. It was at this point, however, that he took his own money and invested in bonds, which failed. For this, even with his professorship, he fell into severe financial difficulties. His parents passed on and left him their money, but once again he was reckless. It wasn't long before most of his inheritance was gone.

During these financial troubles, which he had brought on himself, he met another woman and married her. Marriage was a bright light in his life that could have helped him through his challenging times. Unfortunately, he wasn't kind to her. Instead of working with her, he was verbally abusive and took out his frustrations on her. It was not long before she left him. Once again he did not show good business sense and took what little money he had from his professor's salary and lost it on another ill-conceived investment. He finished his incarnation broke, as a direct result of his own actions.

Here his lesson was in learning how to handle money. He was trying to find a quick way to make money and was too cavalier in dealing with financial matters regardless of consequences. As time went on, he continued to invest with money he did not have, which was where the money karma was generated. On occasion, many of us take calculated financial risks for what we feel is important, and sometimes these risks don't work out; but in George's case, he took his financial risks too far. He did not properly evaluate the potential repercussions of taking such risks.

To his credit, George was not a bad person and his underlying motive was not malicious. His lesson of life was not greed or avarice. He was not stingy with his money. Had that been the case, his karma would have been far worse. His mistake was the mishandling of money and not recognizing its value. This set up the condition for his next life, where he would have to financially struggle to build the life of his dreams, to learn the true value of money. In a future life, he will also have to resolve the karmic situation he created with his wife as a result of his mishandling of finances. This shows that if we are not careful, karma in one area of life can extend into another area of our life.

THE PROSPERITY PRAYER

I conclude this chapter by offering a very effective prayer to increase your prosperity consciousness. The turquoise ray is the spiritual energy to use to help strengthen your prosperity consciousness and redeem money karma. In addition to the meditation exercise offered in chapter 16, this exercise is excellent to do at the moment of receiving and giving money.

Hold the money in your left hand and place your right hand over your left as you ask the light to touch it with the following prayer.

THE PROSPERITY PRAYER

Down-ray the turquoise ray of abundance and supply into this Thy money, increasing, quickening, and multiplying this money one hundred thousand–fold for the good of all concerned, redeeming any and all defiled energies, increasing all present avenues of supply, and opening up new avenues of prosperity. Let this light balance all financial flows incoming and outgoing, blessing the giver and the receiver.

[Say this when receiving money] Let this money be for me to do with as I please.

[Say this when giving money] Let this money be for you to do with as you please.

I hold to the knowing that this energy is already in motion. [Rotating hands clockwise] Immediately, without delay, multiply this money right away. [3 times]

MONEY KARMA REVIEW

Overall, how would you evaluate this part of your life?

Have you had the money you needed or have there been chronic difficulties?

What is your attitude toward money?

Did you grow up having the things you needed or was money always an issue?

Do you feel money is somehow owed to you?

Do you recognize the value of money and are you willing to work for it?

Chapter 5

THE KARMA
OF RELATIONSHIPS

The karma of relationships can be one of the most intense, involving, and demanding of all karmas we face, which means the karmic lessons connected to relationships are some of the most essential lessons of life. If there's one area where you want to build your spiritual power and spend your coin of wisdom well, it's with relationships.

The karmic lesson of relationships sounds simple enough: Love one another. It's a lesson we've heard countless times. Yet learning to really love can sometimes be the hardest thing to do. If love is so essential to our well-being, why do we sometimes have difficulty expressing love to others?

Love is a *power*, one of the most potent powers in creation. Metaphysics teaches that love is the bond that holds creation together. Love is what keeps us connected to one another, to the universe, and to God. In the aura, there is an actual spiritual energy of love. It appears as various shades of pink light, especially deep rose-pink light. This spiritual energy embodies the divine attribute of love. It's one of the most essential energies to have in the aura. Yet all too often there is not enough of this vital deep rose-pink energy in people's auras, which tells us that too often there is not enough love in our own hearts! If we don't have enough love within ourselves, how can we express this love to others? And if we can't express love to others, how can we have healthy, productive relationships?

Your first duty in handling or resolving karmic relationships is to build up your love flow. The wonder of love is that it brings in so many positive attributes. These facets reflect the many lessons of life that love presents: kindness, patience, understanding, affection, forgiveness, happiness for others, joy, compassion, generosity, service, tolerance, sacrifice, care, support, mercy, charity, devotion, and the list goes on. So much is incorporated in that simple word *love*!

Build your love so you feel it from the top of your head to the bottom of your feet. When you go out into the world with such a beautiful energy of love, everyone benefits. Love lifts the spirits of yourself and everyone around you. Have you noticed that when you are around loving people, even if you're not in a loving place, you get into that momentum of love and are lifted by it? It doesn't matter where you are in the expression of your love. Start with the love you have and build from there.

One of the most beautiful energies of love I have seen was my mentor and spiritual compatriot, Inez Hurd. She was the one who prepared me to become a teacher. We often called her Mama Hurd as a term of endearment. She had a magnificent enlightened aura. One of the things that stood out most about her energy field was the degree of love she had developed. She had a gorgeous star formation of pink light emanating from her heart chakra, demonstrating the bounty of love she expressed. She also had this amazing spherelike energy of pale pearl-luster pink above her head. It showered down on her a perpetual pink light, indicating she had reached that state of universal love where she was truly able to love others unconditionally. What a beautiful soul she was and how lucky I was to have known her.

Perhaps the greatest teacher of love the world has ever seen was Jesus of Nazareth. He is considered the prince of peace, yet what was His key message? Love. In a time of bloodshed when the value of human life was very low, He taught us that the most important thing was to love one another. He showed that God who created us is *loving* as well as strong and all-powerful.

He taught us how through loving one another we can begin to love God. And here is the ultimate purpose of loving one another—it opens us up to loving God. God *is* love. There is nothing greater than the love of God. Yet we cannot love God if we do not love one another.

When there is not enough love in our hearts, we are open to all sorts of destructive emotional states, including anger, fear, hatred, resentment, jealousy, lust, greed, and so on. These states of consciousness produce unenlightened conditions in our auras. Cold-hearted people have a lot of gray in their auras, especially around the heart. There can also be a dirty dark blue above the head. Naturally, such lower vibrations are going to have a detrimental effect in our interactions with others. And here is where we generate difficult relationship karma. As a result of our mishandling of others, there is inevitable pain and suffering as life balances the slate and we learn about love.

There are times when love *is* in your heart but you choose not to express it out of selfishness, fear, resentment, etc. You know what love is about, but still, through your gift of free will, you choose to act in an unloving way. If you do not turn things around, you can diminish the love you have through such selfish acts and will find yourself starting over to rebuild your love flow.

When you recognize the opportunity to work your karma out with someone, bless that opportunity. It's not easy to incarnate people together to work out past life karma. The timing can be tricky. One may be ready to incarnate but not the other, or one may be in a completely different part of life and your paths will not cross. So when the opportunity to be with each other presents itself, take advantage of the situation. This is your golden opportunity.

You will be faced with relationships that will test the spiritual qualities you need to strengthen. One relationship may test your patience, while another relationship tests your ability to be kind and generous. Yet in another relationship you may have to sacrifice or be forgiving. Or you may get to enjoy a happy, joyful, affectionate relationship as the result of good relationship karma you have accrued. All of these help to develop and expand your love flow. Each relationship brings out different character traits in you as well as its own joys and challenges.

Love does not work in isolation. You cannot succeed in mastering the art of love unless you interact with others. As you search for people who are meant to be a part of your life—those very people are searching for you as you are part of their destiny. You cannot climb the spiritual ladder without a great deal of love in your heart, no matter how smart or clever you may be.

GUIDELINES FOR RELATIONSHIP KARMA

Through your many incarnations on Earth, you have played out every relationship: you've been mother, father, son, daughter, boss, employee, friend, enemy, lover, wife, husband. In those relationships, you've played out and are still playing out every type of dynamic: you've been kind and cruel, been giving and selfish, been murdered and the murderer, been petty and generous. This is all part of the growing process.

When working out karma, your relationships tend to repeat themselves. For example, if you have created karma in a romantic relationship, you will tend to reincarnate in another romantic relationship to work out that karma. Of course, this does not mean you have not known these people in other types of relationships. You have. Part of the purpose of reincarnation is to have a diverse and well-rounded experience in relationships. It simply means the karma needs to be resolved in the same way it was generated.

The people who play an important part in your life you have almost always known in past lives, usually many times. This is especially true for family. This also means your karma with these souls runs deep, and it can take many lifetimes to work out all the intricacies. However, not every relationship is karmic. It's not always easy to know what is karmic and what is not. The best remedy is always to express love in all your interactions.

Attitude and motive are essential keys in how souls reincarnate together to resolve karma. The karma of someone who is remorseful for their misdeeds is very different from that of someone who has no awareness of the implications of an offense he or she is committing. The graph on page 64 gives you an idea of how this dynamic works.

What happens when person A offends person B?

Scenario 1
If person A can work things out in same lifetime with person B, karma is resolved on both sides and the two people do not have to reincarnate to resolve offense.

Scenario 2
If person A is truly remorseful to person B in same lifetime, but not able to work things out or person B is not forgiving of person A, the two people will generally come back in another lifetime in the same roles so person A can pay back person B.

Scenario 3
If person B forgives person A, person B does not have to reincarnate with person A to work out particular offense. Person A will have to work out remaining karma in another way.

Scenario 4
If person A is not remorseful and person B remains unforgiving, the two will reincarnate in another life to work things out with the roles usually reversed. Person A will now be at the mercy of person B.

Scenario 3a
Sometimes, as an act of grace, person B will permit person A to pay back karma with B even though person B has forgiven person A and is not bound karmically. This usually results in the building of a strong bond of love.

Scenario 4a
Sometimes in the new incarnation, the energy ricochets and person B ends up committing a similar offense to person A. In this case, person A has paid back karma to person B, but person B has created new karma that will have to be worked out.

Scenario 4b
If person B in new incarnation treats person A in a forgiving way, the karma is resolved on both sides with both people learning how much forgiveness counts.

Working Out Relationship Karma

Resolving relationship karma does not necessarily mean that the people involved will develop great personal affection for each other. With more intimate relationships it usually does, but often when the relationship karma is resolved, the situation becomes neutral. Your personal expression of affection to someone is a choice, and that choice has nothing to do with karma. You will have to show love in your ability to work out karma, but the intimacy and expression of love is up to you.

THE KARMA OF FAMILY

Our relationship with our family can be one of the most sublime expressions of love or one of the most painful and difficult experiences that we will ever endure. From the beginning of our incarnations, there is an affinity with souls who have been family-related. As we express free will, karma inevitably sets in and creates complications, many times dramatic. Once the karma is resolved, usually the love flow returns on an even better level. Of our 800 lives to spiritual maturity, we are born into a relatively small circle of souls connected to our family. This doesn't mean we don't have family experiences outside this circle. It simply means that by repeating these relationships, we can explore various dynamics and build truly profound relationships. We share our glories and failures, our right steps and mistakes with one another.

Some families get along very well, while others are dysfunctional. This is most always karmic. Families that get along well together have learned the value of family life from many lifetimes of working at it. They have learned the karmic lesson of how to work as a family unit. Dysfunctional families are usually in the process of learning the lessons of family. It's an important lesson of life to recognize and appreciate the value of family life.

If you find yourself in a difficult family situation or were raised without strong family support, this could be a sign that you are facing family karma. Perhaps you abandoned your family in a past life and are now feeling the effects of what it's like not to have that support system. In such situations, it may be your job to go out and build a family of your own. Many souls have done this. They created a happy family life that they themselves did not experience growing up.

The family unit is not always by blood. There can be strong karmic bonds in families in which the children were adopted or are stepchildren. Again it all depends on the karmic chart. In these situations, there does remain some karma with the biological parents even if they are not the souls raising the children.

There are times when it is your karma not to get married and have a family. This can be due to a past situation where you abused the family life and now feel what it's like not to have a family of your own. Usually people in these situations have a longing for family life. However, people who do not get married are not always paying back bad family karma. Sometimes these souls have had many good lifetimes of family life and recognize its value. It can mean that the soul, in that particular incarnation, is meant to go through other experiences and develop other facets of its nature.

It is important to honor and respect your family to the best of your ability. At the same time, strike a balance between enjoying family life and maintaining your independence. There are some families that hold on too tight and can choke the spiritual life of the various family members. This makes it very hard for individuals to act in a way that is not in agreement with the family as a whole. These situations create their own karma. If you are in such a situation, it becomes your job to break such stifling holds. Regardless of the family you are a part of, your first allegiance is to God. Blood ties run deep, but spiritual ties run deeper. If your family is too close-minded, too locked into the family consciousness, then the lesson there is to continue to honor and respect the family, but go out and fulfill your own destiny.

A Reincarnation Story of Family Karma

This is a true reincarnation story that was told to me by my spiritual mentor, Inez Hurd. It is a wonderful example of family karma and one she encouraged me to share with others.

The story took place in the eastern United States, not long ago, in a well-to-do family. Irene was a good-looking woman, married to a wonderful man named Burch. They had one son, named Raul, who was a fine young man. Raul had caught the eye of a pretty blond girl, Gilda, and unexpectedly eloped with her, surprising both Irene and Burch.

After a while, the newlyweds returned and there was a big celebration. However, the new bride turned a very cold shoulder to her new mother-in-law. The hostility was particularly visible when Irene showed affection to her son. Irene and Burch were disheartened, as they loved their son very much and worried about the woman he married.

A few years went by and things did not get better. Gilda became more and more unreasonably jealous of her husband's affections to his mother. She accused him of hanging on to her apron strings. Irene hardly saw her son, since Gilda did everything she could to avoid visits. Even Burch's death, leaving Irene a widow, Gilda's heart still was not warmed to her mother-in-law.

Then Irene heard the news that Raul and Gilda were going to have a baby. She was delighted at the idea of being a grandmother. She had been lonely since her husband died, and she looked forward to having this new grandchild to love. But when she visited the new parents, Gilda picked up the baby and took it away, so Irene could not even see the child! Raul was dumbfounded and couldn't understand why Gilda was acting that way.

Irene decided not to visit anymore unless she was expressly invited. More years went by. Irene traveled and kept herself busy and tried to forget the pain she felt at being so disconnected from her son's life.

Let us pause to look at why Gilda had such a deep and unreasonable resentment to Irene. Certainly, there was free will at work. Gilda was choosing to act this way. As we look at the elements of this situation, we see that the primary antagonism was Gilda's jealousy of Raul's affections to his mother. But where did this jealousy stem from?

To find the spiritual root to this antagonism, we have to look back hundreds of years to when we see these three souls together again. This time it's in the royal courts of Europe. Gilda, in this past life, was a headstrong and beautiful princess. Her father, the king, had plans to marry her to a prince from another principality. But Gilda had different plans. She had her sights set on a young and handsome lord. This young lord was none other than Raul in a past life incarnation.

What Gilda did not know was that Raul had already fallen in love with the daughter of one of the highest officials in the king's staff. As you may surmise, this girl was Irene in a past life. Raul had been careful in expressing his affections because his uncle, a good man who had raised him as his own son, held a grudge against Irene's family. So Irene and Raul kept their affections quiet until they could figure out what to do.

In this life, Irene and Gilda were best friends. They were raised by the same governess, and even though Gilda was of royal blood and Irene was not, they shared many things and were like sisters to each other. However, when it came to telling Irene about her desire for Raul, Gilda remained quiet, saying only that she had a secret that she would reveal at the right time. Neither girl had any idea that they both liked the same man.

Gilda planned an elaborate horse-riding event with the single purpose of getting close to Raul and winning his affections. Her plan succeeded in that she was able to secure some time alone with him, but when she expressed her feelings to Raul, it became clear that he did not feel the same way. She didn't understand the signals he was sending her, and thought he was just playing hard to get.

When the two met up with the rest of the group, Gilda saw the affection between Raul and Irene. This completely infuriated her as she thought Irene was trying to steal Raul from her. In her rage, she caused Irene's horse to startle, throwing Irene off and seriously injuring her. Everyone was shocked at the open display of hostility. When Gilda saw how shaken Raul was, she realized, finally, how strong his feelings were for Irene, for which she swore vengeance.

When Irene recovered, it was announced that she and Raul were to marry. Gilda asked her father to intercede and block the marriage. The king refused and instead announced that Gilda was to be married to a prince of enormous wealth and power. This made Gilda even more angry and desperate.

Gilda decided to write a letter of forgiveness to Irene, congratulating her on her marriage, but this was just a ruse to put Irene's mind at ease and buy a little time. For a few days all seemed well. Irene had planned a quiet rendezvous with Raul in an adjoining house shortly before the marriage. Gilda heard about the meeting, sneaked in ahead, and hid in the drapes.

When she saw Raul and Irene together, and the tenderness they shared, Gilda's jealousy consumed her; she snapped. She went to her room and grabbed a knife. When she returned to the house, Raul had gone out for a moment, leaving Irene alone. When he returned, it was too late. He saw Irene lying on the floor, her dress stained with blood, dead. Even in his shock and grief, it took him only a few moments to realize what had happened—Gilda had stabbed Irene in the back.

Everyone in the palace was deeply grieved. They knew what had happened but could do nothing about it; Gilda was the princess. So Raul went away, vowing never to look upon her again. When his uncle, who was also very grieved, eventually died, Raul sold everything and left the kingdom for good.

Looking at the karmic ties in this story, we discover the root of Gilda's jealousy toward Irene. In this present life, Gilda is meant to learn to control her jealous feelings. Unfortunately, rather than learning the lesson and showing kindness and love to Irene, she is complicating things by repeating past mistakes. Such scenarios happen often. It often can take several lifetimes to learn our lessons, and in the process we inevitably add to our karma until the lesson is finally learned.

What is also interesting to see is that Irene and Raul in their present life hold no grudge against Gilda. Instead, they seem to show an unusual tolerance given the circumstances. This indicates several things. First, that Irene and Raul have forgiven Gilda for her offenses. This is an indication that the love between them is true, and that it can weather challenges that arise. It also tells us that the three of them have ties that go beyond what happened in the past life when Gilda was a princess. After all, Gilda and Irene were originally very good friends. Ultimately, they will be again.

So how does this story end? Coming back to the present life, one day Irene met a man. The two fell in love and married. Raul was delighted but Gilda

good karma, or both. Karma can go either way, parent owing karma to child, child owing to parent, or a combination. There can be an exchange of roles. In one life you may be the parent, and in another life you may be the child. Either way, you will continue to reincarnate together until the karma is resolved.

Being a parent is one of the most sacred duties a soul can perform. It is a microcosm of the relationship you have with God as your parent. The ability to procreate is one of the highest spiritual privileges. If there is difficulty in this aspect of your life, it can be an indication that there is some type of karma related to bearing children.

The spiritual purpose of parents is to usher in new souls to Earth. By bearing children, you are giving other souls the opportunity to pay their karma and learn their lessons. In turn, the soul coming in as the child is putting their trust in the parents.

Parents have a great responsibility in raising children. Many new parents feel helpless in the role as parent and feel they do not know how to properly care for a child. While it's true that there are many logistical things to learn in raising children, what makes a good parent is the same lesson underlying every relationship—love. A parent has many duties to perform, but the most essential is to love his or her child.

What happens if you mistreat your children? You create some of your heaviest karma. It is imperative to do the best job you can as a parent. You are held karmically responsible for the actions you take in the way you raise your children. It's not about perfection. God understands we make mistakes. It's about your motives and intent in your relationship to your children.

Where does your responsibility begin and end as a parent? You are responsible for your children in the sense that it's your job to help in the development of the soul that inhabits the child's body until it is capable of being responsible for itself. Ultimately, you are responsible for your own soul and no one else's, be it family or friends, but until the child has fully developed, it needs the support of the parent.

This developmental process can best be described in terms of the aura. There are three distinct phases in the spiritual development of the child. The first seven years are crucial. Within those years, the soul in the child's body is still developing and engaging its auric field, especially its mental and emotional powers. At this point, the child is very impressionable. By seven, the basic aura is set, which means the basic personality patterns are also set. It doesn't mean you can't change them, but after age seven it requires more effort.

By age twelve, the soul brings in more of its auric power, particularly the aspects of the aura related to its Higher Self. It is interesting that this moment coincides with the child's entry into puberty. Then the soul goes through yet one more developmental stage when it brings in all of its spiritual power. The aura is fully engaged by around sixteen years old. It is at this point that the child is now an adult in the metaphysical sense. It is now responsible for its own actions and will bear its karmic responsibility.

During the formative years, the developing soul needs the support and guidance of the parents. Here is where you need to show all the love and care that you can for your children. Let them know you're there for them. Instill in them a strong moral character. I don't mean a particular religion necessarily, but good basic morals. Make sure you are a living example of the principles you are instilling. The example you set will have far more impact on your child than any words.

Children need to express their desires and wants yet respect decisions made on their behalf by their parents. At the same time, in making decisions for their children, parents need to recognize the unique qualities and characteristics of the child and nurture them, rather than try to force the child to their own way of thinking. The goal is to teach them to become independent.

From the spiritual point of view, the parental responsibility for the child ends once the soul has fully engaged in its spiritual power. At that point, the official role of parent is essentially over, and the young adult needs to start making his or her own decisions. This does not mean that the karma with the child and parent is necessarily over. Depending on the situation, that karma can continue, but the roles are different. The child still honors and respects the parent, but the responsibility to make decisions for the child has come to an end.

Of course, our relationship with our children continues for the rest of our lives. Many times, an even deeper friendship can develop in later years. But parents need to be careful not to interfere in the lives of their grown children. They should certainly be there to offer support and advice when needed, but parents need to respect the independence of the child. In the same way, the child needs to leave the nest and make his or her own life. Again this doesn't mean the parents are left out of the equation or that their advice or value is less. It means grown children need to stand on their own and forge their own way in life.

How does karma work from the point of view of the child? Do children create karma? Even though there is a full soul in a child's body, the full spiritual apparatus is not fully engaged until the child is sixteen. As a result, children do not create much karma, because they do not yet have full responsibility for their actions, except in extreme situations.

However, the child will strongly feel the effects of its past karma. The condition you find yourself in as a child has a strong bearing on the karma you have built up in past lives. For example, if you physically abused your body in your previous life, you may find yourself born into a weak or sickly body in this life. On the other hand, if you took good care of yourself in the life before, you will most likely be born into good health. The type of life you are born into is of your own making. The people, the conditions, for the most part, are karmic. As you grow, you begin to bear the mark of your own free will and can improve these conditions.

What about accidental pregnancies? Are they part of the divine plan? This is a sensitive issue, but I'll share what my spiritual teachers have shared with me. First, the ability to conceive a child always happens in cooperation with the divine. There is no such thing as a purely biological conception leading to the development and birth of a child without the spiritual dimensions being involved. In the normal course of events, the karmic decision as to who will be our children or parents is decided before we incarnate and is part of the divine plan for us.

Having said this, there are such things as accidental pregnancies. In accidental pregnancies, there is a spiritual fluidness connected with it. The spiritual energy leading to the pregnancy is in the ethers before the act of conception takes place. Once the Higher sees that this particular situation is leading to a physical conception, a decision is made quickly as to what soul will come through. Souls coming through these types of pregnancies are paying back certain karma, while the parents will need to adapt their spiritual path to accommodate the unexpected soul. The wonderful thing is the Higher compensates these situations very well, and many times you can alleviate other karma by becoming an unexpected parent.

What about the karma of grandparents? This can be a sign that at some point the role was as parent/child, especially if there is a close relationship. There can be karma in these relationships, but they are not as intense as with parent/child, and more often these souls have worked things out and have now taken on a less active role. The same holds true with aunts, uncles, nephews, and nieces.

Karma of Siblings

The karma of brothers and sisters is usually not as intense as the karma between parents and children, but it certainly comes into play, for better or for worse. Who your siblings are is no accident. This is all part of your karmic chart.

The spiritual lesson of brothers and sisters is to recognize that we are all brothers and sisters in light. We are all children of God and need to respect one another in that way. The tests and trials in being a brother or sister prepare us for other interactions we will have as we grow up.

It is a great blessing to have good karma with your siblings. This is most often a sign that you have earned that relationship in past lives and now come to enjoy that good relationship and support in this present life. Yet it's all too common among siblings for there to be rivalry, jealousy, even a love/hate relationship. Again this can be a sign of a karmic condition returning.

The bottom line with siblings is to show love and patience. You may not always see eye to eye, but do your best to be there for your brothers and sisters and honor the relationship.

HUSBAND/WIFE KARMA

There can definitely be a strong karmic element between husband and wife. You will most likely be drawn to a particular person and marry that person because of a karmic tie. Often what we think of as romantic love is really a tool to learn and grow. This is why sometimes when we try to make someone fall in love and marry us we fail, because we are not meant to be with that person from the karmic point of view.

As with all aspects of spiritual growth, what becomes paramount in a marriage are the lessons you learn as well as how, together, you serve the divine plan. Look at how you are perfecting yourself in that relationship rather than looking for the perfect relationship. Are you handling that relationship in the best possible way? Are you kind and giving? Or is your love overly selfish?

One of the biggest decisions we make in life is who to marry. Some people recognize the one they will marry very quickly, while for others it's not always easy to recognize the right person. There are times when we miss the boat and marry the wrong person altogether. Many times, these marriages don't last, but sometimes they do, and the karmic chart of each person has to accommodate the new situation. However, you will still have to return in a future life to marry the person you were originally meant to be with.

What kind of karma brings two people together in marriage? The institution of marriage is sacred. In today's world, we tend to think of marriage more as a civil and legal commitment, but it is first and foremost a spiritual union. There is a wonderful connection of two auras between people who marry in love. Each partner brings his or her own strengths to the relationship. It mirrors the dynamic/magnetic attributes of God and life itself.

Perhaps what frightens some people when it comes to marriage is that when you marry, you take on an aspect of the other person's karma. Now what does this mean? This means that you will share in the karmic conditions of your spouse. In marriage, both individuals bear the good and the bad of what is in the destiny of their partner. If your spouse has money karma, or job karma, or family karma, you will share in that experience.

Why is this so? It comes back to love. You do this out of love for the other person. Your willingness to sacrifice and be supportive of your spouse is an act of Divine Love. This is why a good marriage can teach us so much about love. Of course, this doesn't mean if your spouse wants to rob a bank that you should join in. You're still accountable for your personal actions.

It is truly tragic that too many marriages are not happy. Sometimes this is the result of past karma coming full circle, sometimes it is not. There are no simple answers. You must evaluate the situation on its own terms.

If you are in a difficult situation with your spouse, do your best to turn things around. If you have done your best and the situation is still hostile or has moved into a physically abusive relationship, then you have to leave. No one has the right to abuse another, no matter what the karma is. Two wrongs do not make a right. These are unfortunate situations where you may have to leave a relationship when it becomes unbearable, leaving the karma unresolved. In these situations, you will come back in a future lifetime to fully resolve what was left undone. This is why it's so important to do your best to work things out.

The truth is, many people today divorce too quickly. They bail out of the marriage at the first sign of conflict, and if there is karma involved, it delays the resolution of that karma. However, there are times when the divorce can be karmic. It is possible that you are not meant to be with the same person your whole life or you are meant to marry more than one person in a single life. This is something you must search out very carefully in your own heart.

PROFESSIONAL KARMA

Yes, karma extends to the workplace. That difficult boss or employee, that jealous colleague can all be part of your karmic path. To understand your karma in this area, you want to observe how well you get along with others at your job. You don't have to be lovey-dovey with everyone, but it's important that there is harmony with those you are professionally engaged with. Love must be here, too.

As with other types of relationship karmas, you have known key people in your professional life before. If you have a business partner whom you get along with very well, or if you have been blessed with some type of creative alliance that is producing wonderful works of art, you can bet that you have worked with these people before in a successful way. You came back again to build on that success. If you have constant difficulty with people at work, particularly a boss or employer, this can indicate that you are paying back professional karma. Perhaps you were the difficult boss in a previous life, and now you are back to feel what it's like to work for a difficult boss.

The same karmic dynamics apply to professional relationships as apply to other types of relationships. The only real difference is that whereas with family karma you will definitely reincarnate with the same people to work things out, with professional karma it's pretty hard to bring together all the same souls, so usually you will be faced with the karmic condition you need to learn from, but not necessarily the same people.

For example, if you were in a position of authority and denied a person a particular promotion they deserved and you regretted that action, you will come back in another life in a position of authority and complete that task, but not necessarily with the same person. The exception here is if the karma was particularly offensive, in which case you will have to return with that person.

In your work life, you are performing a service. Professional relationships are part of that service. If you are an employee, you are serving God by serving your boss or superior. There is nothing wrong with that. It doesn't mean you are less of a person. By learning how to serve your employer, you are learning how to serve God. Trouble in this area can be a sign that you are letting your ego get in the way of performing your job well.

What if you have a difficult boss? Do your best to show the same respect regardless of what they are showing you. Sometimes, little things help a lot. Years ago, I was working in an insurance company. I had a very difficult boss.

She was very critical and constantly bickering with and belittling me. I could see in her aura a mean person with cocoa brown, gray, and avocado green in her aura. Naturally, she was disliked by everyone in the department.

One day, it came to me to do something to try to soften her up, so I put a white rose on her desk. When she saw the rose, she said, "Who the hell put this on my desk?!" I said, "I did." She didn't say anything after that, but guess what? Things got a lot better, much to everyone's surprise.

If you are an employer, you must recognize that your employees are not underlings there to service you. They are there to service the role of leadership that God has placed you in. If you have difficulties with employees, look to how you are treating them.

In terms of colleagues, recognize that you are not the only one who's interested in the career you're pursuing. It may be your passion to be an excellent lawyer or a businessperson, yet there are others who have similar passions. Some of those people will be further along than you in fulfilling this goal, while others will not be as far along as you. Either way, you need to be as cooperative as you can and try not to compare yourself with others.

If you see someone excel in the professional world, admire and emulate them. They are a teacher showing you what you are capable of. Refuse to become jealous, suspicious, or vindictive. While it's true that some do get ahead by lying and cheating, most often, people who progress professionally have earned that right. And for those who haven't, their day will come.

Having said this, a certain amount of competition is good in the workplace as it keeps you challenged. If there is no one to test you or spur you on, it's too easy to become smug, lazy, or distracted.

THE KARMA OF FRIENDS

It is said that a person rich in friends has the greatest riches of all. With friends, there is no necessity to be together other than a mutual affinity and desire to be friends.

Is there a karma that brings people together as friends? Naturally, we do not have karma with everyone we meet and become friendly with. Part of the idea of friendship is to meet new people and make new alliances. Yet when we meet someone who becomes a true friend, most likely we have known that person before. This is good karma coming back to us to offer support and joy in our spiritual journey.

The past life experiences that bring people together as friends are varied. Many times, our friends have been family members in the past whom we've had a close and lasting association with. Other times, they may be people we've worked with or gone through intense experiences with.

It takes lifetimes to develop deep and lasting friendships. Because of this, the hurt can run very deep when a good friend mistreats us. We have to be especially forgiving in these situations. A friend is precious and we don't want to throw friendships away carelessly.

Some people say they have no friends, but generally this is not true. What has happened is they close off associations, whether out of fear, anger, or resentment. Real friendship takes time to build. What we call fair-weather friends are really those we haven't yet built a lasting association with.

Keep developing this part of yourself. Friendships are one of the greatest expressions of love and are a key indication that you are in your action of expressing Divine Love. As Ralph Waldo Emerson said, "A friend might well be reckoned the masterpiece of nature."

ADVERSARIAL KARMA

We have all had the experience of knowing someone who acted as an enemy. Are such people karmic or are they just people doing bad things? And how do we love such difficult souls?

As with all aspects of karma, not every relationship is karmic. If someone is causing you trouble, this is not automatically a sign of karma. If the conflict is happening on a more impersonal level, chances are this is not karmic. But if this is someone who knows you, perhaps well, or someone who keeps returning to your life, this can be a strong indication of karma. In these situations, there is an unresolved issue between the two of you that is playing itself out.

The truth is, there really are no such things as enemies. We are all children of God. Certainly there are those who wish to cause harm, and we have the right to protect ourselves, yet the same law of love comes into the picture. It can be one of our greatest tests to show love to those we feel are enemies. If you find you are not quite up to the task of loving enemies, ask God to love them for you.

THE KARMA OF ROMANCE

Romantic exchanges can certainly be enthralling and exciting. Yet even here there can be karma!

Dating and romance are part of the spiritual experience. The spiritual lesson of romance is the exchange of energy with others on an intimate level and learning how to open up to others. The fear many people face in having a healthy romantic life is the very lesson they are meant to learn. Some do not know how to open up to others, and this can create romantic karma. This is why it's so easy to get hurt in a relationship; you are opening your heart to the other person. So there are lessons for the one hurting and lessons for the one being hurt.

If you make mistakes in a romantic relationship and hurt someone else, you will have to come back in a future life to work things out with that person, usually in a similar romantic situation. Some people feel unlucky in love, and this can most definitely be karmic. Perhaps that person may have been careless in romance, a Don Juan in a past life, and now is on the receiving end in this present life.

In the arc of our many lives on Earth, we have all had wonderful romantic experiences, but this does not mean we are meant to experience this *every* time we come to Earth. Sometimes, it's not in our destiny or karma to find the love of our life; there are other things we are meant to accomplish. If you deeply desire romantic love and cannot seem to find someone, it may mean you dissipated that energy in another life and are feeling that missing energy.

Through your longing and desire you are generating more power that will eventually find consummation whether in this life or a future life.

An interesting question is: What if you are ready for a mature romantic exchange, but the person you are meant to be with is not ready or has walked in another direction? Perhaps this is the person you are meant to marry and have children with. Unfortunately, this is not an uncommon occurrence. You may be doing everything you're meant to do, but your partner isn't. In these situations, the Higher has to compensate. If it's clear the person you're meant to be with is not going to cooperate for whatever reason, the divine will bring another wonderful person for you to be with. Nothing is lost. In a future life, you will meet with the original person you were meant to be with to fulfill that part of your destiny.

RELATIONSHIP KARMA REVIEW

Identify key people in your life and briefly evaluate your experiences
   with them.

Evaluate your attitude toward them and their attitude toward you.

Are you a difficult person to get along with, or are you more easygoing?

Do you make friends easily or are you more of a loner?

How loving are you with others?

Do you give of yourself in a relationship or are you more reserved?

What relationships stand out the most for better or worse?

How would you evaluate the different areas of relationships, such as
   work, romantic, and friends?

What kind of family were you born into or did you grow up in?

Was it a happy life, supportive or difficult?

Have you created a family of your own? If not, do you want one?

What are the dynamics like with your spouse and children?

Have you been married more than once? How has that experience
   affected you?

Chapter 6

THE KARMA OF CAREER

When I was nineteen, I began producing variety shows in Southern California. It was in the days when television was just beginning to blossom and vaudeville was coming to an end. My younger brother was an actor and worked periodically. Through him, I came to know many of his performer friends. They were young and aspiring yet would constantly complain that they were not getting anywhere in their careers.

After a while, I tired of listening to their complaints. I could see the talent in their auras, so I said let's put on our own show. With the various types of artists I had encountered, it seemed like putting on a variety show was the best idea. To my surprise, we were an immediate success! Our show had comedy and singing and dancing acts, and we were well received wherever we went. Within two years, we had built up the show to involve more than three hundred people and attracted young performers like Red Skelton and Mona Freeman.

One day I was approached by the program director of the Flamingo Hotel, who wanted to take our show to Las Vegas. At that time, Las Vegas was just building its entertainment attractions and was looking for new acts. This was a perfect time to get involved. So there I was, at just twenty-one years old, being offered a lucrative contract to produce variety shows!

I was ready to take the job when I received the inspiration from my spiritual teachers not to take the offer. They told me that entertainment was not what I was meant to do with my life. I was destined to become a spiritual teacher. Of course, I recognized the truth in what the Holy Ones were telling me, yet I felt disappointed as I was having a lot of fun and would have done very well financially. The troupe was bewildered and certainly did not understand the true reasons for my declining the offer.

Yet that turned out to be the best decision of my life. With a commitment to follow my spiritual path, I began an incredible period of training. The teachers came closer to me than ever before and taught me how to use the spiritual gifts I was blessed with in ways I could not have imagined. I was taken to various dimensions in the spirit world and shown the inner workings of life, so that I could teach from firsthand experience. For all there was to learn, I spent the next ten years in intensive training before I was ready to begin my professional life as a metaphysical teacher.

I tell you this story because everyone has a destiny when it comes to career. We dedicate time and energy to deciding what the best career is for us. We may go to school for many years to develop the skills to be successful. Then we spend years at the job getting better at what we do. Yet behind all the activities of pursuing a career, there is a miraculous spiritual process going on.

You are ideally suited for work you are meant to contribute in God's divine plan. Throughout your many lives on Earth, you will engage in many types of careers in order to be well-rounded. You may be a baker in one life, a soldier in another life, an artist in yet another life, and so on. This is by divine design so you receive a varied and rich spiritual education on Earth. Yet through all these jobs and experiences, you will be slowly developing an overriding talent or ability that will eventually become your signature, your mark. When this mark is seen in others in any field of endeavor, we revel in it. Yet what we're really seeing is what we will one day do in our own way. We are all marked for excellence.

The Spiritual Purpose of a Career

We all know how important a career is. A career offers us the opportunity to support ourselves and be self-sufficient. Having a job and being responsible for ourselves gives us a sense of self-worth and personal value. There is great satisfaction in being good at what we do and being fairly compensated for our labors and talents.

The spiritual purpose of a career is to develop your innate skills and play your unique part in the divine scheme of life. In doing so, you are fulfilling a plan that was set in motion before you were born. It doesn't matter where you are in the plan at this time; this is your destiny. This unique contribution exists on all levels of life. From my experience working with celestial beings, I am amazed at how skilled and specialized they are. There are angels of business, angels of healing, angels of peace, angels of music, angels of love, and so on. In other words, these highly developed beings have honed their unique skills through aeons of evolution. You are in the process of doing the same thing.

Your career karma reflects how well you fulfill your career purpose through the expression of free will. If you work hard and stay focused, naturally you progress and reap the good karma of such actions. If you're lazy and procrastinate or lie and cheat to get ahead, or become jealous or destructive in matters of career, there is a karmic price to pay for sure.

The lessons behind all career missteps are the same: Honor and respect the divine gifts and talents in yourself and others. Encourage yourself and others in the unfoldment of these gifts. Refuse to be jealous as all are gifted in one way or another. Strive for excellence in all you do. Be patient and persistent as it takes many lifetimes to fully develop your career potential. Someone who comes into life seemly having it all has certainly earned that right through many lifetimes of work and struggle. Yet as talented as you may be, refuse to sit on your laurels as there are always greater heights to scale.

When it comes to career karma, there is a wide spectrum of activity. Some people are very successful at their work, while others are not. Some know exactly what they want to do in life from a very early age, while others struggle for years. There are those who have exciting careers while many others seem to have simple, uneventful jobs. Some display extraordinary talent in their careers while others show very little. All this variety is part of the drama of our unfolding spiritual powers.

UNDERSTANDING YOUR CAREER PATH

In my counseling work, I am often confronted with people who are confused when it comes to their career. They are not sure that they are in the right career, they are unhappy in their present career and wish to change, or they feel clueless as to what career path they are meant to take.

Confusion is the sign of a spiritual lesson. If you're ideally suited for your life's work but you feel disconnected and uncertain as to your career, then there's something interfering with your connection. There could be many reasons for this confusion: You do not believe in yourself enough, you have diverted your attention from where you should be taking your career, you have taken the easy way out and not fulfilled all you are capable of in your career, or you have simply not put in the necessary effort to succeed. You may have picked a career for the wrong reasons and not looked at how fulfilling this work would be for you, or perhaps you faced a tragedy or adversity that interfered with your rightful path. Whatever the reason, the end result is dissatisfaction in the workplace.

A big reason there can be confusion in regard to career is karma. A certain amount of uncertainty when embarking on a career is normal, but when having difficulty deciding on a career becomes a real issue, often this is an indication that the soul did not fulfill its career task in a previous life and is feeling the karmic effects in its present life.

For example, say you are meant to excel in the world of business. You are born into a good family and given every opportunity to succeed. However, instead of recognizing the privileged position you are in—a privilege you earned from your own good karma—you become cocky or lazy, you squander away your life pursuing personal pleasures, and you never really apply your talents or reach your potential. You end your life in frustration, with many regrets.

What happens karmically? You come back to do it again. You reincarnate to fulfill the career path you were meant to fulfill. Life must balance out. But things will be tougher for you this time. If in your last life you did not honor and respect the career path laid out for you, you will have to develop that in this life through struggle. In your next life, you may find yourself in a home life with few opportunities. You may have to work at menial jobs from a very early age and not be given the educational opportunities needed to excel. There can be many years of struggling to awaken the soul to the true value of work.

Yet even in the midst of this challenge, God will give opportunities. Perhaps good people will be brought into your life who will encourage you along the way. Through your struggles you reignite the desire to do better, to do something with your life. Eventually as you burn out the old karma, a career opportunity will present itself and you will be given the chance to fulfill the career destiny that was yours from the beginning.

Naturally, there are countless variations to this scenario, yet the theme remains the same: one way or the other, you must finish the task God has laid out for you.

What about souls who choose the wrong profession altogether? What karma do they reap? It depends on the reasons for picking the wrong profession, but again, the karma must be balanced. For example, if you were meant to be a doctor but somehow went in another direction even though opportunity was there, you will come back in another incarnation with a *burning* desire to go into medicine, but the conditions to reach that goal will be more difficult.

Taking the flip side of this scenario, if you became a doctor for the wrong reasons and you were meant to become an esteemed professor of biology teaching young souls the mysteries of the human body, you will return to do the teaching work, but again it's going to be more difficult. You may work in the inner city with very difficult and unappreciative students. You may have to deal with a lot of administrative and government entanglements. Yet even here there will be opportunity as your very presence in those difficult conditions will help to make conditions better.

Your achievements in this life carry over into the next life—as do your failures. If you don't make it happen in this life, you have to do it again. So the key is, if you're not happy with what you're doing, you need to do something about it. You're never stuck indefinitely in an unhappy job.

If you find yourself confused as to your career path, work through the confusion. Your talent and desire are still there even though they may be camouflaged. As you work on the task, the desire will ignite. Even though your talents may not jump out at you at first, they are there and you must search them out until you find them.

A Reincarnation Story of Joseph

In this true story, the Higher illustrates the dynamics of career karma. In viewing the Book of Life for Joseph, we see an incarnation where he was born in Alaska, near Anchorage. He was an only child of good and loving parents. His father was a tailor and, while not wealthy, was able to care for his family. In this life, Joseph showed a talent for singing, which his parents encouraged. He grew to be a good baritone. He joined a traveling opera troupe and performed throughout the continental United States. He became popular but did not reach star status. He was a solid type of person, didn't have a big ego, and spent his life pursing his career.

In this life, Joseph completed his career destiny. He followed the path of music and developed his talents as far as he could. He was also willing to live a modest life financially to pursue his art, which spoke well of him. Interestingly, Joseph was actually very good in business; had he chosen a more lucrative line of work, he would have been a financial success. Yet somewhere in his heart, he knew that music was his path, and he refused to sell himself short.

This earned him very good karma. In his next life, we find him in Italy in the early 1900s. He was born in Rome, the youngest of three children. His father was a successful doctor and provided well for his family. In this life, Joseph was given the opportunity to reap some of the good karma earned in his previous life. He was drawn to the world of business and became a clothing merchant. He did not marry, but he became very successful in his trade. As time went on, he became one of Rome's outstanding citizens. He was philanthropic and was involved with many charities.

In this Italian incarnation, Joseph developed another facet to his career path. In his previous life in the United States as a singer, he developed his singing talents and a dedication to his art; in Italy, Joseph developed his business skills.

Today, Joseph is a young child. In this new incarnation, it is his destiny to once again return to his singing talent, but this time it will be his destiny to become renowned on the world stage of opera. We wish him well!

TALENT—ACCUMULATING GOOD CAREER KARMA

Confucius said, "In all things success depends on previous preparations; without such preparation there is failure." The truth is, it takes *many* lifetimes to fully develop your career potential. It can't all be accomplished in a single lifetime.

This brings us to the question of talent. Why does one soul come in with so much talent in a particular field while others do not exhibit that same talent? Why do we call some people geniuses? Science has tried to pinpoint the gift of talent in the brain, to no avail. Talent is a spiritual trait. It is the ability to tap into the creative wellspring of life as the result of many lifetimes of accumulated development.

We marvel at the musical talent of Mozart. What we do not see are the series of lives that Mozart spent developing his gifts. He could easily have spent a dozen *consecutive* lifetimes building his musical talents before incarnating as Mozart. Yet as great as this accomplishment was, his greatest accomplishment was his dedication to utilizing his gifts in his incarnation as Mozart and taking them to greater heights. This is what resulted in the extraordinary music he produced. Had he relied only on past life accomplishments, he would have become a mere footnote in musical history. And this is the lesson for us: We are all meant to take our skills and talents and develop them further, eventually to the level of greatness.

Regardless of your achievements, refuse to sit on your laurels. Great achievement spurs you on to even greater heights. Many years ago my sister and I were traveling through Louisiana. We befriended an older woman, Sophia, who invited us to her house for lunch. My sister and I drove to the address Sophia gave us and found ourselves in one of the most exclusive neighborhoods outside New Orleans. We drove up to a magnificent mansion. As the woman had seemed very modest, we thought perhaps she worked for the people who lived in this house, but on entry we discovered it was hers! She was very gracious, and it wasn't long before she told us her story.

It turned out that Sophia was born and raised not far from there, and she was born to some considerable wealth and position. When she came of age, her parents wished her to marry someone of a similar social and financial status, and had a big coming-out party. There was one particular eligible bachelor they were hoping she would like and want to marry. He, too, had wealth and position, and the parents felt this was a good match. Sophia met the man but felt nothing for him and showed no interest.

It turned out there was an electrical short with one of the lights. Sophia's mother said, "Why don't you call that handyman John down the street to come over and fix it." So John came over, and Sophia took one look at him and said to her father, "He's the one I want." Her father said, "John? But he doesn't have two nickels to rub together. He lives in a basement." Sophia didn't care and insisted, so the two were introduced. It turned out there was quite a romantic chemistry and soon they were married.

Without any hesitation, Sophia moved into the basement with John and wanted to make a go of it without her parents' help. At that time, baseball was just beginning to explode as a national pastime. John opened a little peanut concession stand. One stand became two, two became four, and before long, John became a wealthy man on his own. So by following her destiny, Sophia became wealthy anyway, *and* she found the love of her life.

As we develop our talents, the divine can use us to make great contributions to humanity by bringing forth inventions, artistic achievements, and discoveries to the world. Albert Einstein is a well-known and wonderful example. Here is a soul who clearly earned excellent karma in the field of science. He was chosen by the Higher to bring forth the scientific breakthroughs he brought to the world. When it was time for humanity to receive this awareness, Einstein was the chosen vessel. The beauty is we shall all have our turn in making exceptional contributions to humanity.

A Reincarnation Story of Exceptional Talent

In this incarnation from the Book of Life, the Higher is sharing the story of the famous Russian novelist Fyodor Dostoevsky. Dostoevsky is considered one of the great novelists of all time. While he wrote about Russia and Russian themes, the influence of his writing went far beyond national borders, which indicates that his contribution stepped into the arena of collective or world karma.

Dostoevsky was born in Moscow in 1821, one of seven children. His father was a doctor. His mother died when he was sixteen, at which time his father became increasingly tyrannical and was constantly drunk, lecherous, and cruel. Dostoevsky served some time in the army, where he developed a bad gambling habit that would plague him for the rest of his life. After leaving the army, he had his first literary success, a novel called *Poor Folk*. In those days, novels were serialized. Every week a new chapter would be printed. People looked forward to a new installment as today people look forward to a new episode of a favorite television show.

When he was twenty-nine, Dostoevsky was arrested for being part of a young socialist group. He was sentenced to death, but, literally at the last minute, just before the execution was carried out, his sentence was commuted to prison and exile in Siberia. He went through four very difficult years living in the worst of conditions and in the constant company of murderers, robbers, and other criminals. Yet through this time, he saw a completely different side of humanity, which was to provide much inspiration for future novels.

Eventually, Dostoevsky was pardoned by the tsar. He went to St. Petersburg and resumed his literary career, but his ordeal had left its mark on him. A latent childhood epilepsy now returned with violent attacks. His passion for gambling increased, and he was faced with constant poverty. Still, in spite of his difficulties, he continued to write.

At forty-five, Dostoevsky hit a critical juncture in his life. His problems and ill health had caught up with him. He found himself facing possible ruin and prison—this time for debt. His only way out was to finish a new novel he was working on, but he had delayed for so long, and the deadline was so close, it looked like he would not make it.

At that point, a young woman, Anna, only eighteen years old, came to the rescue. He dictated the novel to her and finished it just in time. The two ended up marrying. She became his constant support, always seeing the best in him, even though he could be the most disagreeable person. Anna was by his side unconditionally, despite his gambling, infidelities, and troubles. During their marriage, Dostoevsky completed some of his most important contributions to world literature, including *Crime and Punishment*, *The Idiot*, *The Possessed*, and *The Brothers Karamazov*. It is said that without Anna, there would have been no Dostoevsky as the great literary artist. He died at age sixty, leaving a legacy that influenced literature, art, and philosophy for generations to come.

So what was in his karmic chart that permitted him to create such enduring works of art? In this study, we will focus on the career and talent aspect of his life, rather than on some of the other complexities.

Although Dostoevsky had many unsavory traits, he was a spiritually developed soul; but he was caught in some negative spirals of activities that almost caused him to miss his life's purpose altogether. Fortunately, with help and despite the many obstacles, many of which were self-created, he managed to more or less complete his life's purpose, albeit with some new karmas he will have to work out in another lifetime.

Dostoevsky was chosen by the divine to help raise the level of literary art and give civilization a more mature understanding of human nature.

Dostoevsky's intense emphasis on the darkest side of human nature was supposed to be tempered with a more mature understanding of the good in human nature. Although this was not quite achieved, he still managed to make the impact he was meant to make.

In looking at Dostoevsky's past lives, we find him in England in the Middle Ages. He is the king of England. He was a good king during a tough time, and he handled those tough times well. Other countries were at war with England and he tried very hard to bring those struggles to rest. Eventually he succeeded in bringing peace. He married and had a happy marriage. Interestingly, he showed literary skills in that life as well, even though he did not pursue them. He accrued much good karma in this lifetime. This is an example of good collective karma, and while it was leadership karma, it gave him the karmic power he needed for the scope of his artistic achievement as Dostoevsky.

Two lifetimes before being born as Dostoevsky, he was born in Germany. Then, too, he was a writer, though not very successful. This was not for lack of talent, but was rather because he wrote stories that were not of interest to others. At the time, romance was in fashion and he liked to write more complex, adventurous stories. His stories were well-written and eventually he garnered some success. Yet at the end of his life, he felt unfulfilled and had a burning desire to do more. This lifetime provided him with the driving ambition to be successful that he later would need.

In addition to this life, there were three other incarnations where he developed his skills as a writer. One life that particularly stood out was an early incarnation in Italy, where Dostoevsky was a very successful poet.

All in all, we see that it took several lifetimes to build the talents, skills, and good karma that culminated in the lifetime as Fyodor Dostoevsky.

ABUSING CAREER PRIVILEGES

What about people who do terrible things in the name of a career? It's one thing for there to be a healthy competition between people. Healthy competition can bring out the best in people. Yet there are too many misguided souls who lie, cheat, steal, or are abusive at their jobs. What karma do they reap? What karma accrues to souls who ascend to high positions, but use their influence and power to further their greedy ambitions and engage in activities such as war profiteering?

If you lie or cheat to get ahead in the workplace, you will have to pay back every false step you took—especially if you deny someone else what they were destined to have. These people don't realize that they cannot take what is not theirs, what they have not earned through effort. Yes, they may seize the opportunity for a time, but that time will pass and they will have to retrace and correct the missteps they took.

In extreme cases where souls are willing to let people suffer or even die for personal gain and profit, they pay a heavy karmic price to be sure. Let us put aside the tremendous personal karma that is accrued through such actions and put our attention on the career karma. The soul of a president of a corporation has earned that position through good karma. That person spent lifetimes building the gift to be a leader in business. But as can happen, such a soul can become seduced by the power invested and greed sets in.

For these souls, it takes *several* incarnations to recognize the error and burn out the desire for greed. They may have to work in a sweatshop for twelve cents a day or face starvation and live in the worst of conditions. Opportunities won't just pop up for them. They will have to rebuild them all over again. The career destiny will still be there, but the journey will be delayed and much tougher as there will be inevitable backsliding until the soul finally wakes up and reclaims the divine path that was laid out for them all along.

What about simply not fulfilling your career destiny? What happens when you do not fulfill your career destiny and express the talents you have? Again, you have to come back and complete the job.

A Reincarnation Story of Judith

Let us take a true reincarnation story, from the Book of Life of Judith, to see what happens when someone does not fulfill her career potential. Judith was born to a good family in a town just outside Florence, Italy, in the early

1800s. Her father was a successful architect, and her three older brothers liked to spoil her.

She was a pretty girl, outgoing and fun. From a very early age, Judith showed an exceptional talent for music and singing. Her family recognized her talents and encouraged her. She received the best education and went to a music conservatory to study voice. She developed into a fine soprano and began a promising career in the world of opera.

When Judith turned thirty-one, she developed a respiratory illness. It became so severe that she had to stop singing. She was sick for five years, and bedridden for most of that time.

When she was thirty-six, her illness finally subsided. Her family, friends, and colleagues urged her to return to opera and resume her career. Unfortunately, Judith was so discouraged and defeated by this experience that she decided not to pursue singing anymore. There was still time to resume her career and enjoy success, but her heart wasn't in it. It wasn't a matter of pride as much as it was simply feeling defeated. Instead she married a very good man, who provided well for her. Although he continued to urge her to take up singing again, she never sang again professionally.

When she was in her fifties, she developed pneumonia. As she lay on her deathbed, she realized her mistake. She recognized that she had let the challenges of life get the better of her and regretted not starting her career again. She saw that tough times happen, but you have to keep going and not give up. She finished that incarnation with a strong regret but also a strong desire to sing once more.

What kind of a life will Judith face in another incarnation? What kind of karma will she reap? As we turn the page on her Book of Life, we find her born in Paris in the early 1900s. She was again a woman. Her parents were poor and she had one older brother. There was love in the family, but there was much financial struggle. Her dad was a machinist and did not make much money.

She brought into this incarnation an intense desire to sing and dance. Her talents were good but not at the level she was at in her previous incarnation. This reveals to us a very important lesson regarding talent: You must nurture and express your talents and gifts, otherwise they can fade. This is what we find with Judith. In her French incarnation, she had to not only rebuild her artistic career but also put more energy into it, since some of her talent had dissipated from lack of use.

Judith's saving grace was her determination. Even though she had no memory of her last life on Earth, somewhere in her consciousness she remembered the lost opportunity and was determined not to let that happen again no matter what.

Her parents were supportive of her and managed to scrape together enough money for her to take singing and dancing lessons. She eventually became a popular singer in various Parisian clubs. She lived the bohemian lifestyle but was smart enough not to get caught up in the indulgences of that lifestyle.

Slowly, and with great care, she built her career and talent. She never married, but became famous in France for her singing and was happy with her life. Karmically, she resolved the debt owed from her last life. She lived to age sixty-two, dying when she was shot by a deranged admirer.

Here is a case where the soul heeds the call of its destiny and works through difficult times admirably. Judith is currently on the other side. It's her destiny to fully complete this aspect of her career path, and in her next life she will become a world-famous opera singer.

Love the Work You Do

Sometimes, you find yourself in situations where you have little choice when it comes to career. Despite your best efforts to rise above the conditions around you, your circumstances seem to keep you in a challenging and difficult place. What is the karma here and how is this karma resolved? What happens if you are born poor with little or no job opportunities? What if you had to drop out of school because you had to work? What if you're living in a part of the world where you're lucky to have work at all? How do you fulfill a career potential in these situations? Is there still hope or are you stuck living out a life of "quiet desperation," never accomplishing much?

If you find yourself in a situation where there is no opportunity to progress in your work because of conditions beyond your control, but you have made every effort to succeed, then positive karma is created. Your opportunity will amply come to you at some point down the line. We have all been through these types of lifetimes as the experiences they present are part of the growing process.

Since it takes more than one lifetime to build your full career potential, clearly there will be times when you find yourself in simple day-to-day work—lunch-box-Johnny jobs, I call them. This is part of your career development. In these situations, you are gaining experience and learning a most important lesson: How you handle the journey to success becomes the key to your success.

The East Indians considered the integrity of actions so important they designed a whole discipline called karma yoga—the law of right action. There is a beautiful discourse known as the Vyadha-Gita, or "The Song of the Butcher." In this discourse, a monk seeking the answers to life receives great wisdom from a local butcher. After listening to the butcher's great wisdom, the ascetic asks, "Why, with all this wonderful wisdom, do you follow such an unclean trade?"

The butcher replies, "My son, there is nothing unclean in life. No duty is impure or low. It all depends on our mental attitude. The Lord has placed me in this position, I have tried to do my duty faithfully and without attachment, and all that I have gained has come through that."

Our attitude to our job is most important. While each of us has a career destiny, and we need to make plans for the future, we must live in the moment. No job is too small or menial. We all have our part to play. As Benjamin Franklin said, "Do not waste your life in doubts and fears; spend yourself on the work before you, well assured that the right performance of this hour's duties will be the preparation for the hours or ages to follow."

There is a time for us to be the bricklayer and a time for us to be the architect. Yet both the architect and the bricklayer must do a good job to build a strong building. Even if you are not in your ideal work, put your heart into what you do. The key to your success is how well you perform the task at hand.

Sometimes, it takes many jobs to get to the right one. There is a story of a man who tried his hand at just about every kind of job and failed every time. Fortunately, he had a wife who loved him very much and believed in him. One day, she saw an ad for auditions for a new play that was being produced. She thought he should try it; nothing else had worked, and maybe he'd have better luck as an actor. He went down to the auditions. As he was older than the other actors, the casting director didn't make an issue when he didn't have a résumé with him (he didn't have one!). As the story goes, he got the part and launched a successful acting career.

Failure doesn't always mean you're bad at something. It can mean you're not where you're meant to be. We will do many things in our life, some successful, others not so successful, but regardless of what we do professionally, we must keep our hearts and minds open to where we are meant to be. Failure urges us onward.

The truth is, despite the challenges of today's world, there are more opportunities to progress in your career path than ever before, and those opportunities will continue to grow. Not too long ago women were kept from working. Today, women are more educated and successful than ever before. We are coming out of a period where certain races have an automatic career advantage over other races. Today we see many nations of the world waking up to their economic potential. This is all part of the divine design for humanity.

CAREER KARMA REVIEW

Have you always known what you wanted to do in your career, or has this area been difficult?

Are you happy in the work you do?

Were you given the opportunity to develop your skills and education?

Are you clear in your career path? If so, are you clear in the steps you need to take to fulfill your career?

Do you get along with bosses, colleagues, and fellow workers, or is there friction at work?

What is your attitude toward work?

Chapter 7

The Karma of the Soul

One of the great mysteries of life is to understand the true nature of who and what we are. As Shakespeare wrote: "What a piece of work is man." Philosophers, psychologists, theologians, anthropologists, historians, behavioral scientists have probed deep into the human psyche. Artists have reflected various facets of human experience through their art. Human nature has been looked at from many angles, yet the ultimate truth of us still remains hidden.

As you solve the riddle of yourself, you are solving the riddle of life itself. As children of the divine, the inherent qualities of life within you gradually unfold through your experiences. The character and personality you express are the result of your innate qualities unfolding and the individual karma you have accrued through your spiritual pilgrimage. Soul karma is the result of your past actions that have brought you to the present moment. There is no clearer expression of free will than in the development of the soul.

Certain parts of everyone's nature are more developed than other parts. You may be kind but too passive, while another person may be outgoing but abrasive. These contradicting qualities are part of our developing soul.

You will keep reincarnating until you master these lessons. If your lesson is patience, for example, you will reincarnate until that lesson is learned; in the meantime, however, you will undoubtedly make mistakes for your lack of patience, which will have their own karmic effect.

Fortunately, you are always given the tools to strengthen and master your weaknesses. This is why it's so important to know what your strengths are. Most of us have more positive qualities than negative but can sometimes let the negative get the better of us, especially when we lose emotional control.

You will find yourself in situations that bring out your weaknesses as well as your strengths. Bless these situations as they reveal where you really are in your character. This is especially true for your faults. When someone or something brings out a weakness in you, that is a blessing as you can see that weakness for what it is and build from there.

QUALITIES OF THE SOUL

You are first and foremost a soul. A soul is a spark of life, a spark of God. Your soul is immortal and can never die. Your soul is not a blank slate. The soul has its own inborn traits, its strengths and weaknesses. More than anything else, this generates the dominant characteristics of your nature.

Many influences impress themselves upon the soul throughout its development. These influences are designed to help bring out the full power of the soul. In the process, they bring in their own set of strengths and weaknesses, depending on how well you are learning the lessons they present. The combination of your soul traits and these various influences creates your rich and varied character. You are truly a multifaceted being. These facets become interwoven with your soul karma. Before looking at how soul karma works, let's look at some of the influences on the soul.

Regardless of the soul's influences, your free will is the overriding force in developing your character. Just as you are never stuck with an aura the way it is, you are never stuck in a characteristic of your soul you recognize is less desirable. You can always strengthen and develop any weak areas in your nature. At the same time, you must be sure you are being true to your own nature and not trying to be someone you are not.

Here are some key spiritual influences in your life that affect the building of your character. They affect your soul karma. Depending on how you interact with these influences, they work for your betterment or sometimes they do not. Ultimately all these influences are designed to bring out your highest and most noble qualities.

These influences include:

Spirit qualities
Temperament
Dynamic/magnetic polarity
Environment (influence of events and people)
Genetics
Upbringing
Planetary influences

Spirit Qualities

Metaphysics teaches that each of us has a celestial counterpart called the Divine Spirit. It's the job of the Divine Spirit to nourish and help develop the soul. It's the spirit that's constantly encouraging the soul to aspire to greater spiritual heights.

Temperament

We may be born of the same God, but clearly we are not all of the same temperament. By nature, some of us are more outgoing, others are more artistic, and yet others more analytical, and so on. There is a fascinating spiritual study related to our temperament. The study is vast, but in relation to character, it basically states that there are seven spiritual temperaments. These seven temperaments are attributes of God designed to bring out the innate qualities of your soul. As you develop these temperaments, you strengthen your character. You are meant to develop all seven qualities, but one will be dominant.

When you are born into this life, your soul comes in on a particular temperament that you are meant to develop. These temperaments are represented by certain spiritual energies that stay with you your whole life. No temperament is better than another. All possess intrinsic attributes. Knowledge of the temperaments reveals something very important: You need to respect the differences in each of us as equally divine. Variety must be respected. This is very true for your children. A parent will come in on a certain temperament ray, but that does not mean the child will come in on the same ray. Parents have the job of raising their children to the best of their ability while respecting the unique character of their children and helping to bring out their special gifts and not try to fit them into the same mold they were cast in.

Dynamic/Magnetic Polarity

Gender brings out certain intrinsic qualities. One of the great tests has been to simply understand the psychology of the opposite sex. While the soul itself is androgynous, you will incarnate into a particular sex to experience that spiritual polarity. The male brings in certain dynamic qualities and the female brings in certain magnetic qualities. You are meant to balance the two forces, but depending on your sex, one will be dominant. This is by divine design to help you learn certain lessons.

These qualities in the aura are expressed through what is called the primary ray. This primary ray is constant throughout your life. For males, it is most always gold, indicating the dynamic nature they come in on. For females, it is most often pink, indicating the magnetic nature they come in on. Sometimes there can be a blue primary ray for either the male or the female and this is a tempering energy to help in the dynamic/magnetic expression. It is most important to honor and respect the male/female polarity as being equal. When these energies are unbalanced, it can create much havoc in our lives.

Environment

Environment can most certainly shape your character for better or worse. By environment, I don't just mean nature, but the influence of people and situations around you: your entire milieu. Whether you endure tragedies or are given great opportunities, your character is influenced by these experiences.

Genetics

It has been known for some time that genetics defines our physical attributes such as height, body type, looks, hair and eye color, sex, etc. What science is now realizing is that personality is also influenced by genetics. This is because the physiology of the body possesses a certain quality of expression that you have accrued based on how you treated your body in past lives. This is part of physical karma. As you experience life, you are meant to develop and improve on whatever genetic traits you have.

Upbringing

We know the importance of upbringing. The influences of your family and childhood you will invariably carry into adulthood. The key with upbringing is that in your youth, you are very impressionable. You don't yet have the defense mechanisms you have when you are an adult. Your consciousness is open, so events and people make deep impressions that will color your behavior. You need this openness in childhood so you can receive and process all the information needed to function in life. As a result of this openness, you will take on many of the characteristics of your parents and those around you. Patterns will be set, and this becomes a major contributor to your personality and character.

Planetary Influences

In today's thinking, one would not stop to think about the influence of the planets on our soul and character. That is delegated to the superstitions of astrology and horoscopes. In the ancient days, astronomy and astrology were considered part of the same study. Pythagoras included the study of the planets and stars as part of his metaphysical training, along with mathematics and music.

From the metaphysical point of view, the sun and all the planets in our solar system play a part in our life and evolution and therefore have a hand in the development of our soul. Just as we need to see the Earth as a living organism, we need to recognize the solar system as a living organism as well. We're not just children of the Earth; we are children of the solar system, which comprises the planets, and we are under its jurisdiction.

Each planet has its own spiritual attribute that influences us here on Earth. The soul comes into physical life on a certain planetary vibration that leaves a strong imprint on the soul at the moment of physical birth. This adds another dimension to the soul experience. As with all aspects of our expression in life, it's our free will that dictates how we will harness the planetary influences.

How Soul Karma Works

In looking at the dynamics of soul karma, let's be clear that not every aspect of our nature is related to karma. As said, the soul has its own innate qualities. There's a difference between bringing in a soul quality that simply needs developing and bringing in a weakness of character due to our own bad habit, misuse, or negligence.

As with other types of karma, it can often take many lives to work out soul karma. Let's say that one of your lessons is to learn tolerance. It is your job to learn from and respect others who are different from you or who do not subscribe to the same way of thinking or acting as you do. This lesson starts as part of your soul growth and is not related to a karmic condition.

As part of your life lesson, you are put in situations where your tolerance will be put to the test. Unfortunately, you may fail your test. Instead of accepting others for who they are, you may continually try to mold people in your own image. As a result, you create some soul karma plus some relationship karma as you will inevitably mistreat people because of your intolerance. In a future life, your soul comes in with an intolerant attitude toward others. Instead of softening and learning how to adapt, you become more intolerant.

You will carry this character flaw with you until you strengthen and master that trait. In the meantime, karma will inevitably accrue. Naturally, the sooner you strengthen the character weakness, the sooner you can turn things around. Otherwise, you could find yourself in a very difficult situation until you wake up. Eventually, illumination comes for us all.

It is not always easy to know if character weaknesses are a carryover from a previous lifetime or are expressions of free will. Generally, the harder the weakness is to change, the deeper the roots. Yet either way, the lesson is to work on your weaknesses when you see them regardless of their roots. If you don't, they will come back in stronger ways and it will be more difficult for you to resolve.

Addictions can clearly be examples of past life habits coming back. If you were an alcoholic in a past life and did not resolve that addiction, you could carry it over to a future life. You can carry over the traits of fears and phobias to resolve as well. If you drowned in a boating accident, you may come back with a fear of the water; or if in a past life you fell to your death from a great height, you may develop vertigo in this life.

A wide variety of experiences over many lives shape your character. If you spend a lifetime in solitude, you may lose some of your communication skills and have to rebuild them in another incarnation. Sometimes we bury our positive traits for a time. If you are born outgoing but let fear get the better of you, you will come back in another life to work out that fear and rekindle your outgoing nature.

In developing your character, you want dynamics. Some people hardly change throughout their life, for better or worse. In truth this is not so good. This means stagnation. Life is dynamic. You want the flower of your life to bloom. It's not easy to develop your character. If it were, we'd all be saints by now. Every opportunity to develop yourself is an opportunity worth taking.

A Reincarnation Story of Marie

In this reincarnation story from the Book of Life, we see how character traits from the past influence present behavior for better or worse. Marie was born in France to a wealthy family. She had one brother and one sister. She was a nice-looking, amicable person, but carried with her a feeling of melancholy. There was no apparent reason for her sadness, but it seemed to run her life. A dream of hers was to become a fashion designer. She had the talent for it, and the opportunity, but her motivation was not there. She worked her way through school and was ready to begin her career but her sadness dampened her willpower in this very competitive field, which was enough to keep success at bay.

Time passed and she met a man who loved her very much. She had had suitors before but they never lasted long because of her lackluster quality. But this man was different. Although she told herself she did not love him, deep down she really did. He pursued her for some time, but she continued to push him away, saying she was not interested in marriage. Eventually, he gave up.

In losing this man, she lost the love of her life, the person she was meant to marry as part of her Tapestry of Life. This experience shook her. It started to dawn on her that this morose habit was destroying her life and that she had to change. She realized how much she loved this man and tried to get him back, but in the meantime he had married another woman and the opportunity was lost.

She tried to start her career again, but found it was not easy as her timing was off and opportunity had largely passed her by. She was playing catch-up to try to complete her life's purpose. These realizations triggered a spiritual awakening. She began to truly find herself again, and she rediscovered the joy in her heart. Life is precious, she realized. She felt as if she had awakened from a long dream. She became spiritual, and sought to understand the mysteries of life. In this incarnation, Marie worked through some old soul karma, but because it had taken longer than needed to come to this realization, the completion of her purpose was left unfinished. She never quite reached the place she was capable of. She was well taken care of for the remainder of her days but would have to make up for unfinished business in a future lifetime.

In this story, we see how a personal character trait can affect the course of an entire life. Not every character trait is the direct result of karma, but many are, as in this case. Marie could have broken her melancholy mood sooner. It was within the scope of her control and free will, but she did not exercise that free will. The good news is she ended her life with a determination to do better, and this will put her ahead of the game in her next incarnation.

To find the karmic root of Marie's melancholy, we opened the Book of Life to an earlier incarnation, in the 1600s in Germany. Marie was a male in this life, Hans, born to a religious family. Hans's father was a minister with a successful congregation. Hans was on the quiet side. He was one of four children. It was a difficult time and the family dealt with many challenges.

Hans became an accountant, but did not apply himself hard enough to excel at his craft and struggled with work. He fell deeply in love and married a very kindhearted woman. When she was killed in a carriage accident, he almost lost his mind. He couldn't sleep and became exhausted, which caused him to be consistently late for work. He eventually lost his job, and he found another job, it was not a very good one and life became a struggle. It was then that he lost his enthusiasm for life. Over time, he developed a morose, melancholy demeanor, a sort of defeatist attitude about life. His friends tried to break him of the mood, but he was stubborn. He never really resolved these issues and ended his life quietly with that sadness about him.

WILL THE REAL ME PLEASE STAND UP

If you were to line up all the personalities of the lives you have lived up to this point, you could ask, "Which one is me? All of them? None of them?"

Throughout your many incarnations, there is an identity of the soul that persists, regardless of the type of person you are in any life. Metaphysics calls this identity the Individuality Ego. When you incarnate, your soul puts on a persona or mask that becomes the part you are to play in that life. This is how you gather your soul experience. Metaphysics calls this persona the personality ego.

When you incarnate, you identify with the personality ego and for the most part forget that there is an immortal part of you. You go through life identifying with the personality even though this is not the real you. As you pass through the hundreds of lifetimes leading to your enlightenment, you put on countless masks as part of your spiritual growth. As you reach enlightenment, one of your biggest jobs is to break through the personality veil and reach the immortal identity that has been with you all along.

So as you go through the various experiences of your incarnated life, recognize that there is always a greater part of you urging you onward and upward. Do your best not to take to heart difficulties and challenges. In the same way, do your best not to overidentify with or indulge yourself in the successes you may reap. All these experiences, good and bad, are part of the road to reach the immortal you.

SOUL KARMA REVIEW

What are your character strengths and weaknesses that stand out?

How would you evaluate yourself mentally and emotionally?

What kind of a person were you as a child and how would you say you have changed as an adult?

What do you like most about yourself? What do you like least?

Do you have any bad habits that you have a difficult time getting rid of?

Chapter 8

THE KARMA OF THE
PHYSICAL BODY

Our physical form is an amazing creation. It is a collection of trillions of extremely well-organized cells all working together to form the extraordinary living organism we call the human body. Our first job when our soul comes to Earth is to learn how to use this marvelous form.

There is a remarkable diversity of physical qualities and characteristics with all human forms. Some people are short while others are tall. Some are naturally slender, while others are husky. Some are unusually attractive, while others are not. There are differences in our skin, hair, and eye color. The list goes on and on. We attribute our physical appearance to genetics and the luck of the draw.

Yet karmically speaking, the body you have is not arbitrary. You earn your physical form through the care you have shown to your body and the respect you have shown to the physical form of others. How well you have done this is what is called physical karma. As Frank Gillette Burgess said, "Our bodies are apt to be our autobiographies."

You are not your body. Your soul *inhabits* your body. The purpose of your body is to act as a vehicle of expression in physical life. Through the body, you learn the many lessons of material consciousness. Throughout your evolution, you incarnate in many types of bodies, both male and female. The kind of body you have affects the type of experiences you have. For example, if you are considered very good-looking, your experience may not be the same as if you are considered less attractive. If you are very tall, you may have different experiences than if you are born very short.

Your body is not yours. You are a custodian of your physical form, and you are held accountable for how well you take care of it. Treat it well and you earn better and better bodies. Disrespect it and you pay a price to learn how valuable the body is. This holds true for others as well. If you misuse someone else's body, then you are accountable as if it were your own body.

EARNING GOOD PHYSICAL KARMA

The Buddha teaches us: "To keep the body in good health is a duty . . . otherwise we shall not be able to keep our mind strong and clear." If you wish to earn good physical karma, you need to take care of the body you inhabit. It's that simple. It doesn't matter what condition your body is in right now, take care of it to the best of your ability and you will build your ideal form. God will take care of the rest. If you are already blessed with an excellent physical form, you have earned this through effort. It's your job to continue to care for your physical form and keep refining its qualities.

Caring for your body includes proper nutrition, exercise, and rest. If you are misusing your body through abuse of smoking, drugs, alcohol, sex, overwork, you deplete the spiritual reserves within your body, and your next body in a future incarnation may not be as good. You pay the price for any type of physical self-abuse. In addition to the basic care of the body, it's essential to attend to the spiritual needs of the body. Make sure your thinking and feeling are in a positive place. Feed your body with spiritual energy as this divine nutrition is more essential than food and drink.

As you care for your body, you rarefy the very atoms of your physical form. This gives your soul more expression. Body and soul can be compared to a piano and a pianist. No matter how good the pianist is, if the piano is broken down, the pianist cannot fully express his or her artistic intent. If our bodies are not in optimal shape, we will not be as responsive to the spiritual impulse as we otherwise could be.

In honoring and respecting the body, be careful not to worship the physical form. There are people who pay *too* much attention to the body. The mistake made here is putting body before soul, and that is not the purpose of the body. The body *serves* the soul.

As part of your learning experience, you may be deliberately given certain bodies to see how you handle the lessons they present. You may be given a strong or good-looking form to see if you will respect that form or take it for granted and misuse it. You may be deliberately given a weaker form to build your compassion for those who are less fortunate physically. In your evolution, you will experience just about every physical type there is so you receive a well-rounded spiritual education.

You will always be tested to see how well you honor the body. Let's say you live the life of a monk or a nun. You took good care of your body even if your body was not the most beautiful or strong. In your next life, you will most likely come in with a better physical form because of the good karma you have accrued. Now comes the test. How do you handle this form? Some continue to respect the form and continue to build its power. This is what happens with great beauty. That beauty is earned over several lifetimes of good physical care. Others, having no memory of the care it took to earn that body, take their healthy physique for granted. They abuse their bodies. They indulge themselves and at first seem not to pay a price, but sooner or later they will. Either in this life or the next, these people will have to start at square one and rebuild their form all over again.

A Reincarnation Story of Physical Karma

In this story from the Book of Life, we turn to China in the 1800s. Ai-ling was a woman born into a wealthy family. Her family inherited a lot of property. She had two brothers and two sisters. She was a good person. She married a good man and they had a son together. Ai-ling was born physically strong and beautiful. She enjoyed herself and traveled around the world. She was good with her money and helped others, although she did not have a career. Her weakness in this life was indulgence in drinking and especially smoking. Because she had such a strong constitution, it seemed like she did not feel the physical effects of her indulgences. At one point, she fell during one of her binges and seriously hurt her hand. For a while she stopped, but as soon as her hand healed, she continued to indulge herself. Eventually she contracted lung cancer and died. However, in this life she did not make the connection between her lifestyle and her demise.

In her next incarnation, Ai-ling was born Peter Fitzgerald in the 1900s. Peter was Irish but his family was living in Paris. He came from a big family and again there was wealth that came from an inheritance. The family was in the clothing business. In this life Peter did not have such a great body. He was fairly good-looking but did not have the looks of his incarnation as Ai-ling, and he was prone to illnesses, especially as a child. Despite this, he was happy-go-lucky and went into the family clothing business. In this life he did not marry and seemed to carry over the desire to indulge himself, and here he also liked living the life of a bachelor. His family loved to drink, and again, Peter unintentionally ended up repeating his karmic pattern of drinking and smoking.

This time his body did not handle his lifestyle well, and he was constantly sick. It put a damper on his carousing, but again he did not get the message that he was abusing his body. As in his previous incarnation, in other parts of his life things were good. He showed good business acumen and was kind and generous with others. So in that part of his life he earned good karma. His fall, once again, was his treatment of his body. As the Higher shared, when we repeat our mistakes rather than resolve them, our karma is compounded.

Peter's body could not tolerate his behavior. By thirty-five years of age, he contracted lung cancer and died. Unfortunately, once again he was stubborn and did not make the connection between his lifestyle and his illness. This indicates that he will face more difficulties in future lives until he learns the lesson of caring for the body.

Peter is currently on the other side, and the Higher has shared that he will be born with a birth defect in his next life. He will have a chronic problem with his eyes. One might ask, here, if he abused his lungs, why would the physical karma come back to the eyes? Actually, he will have to deal with his lungs in yet another life but in this life, he needs to have the vision to make the connection between personal lifestyle and physical health.

The spiritual attribute of the eyes is perception. If you "turn a blind eye" to something that is right in front of you, it is possible that you can develop eye trouble somewhere down the line, and this will be the case with Peter. For his life with a chronic eye issue, he will come to understand how important the body is and how essential it is to properly care for the body. Yes, it is a hard lesson, but caring for the body temple is one of the most important lessons of life.

GENETICS AND KARMA

One of the most dramatic revelations regarding our physical body has been the understanding of genetics. Within each cell in our body is a complete genetic blueprint. The instructions to build our physical form are in this genetic code. We have come to understand ourselves in a whole new light by understanding the part genetics plays in our life. How does karma fit into the picture of genetics?

Your genetic blueprint is part of your physical karma. You have earned the genes you have. Your genetic makeup is not a random biological act. It is a combination of the genetic makeup of your parents and physical karma you have accrued from previous incarnations. Not every single characteristic of your body is karmic, but a great deal is. As you live in your body, you are changing the vibration of your genetic pattern. Your actions affect you physiologically. If you develop yourself in mind, body, and soul, you rarefy the vibration of your genes, and this accrues good physical karma. If you misuse your body, you can degrade the spiritual vibration of your genetic patterns, and this will accrue difficult physical karma. So through your actions and intentions, you have the power to build a more beautiful and spiritually expressive physical form.

Some have asked if we look physically similar in different lives. Is there similarity in the genetic pattern, even though we are in different bodies and born of different parents? The answer is yes. If you were to line up all the lives you lived on Earth, you would look similar in many of them. In the exploration of my own past lives, I often had recognizable physical features, even though the lifetimes themselves were very diverse. However, be careful not to read too much into this and try to discover your past lives by studying features of people from the past. This can be misleading and detrimental in trying to understand your ancient past.

The Karma of Illness and Death

Years ago, during one of my early spiritual training sessions, I asked the Higher why some babies are born with physical deformities. At that time, I did not understand physical karma and it bothered me a great deal to see little ones with such serious maladies. I wondered why God allowed these things to be. The Higher instructed me by saying, "You are looking at the body only. There are full souls in those little bodies and they are paying back physical karma."

On the other side, I was then shown various types of physically deformed children and the karma they were paying back. I was shocked to see so many types of physical challenges souls had to face. I was also shown souls who were waiting to incarnate in deformed bodies. Believe it or not, these souls were eager (if that is the right word) for the opportunity because they were shown how much adverse karma they could erase by going through such an experience. It was heartbreaking to see so much suffering, but it was encouraging to see how hopeful and determined many of these souls were to move on with their lives.

Illnesses that you develop in your life can sometimes be karmic. In a past life, you may have physically abused someone or abused yourself. You may have had an unresolved destructive thinking pattern that did not show up as a physical malady but carried over to your present life. Illnesses can also be rooted in sins of omission. For example, you may be in poor health if in a previous life you were affluent and refused to help those whom you had the privilege to help.

The karma of illness can show up in childhood or later in life, corresponding to the karmic debt to be paid. It's not always easy to tell which of our conditions are karmic and which are not. This is why, regardless of the cause of physical distress, we show care and compassion. Some people have the mistaken idea that if a physical condition is karmic, they should accept the condition the karma presents. This is completely false. Regardless of the reason for the condition we may face, we must do all we can to alleviate our maladies; part of our karma is rooted in our participation in the restoration of health to the body. At the same time, we must show patience as the karmic balancing does have to run its course.

On a mass scale, plagues are most always a form of collective karma. The bubonic plague that wiped out almost a third of Europe was karmic. The AIDS epidemic of today is also an ancient karmic debt being paid off. As with all disease, we must do all we can to alleviate these physical distresses regardless of their root cause.

Karma and Death

When it comes to the karma of death, the first thing to see is that death is a natural process of life. There is not necessarily any karmic connection to the way we cross over. Our days on Earth are numbered according to what we are meant to accomplish. There are accidents and situations that can cause us to go over before our time, but there is an actual plan as to when we are meant to die.

However, if you have taken the life of another or caused serious physical trauma, the way you die can most definitely be karmic. For example, if you drowned someone in a past life or had the opportunity to save the life of someone who was drowning and you did not, you may go through the experience of drowning yourself. Usually the payback for these types of karma is not in the same life but in a future life.

People have asked what to do when loved ones are dying, especially if the dying process is prolonged and painful. It's so hard to see someone you care so much about struggle and suffer without apparent hope of recovery. Is it not sometimes better to have such a death end quickly? My spiritual teachers have been very strong on this topic. They say, "When the apple is ripe, it will fall from the tree." You do not know how much karma your loved one is working out by going through that difficult transition. You cannot play God. You must do everything in your power to help that person, but something like assisted suicide is against divine law, as is any type of suicide.

However, deliberately cutting your life short is very different than if your body cannot function on its own and requires artificial assistance. There is no adverse karma if you decide to let nature take its course and refuse artificial assistance. Giving a "Do not resuscitate" order is within your right if you wish.

Ordering the termination of life support for a loved one is a trickier situation. If the person is incapacitated and cannot speak for himself and has specifically requested not to be resuscitated, then karmically the loved ones should respect that request. If the person is incapacitated and cannot make decisions for himself and did not make his wishes clear, then it falls on the next of kin to make that decision for him. It's up to the next of kin to make that decision for him as if they were making it for themselves.

The bottom line is: Respect death as you respect life. Planning ahead for such contingencies is a good idea, so that everyone's wishes in such matters are respected.

What about doctors who make mistakes that lead to their patients' incapacitation or death? There is no karma on the part of the doctor or staff for failed lifesaving attempts or unintentional mistakes that result in the death of a patient. Medical practitioners are in a difficult position, and deal with life-or-death situations on a daily basis. The divine takes this into account. This of course does not include negligence, carelessness, or deliberate misuse. In such cases, karma most definitely accrues.

If your days on Earth are numbered, can you extend physical life beyond allotted time? Under certain circumstances you can extend your life span, and this can be a good thing to give more time to work out more karma and help others.

The Karma of Murder

Murder generates one of the heaviest karmas. From the material point of view, killing appears as extinguishing life. Someone is lost and never seen again. We all die eventually, but to take a life prematurely is considered by some an unforgivable act. Yet from the spiritual perspective, the soul can never be extinguished. When someone is murdered, that person is robbed of his or her physical form, but the soul survives.

The spiritual offense committed when you murder someone is that not only have you robbed him of his physical body, but you have robbed him of his opportunity to work out his karma and his part in the divine plan that he came to Earth to accomplish. By doing this, you carry a heavy karmic debt and take on that person's karma as well.

The degree of your karmic burden depends on the severity of your offense. Murder in the heat of the moment is not as severe as premeditated murder. Either way, it can take several lifetimes to work out a single offense. You will have to reincarnate with the soul you have murdered to help them finish what you cut short. In another life, you will have to go through the experience of being murdered yourself to understand what it feels like to have your life cut short. You may also have to go through a lifetime where your soul clears the destructive thinking and feeling that generated the murderous act to begin with. It's quite an entanglement.

As difficult as the karma of murder is, it's certainly not uncommon. The truth is, throughout our many lives we have all been murdered and we have all been the murderer. It's part of our experience here on Earth. While it is a very serious offense, murder is certainly not past redemption. Many times when we have done terrible things, we feel we have damned ourselves beyond hope or the very thought of having to pay the karmic price seems intolerable. By thinking in this way, we give ourselves permission to continue to build up more karma and walk further along the dark and difficult road we have set for ourselves.

No matter what we have done, the sooner we turn ourselves back onto the path of God, the better it will be for us and all others concerned. No matter what the karma is, it's much better to face our karma sooner than later.

What about capital punishment? Unfortunately, being executed for your crime does not alleviate your karmic debt. It becomes a sort of double punishment. Actually, it's my understanding that capital punishment is against divine law and becomes part of national karma. You do not necessarily solve anything by killing people. They are going to go over to the other side in the same state of mind they were in while on Earth. For example, if you deal with demented killers by executing them and sending them to the other side, they can actually wander around and influence those who are thinking along those lines. It is much better to keep them locked up and try to rehabilitate them.

There are times when taking life does not generate karma. Murder in self-defense is not karmic. It is your right to defend your life. Soldiers in battle are not held karmically accountable for their actions unless they are reckless and act in an unconscionable way. As mentioned, doctors who do their best to save lives but either make an honest mistake or cannot save their patient are not held karmically accountable.

This brings us to the issue of suicide, which is really an act of murder—self-murder. You will have to come back again and finish what you did not complete, usually under more difficult conditions. Most people who commit suicide are in a very confused state. They feel that by ending their life, they are releasing themselves of pain they may be going through. What they do not realize is that most of the time, people who commit suicide remain earthbound. They go nowhere and cannot begin the process of going to the other side and reincarnating as described in chapter 2 until the Holy Ones can wake them up from their spiritual stupor. On top of that, they have not resolved any of the issues they mistakenly thought that suicide would end.

Once they finally do wake up, they will have to reincarnate to finish what they ended prematurely. It's a more difficult situation than it needs to be. The lesson here is that there may be moments when life feels intolerable. Do your best to work through those times as they will pass and you will be the stronger for it.

A Reincarnation Story of Murder

There are many examples of the karma of murder, some very dramatic. However, one of the most common is murder committed as a crime of passion.

In this story, Laszlo was born in Hungary in the 1800s. His family was well-to-do; they owned a big farm. Laszlo was on the aggressive side and was very ambitious. He was competitive in all he did. He had a fascination for archaeology and contemplated a career in that field, but ended up becoming an architect. He did well as an architect. He married and had one child. He had a happy marriage, a happy home life, and a good job. Unfortunately, his aggressive side got the better of him. A big project came up in which he had invested a lot of time, money, and effort. It was a very prestigious job and an important building, which meant he would rise to a higher level of prominence in his field.

He was in competition with another architect, whom he had seen as his nemesis for a long time, although in truth that was not the case. While it was true that this other architect had been awarded jobs over him in the past, there was nothing underhanded about it. The man was simply doing a better job than Laszlo. When Laszlo heard that it looked like the job would go to this competitor, he snapped. He felt that his whole career was on the line and that it would come to a halt if he lost this project. Again, this was a misinterpretation. Laszlo would have been fine either way. As a matter of fact, even if he didn't get the job, other companies wished to work with him.

At the moment, Laszlo didn't see any of this. He felt desperate. It seemed to him that his life was coming to an end because of this other man. In his panic, he got a gun and shot the competing architect in the street, killing him. Of course, Laszlo went to jail. His family spent a good deal of their fortune trying to get him out of jail, and after six years they succeeded. But he had lost everything. He couldn't go back to architecture. His wife left him and he became estranged from his son. Laszlo deeply regretted his rash action, but was confused as to what he could do to set things right. He managed to find work as a laborer. He ended up dying struggling and alone but genuinely remorseful.

In this case, he was able to pay back some of this karma in his very next life. Usually it takes longer to bring people back together and sometimes it takes a couple of lifetimes for the people to be in the frame of mind to be willing to get together, but because Laszlo had such a genuine desire to redeem himself, the opportunity to reconcile the karmic debt came quickly.

We see him now in Scotland, in the 1900s. Laszlo was then Agnes. She was fair-looking and born into a family of four children. The family owned a small factory. They were not rich but were getting by okay. Agnes met a man at a social function. They courted, became close, and eventually married. This man was none other than the competing architect from the Hungarian incarnation, whom Laszlo had murdered. Of course, neither person had any memory of this past association. At first, the marriage seemed to be on the right track. The husband was a mathematician but he was unhappy at his work. Soon into the marriage, he started taking out his frustration on Agnes. This triggered a subconscious memory of what had happened between them. Even though that memory did not come to conscious awareness, it was playing an active part in their relationship. Unfortunately, he became very mean to Agnes and was verbally cruel to her.

Agnes, on the other hand, was very patient with him. She knew he was a good man. He was actually in the wrong profession. He was meant to be a doctor. He showed interest and aptitude in this area, but somehow was fearful of moving in that direction. She was very persistent and tried to help him make the change. Eventually Agnes played a critical role in helping him become a doctor, and he turned out to be a very good one. He reconciled with Agnes. They had a daughter, and spent a happy life together.

Remember, part of the difficulty in murdering people is that you take on their karma. In this Scottish life, Agnes had to put aside her own wishes and dreams to help her husband. It was her efforts that helped her husband complete his life's task, and this was how she helped pay back some of the karma created in Hungary. Her own life path was temporarily suspended in order to resolve this part of her karma. It was to her benefit that she stayed on track despite the challenges. Had she left him without doing her best to make things work, she would have left this karma unresolved, and she would have to face it further down the line. In her next life, she will resume her own destiny, and she will hopefully have learned one of the most important spiritual lessons.

THE KARMA OF SEX

Without a doubt, one of the most confusing areas of metaphysical work is the relationship of sex to spiritual activity. Sex is a form of creative power and expression. The energy of sex has a definite presence in a person's aura. As with any type of energy, if this energy is used as it was intended, it enhances our life. The healthy use of sex is a blessing and allows you to participate in the procreative process of life, which is one of the most sacred blessings God has given you.

If you misuse the sexual energy, you inevitably pay the price. You deplete the power of your physical form and can throw off your spiritual development. When it comes to sex, you have to look at your motives. And you have to be very careful whom you invite as your partner. The closest two auras come is through sexual intimacy. So you want to make sure the person you are with is of a positive vibration.

Remember that sex is part of your human, physical experience. At a certain time in your spiritual evolution, there will come the need to abstain from sex so that your creative powers can be completely redirected to spiritual purposes. But until that time, it is not necessary to abstain from intimate activities.

Is there a difference between sex in a married state and romantic sex? In the aura, there is a distinction between the two that will have its karmic effect. When two people marry out of love, there is a beautiful blessing of a white star that can be seen in each spouse's aura. This is a special blessing to sanctify the sexual act, whether for procreation or not. When in the married state and having sex, there is a beautiful blue band that surrounds the aura of each person, to help in the spiritual bonding of the couple. These blessings simply do not come into the picture outside the marital state.

Watch your sexual activity. Treat this part of you with the reverence it deserves. Sex is an energy just like everything else, and it can move on the higher ranges of light or the lower ranges. The key is to balance it with other aspects of your life. Your goal is to live the spiritual laws of life to the best of your ability. If you do, the sexual part of you will fall into place. Effectively harnessing this power can greatly quicken your spiritual progress.

KARMA AND WORLD POPULATION

An argument made against reincarnation relates to population. The question is, "If there is such a thing as reincarnation, why is it that there are more people on Earth today than ever before?" The line of thinking goes that if we are, essentially, being recycled back on Earth, wouldn't there be the same number of people returning again and again?

As we explored in chapter 3, there are far more souls on the other side than there ever are on this side. Earth is a schoolhouse, and once we earn our diploma, we move on. As in any school, as some students graduate, other students begin their education. The number of souls on Earth at any given time works in a similar way.

Why is it that there are more souls on Earth today than in days past? As of this writing, there are approximately 6.8 billion souls in the world and that figure is climbing. The unusual increase in population growth began in the twentieth century and is largely attributed to advances in medical science, quality of living, and agricultural productivity.

Many are concerned that our Earth is overpopulated, creating many of the problems in the world. Certainly with more people on Earth there are going to be new challenges. But the population of Earth is not just the result of better living conditions.

The reason there are more people on Earth today is primarily the result of karma. More people are here to work out their karma. The better living conditions allow for this to happen. There is what you might call a backlog of karma to be worked out. However, this backlog of karma is not part of the divine plan. It is the result of too many people not paying attention and generating repeated karma. Too many people are not learning the spiritual lessons they are meant to learn, and this has created the population explosion we see today.

The divine has worked it out for more of us to be here in order to be given the opportunity to resolve our karmic issues. So the real problem today is not too many people on the Earth, rather it is too many people who are not paying enough attention to their life's lessons. This is creating a world population that is greater than there otherwise would be.

PHYSICAL KARMA REVIEW

How would you evaluate your overall health?

Did you have to deal with health issues as a child or at certain points in your life?

Are there chronic health issues you are dealing with right now?

How do you treat your physical body? Do you give it too much attention? Too little attention? Just the right amount?

What is your attitude toward your body? Do you like the way you look, or are you critical of your physical appearance?

Chapter 9

THE KARMA OF NATURE

Nature is God's handiwork. Its glory is a continual source of inspiration and wonder. We are a part of nature. It sustains and supports us. The more we understand nature, the more we appreciate life and the more we see life as a connected whole. When we open our hearts to nature we can, as William Blake puts it, learn

> To see a world in a grain of sand,
> And a heaven in a wild flower,
> Hold infinity in the palm of your hand,
> And eternity in an hour.

As remarkable as the nature we see is, there is an even more incredible process of life going on every moment of every day that is hidden from physical sight. If we are to understand how the karma of nature works, we need to better understand the spiritual side of nature and our relationship to it.

When we behold the breathtaking vistas of mountains and valleys, or breathe the fragrance of a flower, when we behold the fish of the seas or the animals of the forests, we are experiencing nature at work and play. Yet nature is not alone. Behind nature is an incredible network of spiritual beings who are guiding the entire evolution of nature. There is a spiritual hierarchy for all the kingdoms of the Earth: mineral, vegetable, animal, and man. These beings range from tiny little curlicue devas and playful fairies to majestic and colossal king and queen devas who guide over entire mountain ranges and oceans.

At different times in my life, I have had the privilege of seeing these incredible beings. They don't present themselves readily to you. Often they are rather suspicious of humans, but if they like your vibration, they will show themselves and perhaps even bless you.

There are wonderful devas that play in the fields of grain without which the Earth could not produce her harvest. We see the sun reflecting on the water, forming diamond points of light, yet dancing upon these waters are countless little devas working on the life force within the water. The fresh scent of pine is sweetened by devas and is considered one of nature's greatest gifts to humanity, as it is the symbol of life on Earth. We value precious gems that took millions of years to evolve, yet what we don't realize is that there is a life force in each of those precious gems, a life force to develop its own soul structure.

In understanding how spirit vitalizes nature, we need to see that physical life was not born of nothing. All living organisms did not come into existence by accident or by a random concurrence of organic material. Every species on Earth is part of the divine plan, going through its own process of evolution. They were first *objectified* on Earth and then began a process of physical evolution, refining and adapting their form but always guided by the divine.

It is our job in the human kingdom to contribute to the spiritual development of nature. Being a product of nature from past cycles of evolution, it's now our turn to help elevate all forms of life on Earth. We are meant to work in harmony with the devas of nature and the spirits of the animal world to uplift nature. The Bible speaks of man's dominion over the Earth, but this dominion is meant as a spiritual service, not to rule over for personal whims. All life is equally precious regardless of its level of spiritual evolution. As the higher forms of life help us, we in turn help the lower forms of life. This completes the evolutionary chain of life. The mineral kingdom is in its own realm, the plant in its own realm, the animal in its own realm, and the human in its own realm. The human is the highest of all the kingdoms on Earth. This means it also bears the most responsibility, spiritually speaking.

Your karma to nature—and you can definitely create karma with nature—is how well you tend to life on Earth and help in the evolutionary process. We in the human kingdom have a spiritual responsibility to help evolving souls in the lower kingdoms. As explored in chapter 3, there is evolving life at every stage of development—mineral, vegetable, animal, and human. The biblical notion of man's dominion over the Earth was not meant to concern man's pleasure in nature, but was meant to imply responsibility to serve and to help. Just as the higher kingdoms of life, including the angels and archangels, have dominion over us to help in our evolution, humans have dominion over the animals, plants, and even minerals to help in their evolution. How successful you are in this process will generate nature karma accordingly. Enhance your part in supporting nature and you generate good karma with nature; misuse nature and you generate negative karma for which you have to atone.

EARNING GOOD NATURE KARMA

There are many ways we can generate good karma with nature. The first is to simply respect nature and its place in the spiritual unfoldment of life. Nature isn't something we can do with as we please. We have a *relationship* with nature, and as with any relationship, we are held accountable for our actions in that relationship.

For example, domestication is one of the key ways of helping the animal kingdom. When we take in an animal as a pet, it's not just for our pleasure. We are giving that animal an opportunity to develop spiritually. By interacting closely with humans, the animal soul is quickened, which accelerates its evolution. Animals are like spiritual sponges: they absorb the love you give them. If you have a farm or a ranch, you have an even better opportunity to help the animal kingdom. Organizing a rescue shelter or an adoption organization for animals and becoming a veterinarian are ways to contribute to the welfare of animals.

In the same way, we help the mineral and plant kingdoms every time we till the soil and plant crops. Gandhi said, "To forget how to dig the earth and to tend the soil is to forget ourselves." When we tend to a garden, we are helping the plant life in that garden. Preserving land for national parks is greatly helping the nature kingdom. Forest rangers whose job it is to tend those parks are contributing to the welfare of nature.

When we generate good nature karma, we receive a beautiful blessing of light, especially white light, which helps our evolution. We are blessed by the nature kingdom itself. Perhaps best of all, by helping the lower kingdoms, the higher kingdoms help us. There may be a time when we find ourselves in a difficult situation and, because of good nature karma accrued, we receive extra help from the divine that we otherwise would not have earned. This is all because we have contributed to the chain of life that we are all part of.

The story of Androcles and the lion is a wonderful example of cooperation between the human and the animal kingdoms. Androcles was a runaway slave during the days of ancient Rome. He hid in a cave that turned out to be the den of an injured lion. Androcles pulled a large thorn from the lion's paw and tended to the wound until the lion was well. As a result, the lion became tame to him and behaved like a pet, even wagging its tale when it saw him, and it shared food with him.

Years later, when Androcles ended up back in Rome as a slave, he was condemned to die by wild animals. The most imposing of the beasts he was confronted with was none other than the lion he had befriended years earlier. The lion immediately recognized him and showed the same love to the man who saved his life. The emperor pardoned Androcles in recognition of the power of friendship, and Androcles was given the lion. This is the kind of bond we are meant to develop with nature.

Paying Back Karma to Nature

In recent times, we have become more aware of the effect humanity has on nature. Whereas before we saw nature more as something inexhaustible and constant no matter what we did, a commodity to use as we pleased, now that the world is getting smaller, we can more readily see the impact we have on nature, for better and worse.

It is tragic to see that as we are advancing as a society, we have yet to show the same advancing treatment to nature. While nature is meant to give to us, it's not a commodity. It's as a partner in the great plan of life. As a result of our mistreatment, we can unbalance nature, creating much work in the spirit realms to keep things in equilibrium.

When you mistreat nature, you create negative karma and have to pay it back. If you mistreat an animal, you will have to pay back that karma through caring for another animal. By mistreating that animal, you have deterred rather than aided its evolution, so things must balance out.

If you mistreat animals on a larger scale, there is a human debt as well. You still owe karma to the animal kingdom, but you will also have to perform some type of humanitarian act. This is because to redeem your destructive actions, you must build more spiritual power and compassion by contributing to those in need on a human level. Offenses to the plant kingdom through the abuses of the elements of soil, water, and air are paid back by being of service to nature and also performing humanitarian acts.

Some schools of reincarnation teach that when a human commits a terrible crime, he can actually reincarnate as a lower form of life, reverting back to an animal, but this is not true. Once a life soul has passed from one kingdom to the next, it cannot revert back to a lower kingdom, no matter how serious the offense. It has to redeem itself in its own kingdom.

Some have asked what happens to animals that have been severely abused, such as those used for laboratory experiments. When they go to the other side, the divine tends to them very lovingly until they can be released from the effects of the trauma they endured. It's heartbreaking to see what some animals have had to endure. Perhaps their saving grace is that animals do not yet have a sub-conscious mind. While in physical life they remember through their own instinctual levels, that instinctual memory fades once they drop their physical body. Once the negative energy is cleared, their soul absorbs the lesson that experience taught them and they are free. So they hold no grudges or resentments.

Does nature seek revenge when we offend it? No. Nature doesn't work that way. Sure, if someone is of a dark vibration, animals will sense that darkness and be repelled, but that is not old karma coming back. Karma in the lower kingdoms does not work the same way as in the human kingdom because it is only in the human kingdom that there is self-awareness and free will in the sense that we understand it.

There is drama within nature itself that is not directly related to us, but we will feel its effects. As nature is developing, it will at times bellow and belch. There will be floods and natural cataclysms, but this is not karma. It's part of the natural process of life. Some of these natural disasters are fairly tame while sometimes they can be catastrophic, as science is discovering in unlocking the history of Earth's long past. Yet again this is nature going through its own growing pains.

Can nature correct humanity's misuses? Of course it can. Even though we have developed to a point where we could have a devastating effect on nature, the divine will not permit this to happen as some doomsayers predict. This is not to say that there have not been devastating effects on nature by humans. For example, we have caused some species to become extinct before their time, and this is a heavy karma to bear. Although it's part of nature that some old forms die out so that souls in those forms can incarnate into better, more refined forms, the endangerment of many species going on today is largely due to human intervention. The abuses of animals on a mass scale and the use of animals for testing generate serious nature karma.

More than ever, the misuses of nature will have to be balanced. Yet overall, despite present challenges and global concerns, nature is heading toward a golden age. Just as humanity is on the brink of a spiritual renaissance greater than ever before, so is nature. The Earth itself and all living forms are in the process of a dramatic shift in spiritual consciousness and evolution.

NATURE GIVING BACK

In respecting and earning good karma with nature, what about eating animals for food or cutting down trees for lumber in order to build homes? Is it spiritually wrong to engage in these kinds of activities, even if done in a humane way?

This brings us to a very important point about our relationship with nature. With any type of relationship, there needs to be an exchange. We help nature and in turn nature helps us. Nature is meant to give of itself and we are meant to partake of the bounty of nature. This is part of life and is how nature grows. In one way or another, form is meant to sacrifice itself to spirit. The life spirit in the mineral kingdom gives of its form so that plants may take their minerals and grow. In turn, the life spirit in plants gives of its form so that animals may grow. Animals will give of their form to one another and to the human kingdom as part of their act of sacrifice. In the human kingdom, there is sacrifice, too, as we will give our life's blood in service to the divine creative plan.

There is a humorous story about the famous actor John Barrymore. As well as being an extraordinary actor, he was well known for his adventures and had a strong affinity for animals. One time, he was encouraged by his friends to go fishing. He didn't like the idea of catching the fish and seeing them die, so when he caught one he would throw it back in the water. At one point, he caught a huge fish. When he was releasing the hook from its mouth to throw it back in the water, out came all these little fish. Barrymore exclaimed, "Well, if you eat each other, then I'll eat you!"

It's understood that we will take from nature to sustain ourselves. There is nothing spiritually wrong with eating animals for food. I know there are many who feel eating animal flesh is wrong. I went through a period when I was a vegetarian, but the Higher urged me to stop, as it did not agree with my constitution. Certainly, this is a choice. Some do it for health reasons, others simply don't like to eat meat, but you do not create bad karma by eating meat. What you do want to do is bless the food with the Divine Light before eating, to honor the kingdoms of the Earth that produced the food. (See the appendix.)

Even the killing of animals on a mass scale to feed nations of people is okay, karmically speaking. Where the offense comes in is if the animals are mistreated. There are too many horror stories of animals living in terrible conditions and being severely mistreated, all in the name of feeding people. Clearly, this is terribly wrong and carries a heavy karmic burden. Fortunately, a growing number of farms and ranches are realizing this and treating the animals more humanely, but much more still needs to be done.

In the same way, there's nothing wrong with chopping down trees for lumber, but the reckless chopping without thought of effect or replanting again creates karmic situations and hurts nature. The key is balance. How much can the Earth give? I have asked this question of the Higher several times. While it is true that we can deplete certain of nature's resources and are doing just that, overall the divine keeps things in balance in spite of humanity. This does not let us off the hook, but it does mean that just as our life is in God's hands, so is nature.

HONORING NATURE

Every living thing is striving to be a reflection of the Creator. Each kingdom of the Earth serves a purpose. To best appreciate nature, spend time in it. Let your bare feet touch the soil. Breathe fresh air deeply. Wherever you can, help nature. Your connection to nature keeps you connected to the whole of life. Divorce yourself from nature and you cut yourself off from your full participation in the process of unfolding life. "Man's heart away from nature becomes hard," the Native American Indian chief Standing Bear tells us.

Your soul grew up from all the kingdoms of nature. You are its crowning glory and must wear that mantle well.

Blessing Your Food

I would like to conclude this chapter by offering a very effective food prayer given by the Higher. Blessing food before you eat it is a tradition in cultures across the world. This food prayer is a wonderful way to ask the Divine Light to go into the food you eat. As you know, there is vibration in everything, and there is a strong vibration that goes into food. You are ingesting this food, so it is critical that the light blesses the food before you eat it. It sends the light strongly to the source from which the food came, to give thanks and to bless it.

FOOD PRAYER

Heavenly Father, Holy Mother God, down-ray Thy light into this Thy food to remagnetize, reenergize, and revitalize my physical body. Let it flow into each and every kingdom of the Earth: mineral, vegetable, fish, fowl, winged creature, animal, and man, and into a reservoir of light to feed the souls as yet unborn and all around the planet to feed the hungry.

Let it flow like manna from heaven multiplying this Thy abundance and supply—the ambrosia, the taste, and the nectar—in a variety of ways. Each and every bite to Thy everlasting Glory. Amen.

Nature Karma Review

How would you evaluate your attitude toward nature?
Do you honor it or see it as something to do with as you please?
Do you have pets? How do you treat animals?
Do you have a garden?

Chapter 10

Spiritual Karma

There comes a time in the evolution of every soul when it turns its attention to God. Through its involvement in the affairs of the world, the soul is growing all along. Yet at a certain point in its maturity, the matters of the world seem less important than putting attention on God and the divine process of life. At this point, the growth of the soul takes on new dimensions.

Many call this epiphany the spiritual awakening. Every soul has this awakening sooner or later. Once the lightbulb goes on, the next question is how best to live your spiritual life in a conscious and direct way. I often see this spiritual awakening in the aura as an ethereal blue light around the heart chakra. This blessing is an indication that the person has been quickened by the divine and is ready to begin his or her spiritual quest.

Each human soul is born with the gift of free will. We can use that will any way we like. Yet the ultimate purpose of free will—our coin of wisdom—is to choose God. We choose God in the way we live our lives. Many times, we choose God without even realizing it is God we're choosing. It just seems to be the right thing to do. Yet when we choose God in a conscious way, the dynamics of our life dramatically change as we recognize that there truly is a greater life that we are a part of.

As an awakened soul, it's your job to demonstrate the spiritual life in all you do, to bring out the spiritual dimensions in your job, relationships, and finances and everything that's going on in your life. This takes great concentration because naturally there will be distractions and temptations that can easily cause you to deviate from your spiritual path. Yet as you hold strong to your spiritual path, you grow quickly.

The day and age we live in offers some of the greatest opportunities to grow spiritually and to make some of your greatest spiritual leaps. These spiritual opportunities are available as long as you follow through on what is being offered to you. Many today have walked the spiritual path in other lives and are picking up where they left off to continue their spiritual journey.

Heeding the Spiritual Call

If you get the spiritual prompting, follow it. It is your destiny calling on you. You don't know how many lifetimes it took your soul to reach the place of being ready to open to your enlightened spiritual path. It is exciting to see more and more people are heeding the spiritual call, but still, there are many wonderful people who are ready for a more mystical life yet hesitate to actually follow through on the promptings they are being given. This is a great shame as it's a spiritual opportunity being lost.

It's not easy to follow the spiritual path. Anyone who thinks the path of light is all wine and roses does not understand what the spiritual life is all about. There are many tests and challenges walking the path of light, yet the rewards are enormous and worth every sacrifice and effort.

At the right time, we are all tested to see if we are ready for the higher life. Sometimes people fail their spiritual tests because they have allowed the cares of the world to get the better of them. Their spouse may discourage them from continuing or they are comfortable where they are in life and do not want to disturb that comfort. Some do not quite recognize the full value of the opportunity being presented. The spiritual path may be a desire for them but not a *burning* desire.

If you do not follow the spiritual call presented to you, you do not accrue bad karma, as this is a personal choice. It doesn't mean that you have acted wrongly, but only that you have missed a spiritual opportunity and delayed your spiritual progress. You will have to return in a future life to complete the task you were meant to complete in this life.

For those who follow the spiritual call, it becomes your job to understand the road you are to follow. For some, heeding the spiritual call means learning how to incorporate the spiritual life into your daily life. For others, the spiritual call can be more dramatic. We all know the story of Siddhartha, who became the Buddha, and how he left fame, fortune, and family to follow his spiritual call. This had nothing to do with karma. Rather, it was the path to the destiny he was meant to fulfill.

It goes without saying that the sacrifices you make in fulfilling your spiritual destiny offer you some of the greatest opportunities for spiritual advancement. In saying this, I do not want you to think you must give up everything in an effort to make leaps in your spiritual progress. Rather, I wish you to look more closely at what you know in your heart you are meant to accomplish and make sure you are doing everything you can to accomplish the task at hand. God does not ask you to make needless sacrifices, only to let go of that which becomes an obstacle in your spiritual path.

A Reincarnation Story of Enlightenment

This reincarnation story starts in India about three hundred years ago, in a small town outside Calcutta. A child was born into a modest home. This child was an advanced soul of good nature. His name was William. (This is the name used in a future life but used here for consistency.) William was an only child and had good parents who loved him. William had earned a great deal of accumulated good karma. This was a very special life for him, as this was the lifetime in which he could reach enlightenment and step into a whole new level of awareness.

William's parents were metaphysically minded, and from an early age, William showed a devotion to prayer and meditation. William grew into a tall and handsome young man. He was outgoing but on the serious side. His parents wanted him to marry and continue in the family business, but William sensed his destiny lay elsewhere. He chose not to marry, and he became a professor of literature in a university in Calcutta. His parents kept trying to pull him back to the town he grew up in. William showed tolerance as he loved them very much, but as his own spiritual awareness blossomed, he did start to look down on them a little, sort of putting them at a lower echelon than where he was.

Here was one of the few karmas he developed in this life, as this caused him to pull away from his family and not work with them. His lesson here was to recognize that no matter where a soul is in his or her development, we are all equal in God's eyes and must respect that equality.

William was a bit of a loner in this life but did a lot of good things for those who were less fortunate than he. He gave of his time, energy, and resources. He helped the untouchables. His spiritual nature started to blossom more and more. He received visions and inspirations and sensed he was getting close to the enlightenment he was destined to reach.

One day, when he was in his late fifties, he retreated to the mountain to meditate and commune with the Higher. Unfortunately, as he was climbing up a mountain pass, some rocks came loose. He lost his footing and fell to his death. In this incarnation, we see a very good person who has the full potential to reach enlightenment, but because of conditions beyond his control, he dies prematurely and is unable to complete the task given to him. What happens to a soul in this situation?

First we see that William came in with a lot of good karma and continued to accrue good karma. The fact that he did not finish his purpose in life was not something of his own doing. In these cases, the soul reincarnates quickly and is given the opportunity to finish what was started.

And this is what we find with William. He spent about twenty years on the other side, which is not a long time by the standards of the Hereafter. He reunited with his parents from that life, as they, too, had passed on, and resolved the little remaining karma they had with each other. Then, before long, he reincarnated in the United States shortly after America gained her independence.

William was born into very similar circumstances as in his Indian life. He was born an only child to parents who were farmers outside Philadelphia. William's parents were also metaphysical and started teaching him spiritual truths from a very young age, which he gravitated to immediately. William grew into a fine young man. Once again he chose not to marry and was again drawn to teaching. This time he became a history teacher at a college in Philadelphia. And again, there was some friction with his parents as they wished him to stay and be a farmer. There was also a little jealousy as they sensed William had special spiritual gifts. In this life, William didn't look down on them as he did with his parents in India, but he did show some intolerance and found it hard to forgive their not understanding what it was he was meant to do.

Here again we see a little karma brewing. One of the areas where he was meant to show the greatest tolerance was his family. Even though he did not always see eye to eye with his family, it was his duty to let slights go by and be forgiving. The truth is, it really didn't matter what his family was doing. It mattered far more how he was treating his family. And this is a lesson for all of us. If your parents or siblings don't understand you or the spiritual journey you are on, be patient and kind. Love them anyway.

As William matured, he became very in tune with the divine. Although he was without the guidance of an earthly spiritual teacher, he had already advanced far enough to receive strong direct guidance from the Higher and clearly understood his mission in life. He showed a strong determination to reach the spiritual heights he was capable of reaching.

As he reached into his fifties, he went through the tests and trials that preceded the enlightened state. He passed his tests wonderfully and became enlightened. He then became a teacher of metaphysics and held classes and taught privately. He still did some teaching at the university but his energies were primarily focused on metaphysical work.

His evolution did not stop there. Once he completed the task from his Indian life, he continued to climb the spiritual ladder to reach the full potential of his American incarnation. He did very well in his spiritual ascent. Ironically, when he was in his sixties he was in retreat in the mountains during winter and died in an avalanche. He once again died prematurely, just a little bit short of fulfilling his destiny.

In this story, the Higher teaches that we are always given a second chance at life. If somehow things don't fully work out like they should, don't worry. Life will balance things out. It may be delayed, but you will complete the destiny that was yours from the beginning.

Our Arc of Development

The road to enlightenment is not a straight upward line. As you incarnate from life to life, it is the hope that your next life will be better than the life just lived. We all want to think in terms of moving ahead, rather than backward. In practice, however, you have had incarnations in which you progressed and gained spiritual ground and also lives in which you generated negative karma and lost spiritual ground. This is an inevitable and natural part of the growing process. Your ascent actually looks a little like a stock market graph—up and down. This up and down goes on for some time until the soul decides it's had enough and is ready to make a consistent effort to finish its laps on Earth and get off the wheel of necessity.

What usually happens is, you go through a series of lives in which you gain spiritual ground and build up spiritual power. The gifts you develop through these lifetimes reach their pinnacle at a certain point. It is often here that you are tested. At some point, you will fall prey to the temptation to use the gifts you have accrued over lifetimes of effort for selfish gain and not to serve humanity and God. This fallen lifetime will cause you to lose spiritual ground and you will not only have to pay back karma accrued but also have to rebuild the spiritual power lost.

For example, say you have spent lifetimes building up good money karma. Then there is one life where you incarnate with enormous wealth and opportunity. You find yourself in a position where you wield tremendous power and influence in money matters. Even though you earned this from many lifetimes of good work, in this present life you become intoxicated with the benefits that such wealth brings. Instead of using that wealth for the greater good of all, you become self-absorbed and eventually ruthless in money matters. You use your influence and position to satisfy your greed and lust for power, regardless of how many others are hurt or even die as a result of your greed. Your concern is to make more money. In this scenario, you have made the fatal mistake of misunderstanding that your wealth is not your own. Regardless of your good karma in earning such a privileged position, you still remain the steward of God's riches. Of course, your actions will generate heavy money karma that will cause you to start over again rebuilding good money karma.

We have all made mistakes in our many incarnations that have caused us to retrace our spiritual steps. Some have made more mistakes than others. But it's part of the experience to spiritually fall from time to time. Regardless of how we may fall, the basic lesson is the same: Gifts we have earned are not our own, they are ours only to better serve God and the creative process of life. Anticipating these potential mistakes, the Higher has already made accommodations in our 800 lives to spiritual mastery.

THE KARMA OF SPIRITUAL OFFENSES

Your enlightened lifetimes will naturally be some of your most glorious moments on Earth. When you consciously walk the path of God, you earn some of your best karma. Day by day, you understand better how life really works and are living in harmony with nature and the divine. However, when you misuse spiritual gifts and opportunities offered in these lives, you can generate some of your heaviest karma. These are the karmas of spiritual offenses. They fall under three broad categories:

The spiritual con man
The misguided spiritual teacher
The black magician

There are con men in all walks of life. If there's a dollar to be made, there will be those who try to make it by any means possible. However, those who con people in the name of God commit a serious spiritual offense. These impostors have built themselves up to be great spiritual leaders. They may possess charisma or charm that is appealing, and some people fall under their spell.

What makes this type of con more serious than others is that they are misrepresenting the divine and are interfering with the evolution of the souls who are under their influence. In other words, if someone cons you into buying a vacuum cleaner that you don't really need, you are out just the money. But if people con you in the name of God, not only may they rob you of money, they have steered you in the wrong spiritual direction, which diverts you from the spiritual path you were meant to take. The divine does not look upon this kindly. When these souls cross over to the other side, they are taken to a special tribunal and shown the karma they have accrued and what they will have to do to balance the karmic slate.

In these situations, there is a test for those who follow such leaders. There can be blind faith where the devotees are not really putting the teachings to the test and are letting someone else do the thinking for them. Often these souls do not really understand the actual steps it takes to walk the spiritual path. Or it could be ego, where one might join such groups to feel better than others or more privileged. Often in these situations, the aspiring soul is looking for the quick and easy way to enlightenment, which doesn't exist. In other situations, people have been hurt and are seeking support without taking the time to evaluate the kind of people being dealt with. Or it can be the other way around, where people did something bad and are trying to atone for their misdeeds but are letting guilt get the better of them. In all these situations, there will be warning signs that the people they are dealing with are not what they claim to be, but unfortunately these warning signs are too often ignored or misinterpreted. It ends up taking a dramatic or shocking experience to wake up such souls to the truth.

Then there are the misguided spiritual teachers. These can be good-natured people who wish to help others, but have put themselves on the teaching platform before they were ready to teach. They do this either because they were encouraged by others or because they have a burning desire to be in a spiritual place where they have not yet earned the right to be.

What many do not realize is that you are held karmically accountable for misleading any soul, whether intentionally or unintentionally. When the Higher first encouraged me to become a spiritual teacher, I hesitated, not because I didn't see its value, but because I understood the responsibility involved and I wasn't sure I was up to the task.

In today's growing metaphysical arena, there are many people who want to teach. This is noble, but my strong advice is to wait until you are ready and prepared for such responsibility. Don't rush in half-baked. The last thing you want to do is inadvertently generate negative karma in your effort to help others. If you are meant to be a teacher, you will be. But first go through the necessary steps.

The karma of the black magician is one of the worst karmas of all. This is the karma of evil. What is a black magician? A black magician is a soul who has climbed high up the spiritual ladder and accumulated many spiritual gifts through many lifetimes of spiritual development. They are destined to be great spiritual emissaries, but become so entranced by their own splendor that they end up using their great gifts for selfish ends. Not anyone can be a black magician; they have to have first reached a great spiritual height.

Such souls end up doing the most terrible things, causing great misery. What makes their offenses so severe is that they are done with conscious awareness of their actions. When these souls cross over to the other side, they have forfeited so much spiritual ground that they lose their spiritual gifts and status and have to rebuild them all over again. And of course, they have to pay back the souls they misused. It takes centuries to pay back such karma.

Again, the lesson here is to remember that no matter how high you climb up the spiritual ladder, your power and glory still comes from God. The fact that such spiritually advanced souls can still fall from their state of grace tells you that you can never take your gifts and talents for granted. Free will exists on all levels of evolution.

Your Responsibility on the Spiritual Path

The spiritual path is not an escape from life; it's the fulfillment of life. Regardless of whether you are walking the spiritual path alone or with the help of a spiritual teacher, you are always responsible for your own actions and conduct. Before accepting a spiritual principle, put it to the test. Make sure it rings true for you and brings out the highest and most noble part of you. Refuse to participate in anything that compromises your highest morals or goes against your own common sense. It is true that in your metaphysical study, there will be things that are taken on faith until you can reach a place of inner knowing. Yet this is not a blind faith where you accept things without thinking. This is true faith where, as the Bible says, you are "giving substance to things not yet seen." True faith is the path that eventually leads you to spiritual knowing. With true faith you are still using your intuitive as well as rational skills. In addition, with true metaphysical teachings, there is almost always an immediate practical use that requires your application. For example, it may be difficult at first to fully realize how a lack of forgiveness can cause you to reincarnate with the person you have not forgiven. Yet if an understanding of this principle gives you more courage to practice forgiveness right here and now, you will immediately experience its beneficent effect. This is what is meant by putting spiritual principles to the test.

Spiritual Karma Review

Do you see yourself as better than others because you have had spiritual experiences while others may not have?

Have you heard a spiritual call? Are you following through on that call or letting other things get in the way?

Are you trying to direct people in their spiritual path?

If you are teaching, have you gone through the necessary steps to become qualified to teach?

Are you putting teachings you are receiving to the test or accepting them blindly?

What is your motive for following a particular teaching?

Have you been hurt and are looking for solace, or do you wish to feel a sense of self-worth?

Are you genuinely giving of yourself or looking for what you are getting from your spiritual quest?

Do you have a desire or a burning desire to walk the spiritual path?

Part Three

Our Collective

Karma

Chapter 11

THE KARMA OF NATIONS,
RACES, AND RELIGIONS

If there's one thing that the laws of karma demonstrate it is that there's *always* justice, even in what too often appears to be an unjust world. Yet there are many times when we are caught up in events that are beyond our control. Countries go to war against our wishes. Governments enact laws we must abide, even when we do not agree with them or feel they are right. Companies make decisions that can make work life for employees difficult. Even with families, parents may make decisions that work against the welfare of their children, but the children have little choice but to go along. In all these scenarios, how does our free will work? How does karma work when the welfare of many people is involved?

Up to this point we have been looking at the ways karma works on an individual level. In this section, we explore the unique way that karma works on a group level, and how we spend our coin of wisdom collectively.

In the arc of our spiritual evolution, we have reincarnated in many different countries, experienced just about all the various races, and participated in most of the major religions of the world. This has been to experience life in its variety, to work out our personal karma, and to participate in the activities of society as a whole. In part, the history of civilization is a history of ourselves. The effect of our participation in the various aspects of society is called collective karma.

Collective karma simply means a group of people sharing the same karma. But not just any group. An angry mob may generate an action, but this does not make it an example of collective karma. For the purpose of understanding collective karma, we will define a group as an organization of two or more people that is imbued with its own divine power, thereby giving the group a spiritual life of its own. At this point, the group becomes part of the divine plan and begins generating karma as if it were an individual.

Collective karma is part of life because this is how we learn to work together in an organized and productive way. It's people working together who produce civilizations with their various cultures and societies. All the great achievements of humanity are the result of cooperative efforts in one way or another.

Organization is one of the defining characteristics of the spiritual life. The spirit world is extremely well-organized. There is a divine government administered by the spiritual hierarchy that works in an unparalleled and cooperative way. The same is mirrored on Earth. The civilization we live in today was built on the divine inspiration of generations long past, and we are the precursor to greater and more spiritual civilizations yet to come.

The laws of karma work the same way for groups as they do for individuals. If a group initiates a destructive action, it will pay the price. If it generates a positive action, it will bear the fruit. The difference is the group is its own self-sustaining entity. Individuals add or subtract to the welfare of the organization, but it is the group itself that bears the karmic mark. In other words, if a leader of a nation initiates an action that is detrimental to the country, the country as a whole will bear the burden of that leader's actions.

Collective karma works a little like a public corporation. A public corporation is owned by no one. It is its own entity even though it was started by people; people own stock and it has a management and employees. If a corporation is run well and serves a purpose, it outlives its founders and continues to thrive and, as long as it serves a spiritual purpose, even generates collective karma.

There is collective karma with families. When two people marry, there is a sanctifying by the divine to bless that marriage. Among other spiritual benefits of being married, the couple starts operating as a group, which means they start generating collective karma. If the couple builds a family, all the children within that family also become part of the group karma. The family unit is an essential part of any society. The healthier the family unit, the healthier the society. From the point of view of karma, family is the uniting tie between our race and our country.

Not all groups serve a spiritual purpose, in which case they are not imbued with their own divine power. Terrorist groups, for example, are not part of the divine plan, in which case there is no collective karma but there is most definitely individual karma. These groups do have their own group energy but it is a dark energy, which is why some are swept up in their allure. They confuse that dark light with divine power. Loosely organized groups are not part of collective karma either. For example, cultures do not generate karma of their own but work under the race and national karma they are a part of.

A great irony of collective karma, especially when we speak of nations and races, is that the full effects are often felt generations *later* by people who had little or no connection to the people who started the karma to begin with! This has caused great confusion as to how God works out divine justice. On an individual level, if you create bad karma, it comes back to you, not to those around you. But if the government of a nation initiates a destructive act, the country will often not feel the karmic effects until *later* generations.

Why do we have to pay the price for the sins of our forefathers? At first glance, this may seem unfair, but there are many reasons why the divine works this way. First, even though karma generally swings back sooner rather than later, the bigger the group, the longer it can take the karma to come full swing. So it is often not possible for the karma to come to fruition in the same generation. Second, the law is impartial. With collective karma, we pay the price *and* bear the fruits. Third, if individuals were held personally accountable for collective actions, the group's leadership would never be able to carry such a karmic burden. We have seen how much karma we can create by our personal actions. It would become unbearable if we multiplied that many times over. Remember, no matter how those in power may be perceived or exercise their power, they are still *representatives* of many people.

And finally, collective karma actually *protects* individuals within the group. Remember, karma is a harmonizing law. The pain we may feel when karma swings back to us is how the divine brings itself back into balance. Take the analogy of the human body. It takes many cells joining together to form and preserve a human body. Regardless of the activity of individual cells, our body thrives because of the collective effort of many cells. If malignant cells get the better of certain parts of the body, we can develop diseases like cancer, which can affect not just individual cells but potentially the life of the entire body. So by keeping the body as a whole in harmony and balance, we are protecting the life of the individual cell. In the same way, it is the job of collective karma to maintain harmony and balance for the group as a whole, which serves to keep its individuals healthy.

Does collective karma mean that individuals are not accountable for their actions? While it is true that you are not held personally accountable for the group's actions, you are always held accountable for your individual actions. If you work at a company that's involved in illegal activities, you are not held karmically accountable for the company's actions even if you're aware of what the company is doing. But if the company asks *you* to participate in something illegal and you do, then, of course, not only are you bound legally, you are bound karmically as well.

Another very important feature is the Higher will use collective karma to work out individual karma. Say you've generated negative money karma. You may find yourself incarnating in a country going through a heavy collective money karma to pay back that karma, even though you had nothing to do with the country being in that situation. Through that collective karma, you are being given the opportunity to work out your own money karma. Despite appearances, God always works things out to your benefit. Through that difficult experience, you are given the opportunity to learn your lessons and rebuild your life. Nothing is really lost.

NATIONAL KARMA

My spiritual mentor, Inez Hurd, was an eloquent speaker on many spiritual topics, including karma. When it came to national karma, she taught:

> Let us understand the karma of all nations on the Earth as each one of us owes a karmic debt to our nation, to our state, county, and to our city, and we owe this karmic debt through our government. This is our karma to civil law.

National karma is a form of *domestic* karma. It deals with the internal affairs of a country. This means that as we live in a country, state, and city, we partake of its collective karma, good and bad. It also means we owe it to the place we live in to contribute to its betterment.

Although we will use the words *country* and *nation* interchangeably, they are not actually the same thing. A country is a self-governing political entity. A country has its own internationally recognized land and its own sovereign government that can administer public policy and affairs without outside interference. A nation, on the other hand, is a culturally tight-knit group of people, but a nation does not necessarily have its own land and sovereign government. When it does, we call it a country, or a nation-state. And it is at this point that a nation generates its own national karma.

To better understand national karma, let us step back for a moment and look at the spiritual purpose of a nation, and for that matter, civilization itself. Richard Overy, author of *The Times Complete History of the World*, writes that anthropology and archaeology teach us that "the transformation of humankind . . . from hunters and fishers to agriculturists, and from migratory to a sedentary life, constitutes the most decisive revolution in the whole of human history."

Yet this monumental transformation of humanity that led to the development of cities and nations as we know them today did not happen by itself. At every turn, the divine has lovingly initiated every phase of human development. Civilization itself was born of the divine impulse to facilitate the development of humanity's blossoming divine powers. Even now, working behind the scenes, the divine is guiding the development of civilization. There's a balance between the spiritual influence and human free will, and here is where karma comes into the picture.

The spiritual purpose of a nation is to contribute to the management of civilization as a whole. Countries act as a checks-and-balances system to other countries. This serves to keep the activities of civilization moving in the right direction and prevents one country from getting too much power. It was not always this way.

When civilization first developed, humanity worked together as one people, one nation, one voice. This was a golden age. Unfortunately, humanity did not handle the power that civilization brought very well. As the biblical story of the Tower of Babel alludes to, humanity became tall with pride and committed terrible offenses, accruing heavy karma very quickly. The divine chose to break up humanity into smaller, more manageable groups. Out of this period of struggle, the first nations of the world were born.

The Dynamics of Nations

Why is it that some nations thrive while others struggle? Since nations act as a collective whole, their spiritual destiny works the same as it does for any individual. There are three determining factors that strongly affect the development of a country. All three elements work together to form the dynamics of a nation.

They are:

- The purpose a country serves in the divine plan
- The overall development of people within that country
- The national karma that country faces

Some nations are designed to nurture younger souls. By younger, I mean souls who have not gone through as many cycles of incarnations as other souls have. Naturally, these younger souls will reflect in the collective karma of those nations. There is nothing at all wrong with nations in this state of development. They serve an essential spiritual function. The challenge many of these developing nations face is that they are taken advantage of by aggressive leaders and other nations who exploit their resources and people.

There are nations whose destiny is to be at the vanguard of civilization. Naturally there will be more developed souls in these countries to facilitate their purpose. Once these nations fulfill their purpose, they may fade or continue to be an example of what humanity is capable of.

Then there are nations that reached great heights but fell, then, into a period of decline for some national karma, only to rise again once that karma has been paid. Some countries disappear altogether or are assimilated into other nations, and these are examples of heavy national karma or the spiritual purpose of that country coming to an end.

Civil war is a dramatic form of national karma where there is an irreconcilable division within a country's government. Revolution is an extreme case of national karma where the government itself becomes so corrupt or inept that its people have to take matters into their own hands. These types of karma can move nations for their betterment or complicate matters further, sometimes generating new karma.

Civil Laws and Divine Laws

The government of a country is responsible for taking care of its people. It has a moral and a karmic obligation to do so. Since it is the force that guides the collective destiny of its citizens, a government is responsible for such things as job opportunities, providing a stable economy, social services, education, cultural advancement, religious and personal freedoms, equality among its citizens, health care, protection against invaders foreign and domestic, and so on. It accomplishes this through its form of governing: the laws it enacts and the way it enforces those laws. All branches of government are part of the collective whole and share in national karma.

From the spiritual perspective, no single form of government is better than another. The type of government a nation has is more a reflection of the temperament of its people and its spiritual destiny. A theocracy or monarchy can work as well as a republic or democracy if it is run well and not corrupted. So the defining factor in the success of a government is the quality of its people and leadership. If a government truly serves its people, then it will thrive.

Our earthly governments are meant to be a reflection of the divine government. The closer the Earth government reflects the divine, the more it lives up to its potential. In addition to the moral fiber of the people, a government accomplishes this through the laws and policies it enacts. Civil laws are meant to reflect divine laws. When they do, a nation prospers, and when they don't, a nation suffers. Fortunately, we are not held karmically accountable for civil laws that work against divine laws if we have no choice in the matter. The divine does not ask us to break civil laws. However, we are accountable if we have a choice.

There are examples of people engaged in activities that serve the country but that do not bear personal karma. Soldiers going to war are under the authority of their commanding officers. They bear no personal karma as long as they do not act in an unconscionable way. Lawyers do not generate karma for defending guilty clients even if they know the client is guilty and manage to win their case, because those lawyers are preserving the right to a fair trial. But if a lawyer has ulterior motives, manipulates the court, takes bribes, then karma accrues heavily. Police generate no adverse personal karma when performing their job, as long as they are not corrupt.

KARMA OF LEADERS

It is an honor and privilege to be in a position of leadership. From the point of view of collective karma, a leader is someone who guides the actions of the group. Because groups that generate collective karma are part of the divine plan, leaders are very much a part of the divine plan as well. When Jesus was on trial, Pilate, not wanting to condemn Him, urged Jesus to speak out in his own defense, saying, "Knowest thou not that I have the power to crucify thee, and have the power to release thee?" Jesus answered, "Thou couldest have no power at all against me except it were given thee from above."

The power of leadership comes from God. The leaders we have are *meant* to be our leaders. It is rare that someone becomes a leader who was not meant to lead, and if they do it's for a short time. We may complain about a leader's performance or decisions, but it is our collective karma, good or bad, to have the leaders we have. Of course, we must still go through the process of selecting our leaders, but in doing so what we are really doing is fulfilling our part in the divine plan.

When a leader takes his or her oath of office, a special Divine Light is bestowed upon them. This light helps them in their term of office and in dealing with their work on a karmic level. It appears as a beautiful white sphere in the heart center and acts as a contact point for the Higher. Leaders receive special help from the Higher to assist them in accomplishing their goals. They are carefully watched, and are inspired to make right decisions. Yet even here, free will comes into the picture.

A group may have earned a great national leader such as Abraham Lincoln or an enlightened race leader such as Mahatma Gandhi. It may have earned a leader who is very liberal or very conservative. Once in a while, the collective karma will be so heavy that a lowly or evil soul will be allowed to be a leader, resulting in a dictator taking control of a country. Germany experienced this during the days of Adolf Hitler.

The big question so often asked is: Are leaders held accountable for their actions? It is tragic that too often leaders do not live up to their potential and this distorts the true meaning of leadership, which causes a great deal of adverse karma. Of course leaders are accountable for their actions. No one is exempt from the spiritual laws of life. Yet because they are leaders, we must consider the collective and personal karma that is involved. Remember, collective karma means the *group* is the individual, not any single person. Regardless of what individuals do, the group bears the karma.

Take a president or king who sends his nation to war. National leaders will tell you that the most difficult choice to make is to send troops into harm's way. There are times when war is just and necessary. In such cases, there is no adverse karma to the leader whatsoever, even though that leader knows he or she is sending troops into battle.

If a president or king initiates war as an act of aggression for vested interests with little or no thought of the consequences of his or her actions, then both the country and the leader will accrue karma. The country may go through tough economic times or be ruthlessly attacked in a later generation.

The leader accrues one of the heaviest personal karmas. For one, that leader will have to reincarnate in the worst of circumstances to experience what it's like to live under an oppressive ruler and lose your life in the process. That soul will have to go through other lifetimes of rebuilding his or her character, plus repay any other personal or relationship karma that will undoubtedly have accrued. It will take centuries of incarnations to fully resolve such actions. This is why the divine is so careful when it comes to the karma of leaders and does everything it can to avoid such a tragic outcome.

On a collective level, that person had karma as well. That leader will someday have to reincarnate as a leader again, perhaps in difficult times, to pay back the collective debt he or she owes. They don't necessarily pay back each person offended from the past collective action—that would be near impossible—but they will have to redeem their actions as a leader in a situation commensurate to the offenses they made.

Motive is always an important component of how severe the karma will be. For example, a president may go to war thinking that is the right thing to do but in fact it is not. The national and personal karma remain but will not be as severe. Or there may be a situation where war started as a necessary step but quickly spiraled out of control, as in the case of a country interceding on behalf of an oppressed country, only to then take advantage of the situation to pursue its own vested interests, thereby creating karma rather than resolving it.

In practice, leadership karma, especially leaders of countries, is one of the most complicated karmas because so many factors come into the picture, including: the destiny of a nation, its past collective karma, what it is still meant to accomplish, the actions of its people and leaders, and how it interacts with other nations.

What can we do as citizens when leaders act in ways that are not in the best interest of the nation? If you disagree with the actions of a president or government, it is your duty to express that displeasure. It is important to be civic-minded and contribute to the betterment of society. At the same time, it is most important to respect the oath of office the leader has taken. Regardless of your personal feelings, that leader is still in the position of representing the whole nation.

From the point of view of karma, you must take your own stand regarding the issues and decisions being made on behalf of the nation. You may not be able to change the collective outcome, but by standing by your beliefs, you maintain your integrity and do not generate any *personal* negative karma.

For example, take the terrible situation in Germany shortly before World War II. Let's say you are a citizen of that country and do not agree with the politics of the time. As long as you remain in the country, you inevitably share in the national collective karma. However, even though you may be forced to become part of the drama of that period, if you maintain your integrity and disagree with what is going on, you do not accrue any personal karma. Yet if you were to agree with the skewed politics of that era, not only do you share in the collective karma but you generate personal karma as well.

You may not be able to change the direction a nation is going in, but you have complete control over the role you play in the affairs of a nation, and that is the part you are held personally accountable for. Do you see the difference?

The bottom line is: Do your best to inspire and influence your leaders in a positive, constructive way. Get involved in the affairs of your city, state, and country. You make a difference. Recognize that there is a national karma and destiny you are a part of. You are responsible for how you participate in both. Make your own decision as to what is best and what is the most moral and noble road to take in any situation or issue of the day. Remember, we are not doing this on our own. All nations are under God, and the divine works diligently to direct national and international affairs. Pray for our leaders. It is not an easy job to lead effectively.

Leadership karma works the same for those in all types of collective decision-making positions: CEOs defining company policies, religious leaders deciding religious codes, judges and juries reaching verdicts and sentences, lawmakers passing new laws or revising old ones—all are accountable for their individual actions, but the collective karma is owed by the group itself. Always remember, people working on behalf of a collective whole never work alone. If an organization of people has earned its own divine power ray, it has become part of the divine plan of life and is guided carefully by the divine. This means the divine is there managing every court case, every law passed, every action of the group according to the karma limits of the situation.

We are all given the test of leadership at one point or another. It's part of our spiritual growth to pass the test of leadership. If you find it is your turn to be called into service, honor that call and do your best to serve those entrusted in your care.

A Reincarnation Story of a Tyrant

Let us now look at an incarnation from the Book of Life and see how karma works when dealing with a leader. In this story, we will look more at the personal ramifications of karma and its connection to leadership rather than the collective karma.

This incarnation takes us far back to the Old Kingdom era of Egypt, to the Fifth Dynasty pharaoh Djedkare Isesi. At this time in Egypt, there was unrest. There were several domestic issues plaguing the country, but a key problem was a severe drought that was causing poor crop production. This was creating unrest among the Egyptian citizens.

Djedkare started as a young pharaoh. His intentions were good and he began his reign with high hopes of making his country better. Unfortunately, when difficulties arose, his approach was too often not well thought out. Over time, he became more strict and tyrannical. Some people continued to be loyal, but many started to hate him when he laid down laws that were difficult to follow. In an effort to control population and food usage, he decreed that couples could have only two children. He ordered people to death without just reason, in order to quell dissension. His advisors had good ideas, which he did not implement. At one point, his high minister gave him sound advice in negotiating with a neighboring country. In a fit of rage, Djedkare stabbed the man to death—an action he later greatly regretted.

These tactics put the country into more trouble rather than making things better. Djedkare thought that being tough was the way to solve problems. Another issue was a religious reformation going on in the country. This aided in the decentralization of power, with some of the influential classes in society gaining power and momentum. Rather than see that this was something good for the country, Djedkare felt threatened and tried to tighten his grip. Even though he died relatively young, he had a long reign. The next pharaoh did better, but other conditions also changed to improve life in Egypt.

There is almost always national karma when it comes to deciding who will lead a country. Leadership is not happenstance. Sometimes it's the national karma to have a difficult leader. But this was not the case with Djedkare. He was meant to lead differently than he did. In the beginning, he was on track and led his country in the right direction. He was intelligent and full of ambition to do well. It was when difficult times came that he started to make mistakes. Like all of us, he had his own personality tendencies and, unfortunately, some of the less desirable character traits were triggered, causing this downward spiral in leadership.

Several lives were involved in his becoming the leader he was. A key lifetime was a previous incarnation in ancient China, where he ruled a province. It was on a smaller scale than the later one in Egypt. Yet in this life Djedkare did a very good job and ruled well, earning very good karma. He was benevolent, and, interestingly, there were tough times in that era as well. Similarly, there were domestic problems dealing with the land, but this time he did a good job. He turned things around and got that part of China moving on the right track. Part of his job as pharaoh was to apply the same talents and skills in Egypt but on a larger scale.

So what happened? What turned this good leader into a tyrant? First it must be seen that despite his harsh rule as pharaoh, his intentions were good. His motivation was to serve his country. Had he ulterior motives, vested interests, his karma would have been very different. What flipped him was soul karma from two lifetimes earlier where he was again born in the Middle East, but was a very successful merchant. He had an air about him that he wanted to be above everyone else. He was very tough in his business dealings, not cruel but ruthless, and although he progressed and became wealthy, he accrued soul karma. The stresses as pharaoh triggered this character flaw. It was inevitable that this character flaw would surface, but it was fully within his ability to master this part of himself if he put his attention there.

How does Djedkare work through this karma? Again we must separate the collective karma from the personal. Depending on his motives, he was not as bound karmically to his collective actions as he was to his personal actions. There were exceptions made as a leader, but as a man he was like everyone else, responsible for his actions. Because his motives were good, his karma was not nearly as bad as it would have been were he simply out for his own selfish interests. Yet naturally he generated karma.

In his life after being pharaoh, Djedkare was born in ancient Syria. Again, the country was in a very difficult period. He was born into luxury, but was part of a group that was not in favor with the people. There was almost a civil war. He did not show a good character in this life. At one point, he killed a woman he loved out of jealousy, creating more karma for himself. He was not happy, and as the unrest worsened he lost his fortune and wound up living a destitute life. While he was still rather young, he was killed because of his political affiliations. In this life, Djedkare learned firsthand what it is like to suffer at the hands of someone else's misguided rule.

Soon after, Djedkare had an incarnation in ancient Rome. This was the lifetime where he was meant to work through his personal karma of being too tough on people. Again, he was born into a life of wealth. He did a lot of commerce and trade. At first he seemed amicable enough, but soon became bored with life. In his personal life, he started taking advantage of people financially.

He had two disastrous love affairs and this helped him see the error of his ways. He changed and made an effort to become softer. He did his best to make up for his past mistakes. Some years later, he met a woman who was very helpful to him. They married and had a child together. It was a happy marriage and a happy home life. By the end of his life, he had worked out this character flaw and resolved this personal karma.

In yet another incarnation further down the line, Djedkare was in Gaul, or what is southern France today. He was a man who married and cared for a woman who, in a past life, was the Egyptian minister he murdered. Actually, they had many good lives together. Djedkare deeply regretted killing him and was more than willing to make up for it. He helped the woman through a very difficult time and made many sacrifices for her. This helped to pay back the personal karma he had generated. The person he murdered as pharaoh was not part of his official act as a leader. It was a personal act of rage and was treated as personal karma. Those who were executed or killed as part of an official act of State were generally under the collective karma, unless there was an abuse of power.

COLLECTIVE RELATIONSHIP KARMA

We know that countries and other groups don't work alone. They constantly interact with one another in the same way that individuals interact with one another. This means that just as there is such a thing as relationship karma between people, there's such a thing as relationship karma between groups.

The same lessons of love apply to groups as they do to individuals. It is our job to honor and respect other groups. Groups must learn to get along with one another, to be able to work together and respect one another's differences. When we bully, trespass upon, cajole, unduly influence, or manipulate other groups, karma accrues.

There is collective relationship karma regarding how similar groups interact: country to country, religion to religion, race to race, corporation to corporation, and family to family. Then there's the collective karma of how varying groups in society interact with one another: political, economic, religious, racial, cultural. Each sector of society is meant to play a part in the scheme of civilization, with one complementing the other. When things work well, a wonderful synergy occurs and good karma accrues. Government offers equality to people through civil law. Religion and cultural groups offer free-dom of personal belief and expression. Business groups bring about coopera-tion and working with others to produce the material needs of society.

What makes relationships between groups successful is *motive*. Ideologies are only as good as the quality and integrity of the people employing them. Groups need to adopt the Golden Rule—Do unto others as you would have them do unto you—in their interactions with other groups if they wish to be successful. This win-win scenario is the only way that groups can learn the spiritual lessons collective relationship karma teaches.

For example, let's take the relationship of Church and State. In most coun-tries today, there is a distinct separation of Church and State born out of centuries of contention and strife. Yet there are some societies that welcome this relationship. So how does collective relationship karma work here?

First let us make a distinction between Church and spiritual ideals. In our definition of Church, we are referring to a recognized, organized group. The relationship of Church and State refers to a particular religious organization and its interaction with a particular government. This is different from a country basing its society on spiritual or religious ideals and different from State religions.

For example, the United States was specifically designed to keep matters of Church and State separate. It also was specifically designed not to have a State-sanctioned religion in order to offer freedom of religious expression. Yet the United States was strongly founded on spiritual ideals, particularly Christian ideals. The concept of "one nation under God" is at the bedrock of what the United States is all about. And this has been reflected in the moral life of the nation.

If a country is set up where there is a distinct separation between the religious organization and the activities of government, then each group must respect that difference. If one group unduly influences the other, then negative karma accrues. We have seen examples where the leaders of a religion have unduly pressured and influenced governments, and this creates negative karma.

However, if a government welcomes religion in the affairs of government, then there is a marriage between the two groups and no negative karma accrues. There is nothing karmically wrong with a government being set up this way. There have even been societies where the religious leader becomes the political leader and runs the country as a president or king would. In these situations, the karma switches. The religious organization or leader now becomes the political leader. The collective karma now works on a civil level. Of course, the leaders are still answerable to divine laws. If they wield their power for personal gain, collective karma most definitely accrues.

THE KARMA OF WAR AND CONQUEST

One of the most dramatic forms of collective relationship is the karma of war. We all know how terrible war is in any form, yet even here there are spiritual dynamics. War is man's own evil, sometimes a necessary evil. Sometimes war ironically leads to progress, other times to decay. It all depends on the motives behind the acts of war.

When wars are started as an act of pure aggression and conquest, naturally this creates disastrous karmic effects for the country initiating the aggressive action. Usually, the country will end up going through the experience of being invaded itself in future generations. However, when war is used as a defensive action, there is no negative karma. Just as we have a right to defend ourselves on an individual level when attacked, a nation has the right to defend itself when attacked by another nation.

There are times when it is necessary for one country to intercede on behalf of another country. If country A sees country B treating its citizens horribly, then country A has the spiritual right to go to the aid of country B, even if it means military action. I don't mean interfering in the national affairs of a country for vested interest. I'm talking about interceding if the government is committing acts of genocide, enslaving its people, or brazenly invading weaker countries around it, etc. Such actions actually help create good karma for the country helping out. However, the country interceding must have the military means to be able to help. Otherwise, it's putting its own welfare in danger.

What about times when war and conquest seem to further civilization, even though it's a terrible thing? We have seen how the conquests of Alexander the Great, the Roman Empire, Genghis Khan have actually helped to further the cause of civilization. Through their conquests, they united parts of the world. Charlemagne in his Christianizing of Europe was able to quell barbarian hordes, which allowed for the blossoming of the continent. What is the karma in situations such as these?

These are intricate situations and one cannot make sweeping statements about them. Yet there are times when God permits conquest and war to occur as a way to further the divine plan for civilization. We must remember that there are groups that unfortunately will respond to nothing but the sword. When a Viking takes the name "Skull Splitter," you cannot ask such a soul to quietly lay down his weapon and take on a new mode of living, even if that modality is for his betterment. Sometimes the growing pains of civilization are violent. In these situations, personal karma still accrues, for these are still acts of aggression. But the interesting thing is usually there is no negative collective karma. The nations themselves can prosper and even blossom.

RACE KARMA

The karma of race is a fascinating study as it touches on one of the most ancient of all collective karmas as well as the history of human evolution itself. Before there were civilizations or religions, there were people. Anthropologists and paleontologists have done a remarkable job opening new doors in understanding the complex history of our species from very piecemeal evidence. Although it's a long way from complete, what emerges is a rich history of life going back millions of years.

The term *race* refers to the idea of dividing people into groups according to their characteristics and common ancestry. Through the ages, the understanding of why humans are different has varied greatly. Today the whole idea of race has become controversial. The question asked is whether races are really distinct from one another biologically or is race more a matter of environment and a sociological construct to understand physical differences in people or people who developed in different cultures.

The point of view of metaphysics is that although we are all of the same species, in fact there are definite, distinct races that all play a crucial role in the evolution of the human soul. Each race is holy and divinely designed to accommodate the temperament and evolutionary plan of the souls in that race. All races are equal in the eyes of God. Each serves a spiritual purpose and has its own divine destiny.

So that you can better understand how race karma works, I would like to give you a very brief outline of the spiritual history of the races as metaphysics teaches it. This is a vast and noble topic and one that introduces many principles that science does not currently recognize.

In a nutshell, metaphysics teaches that the human body was designed by God and is going through its own process of evolution and refinement. There are seven grand cycles in the physical design of the human form. These cycles are generally known as root races. The term is a good one but can be misunderstood, as we are not speaking of a particular race of humanity, rather an entire epoch, or cycle, of physical development that all fall under a broad classification of a root race. As part of each epoch, there are seven successive sub-races. It is these sub-races that are the actual races that have developed as we understand them.

The individual races that developed out of the first two root race cycles were primitive nonphysical forms yet still operated in the physical world. These races passed away long ago and nothing remains of them today. It was in the middle of the third root race cycle, known as the Lemurian epoch, that the first physical human forms appeared on the Earth. This was a gradual process that began approximately 18 million years ago. Although these first human forms did resemble apelike creatures, they were not of the animal kingdom. From the beginning the human form has had its own evolution separate from other organisms on the Earth, including apes.

Of the seven root races, it is said that we are currently in the fifth cycle, or fifth root race. The term *Aryan* has been applied to this root race, but there has been a gross misunderstanding and misrepresentation of this term.

Ethnologically, Aryan means "noble" in Sanskrit and refers to the original Indo-European or Proto-Indo-Iranian nomadic tribesmen. In terms of the fifth root race, the word *Aryan* is used not just as a name for the fifth cycle of races, but includes *the entire epoch of human development through the fifth cycle*. Spiritually speaking, *all* humans today are Aryans because we all are partaking of the fifth epoch of physical evolution regardless of where we are in our spiritual development.

After the fifth root race, there are two more cycles to go in which the physical body will continue to become more and more refined to the point that Earth will one day become a planet of spiritual adepts.

These cycles of development overlap, and here is where you have the races of humanity as we see them now. Today's races developed out of the fourth and fifth race cycles. The oldest ones of course have refined their forms through many millions of years of evolution and the newer ones bring their own characteristics and qualities. (See the graph on page 167.)

So to return to karma, do races generate collective karma? Yes, they most definitely do. Because races are distinct groups imbued with their own divine power ray and are part of the divine plan, they generate collective karma. Race karma essentially works the same as other collective karmas. The actions of individuals within races affect the collective karma of the race as a whole. Race dynamics also work the same as other group dynamics. You are born into a race as part of your divine destiny, to learn particular lessons that race offers and to become part of the race karma.

Just as national karma pertains to a country's domestic issues, race karma relates to how people work together within that group. As we know, there can often be conflicts between various tribes and groups within the same race, and these are examples of race karma.

With race karma, there are some differences from other collective karmas. For one, you can leave a country or change your religion, but you can't change your race. You keep the physical form you inhabit for the duration of your incarnated life. Good or bad, you have to go through your experiences in your race cycle. Also, other forms of collective karma are strongly tied into the leadership of that group. With race, you may have leaders that emerge,

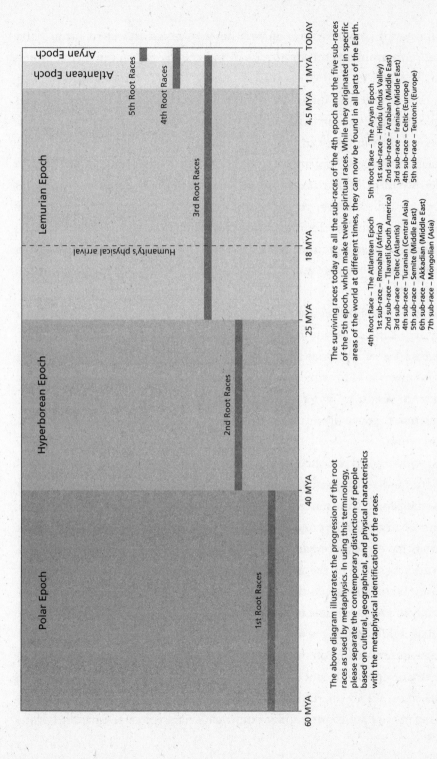

The above diagram illustrates the progression of the root races as used by metaphysics. In using this terminology, please separate the contemporary distinction of people based on cultural, geographical, and physical characteristics with the metaphysical identification of the races.

The surviving races today are all the sub-races of the 4th epoch and the five sub-races of the 5th epoch, which make twelve spiritual races. While they originated in specific areas of the world at different times, they can now be found in all parts of the Earth.

4th Root Race – The Atlantean Epoch
  1st sub-race – Rmoahal (Africa)
  2nd sub-race – Tlavatli (South America)
  3rd sub-race – Toltec (Atlantis)
  4th sub-race – Turanian (Central Asia)
  5th sub-race – Semite (Middle East)
  6th sub-race – Akkadian (Middle East)
  7th sub-race – Mongolian (Asia)

5th Root Race – The Aryan Epoch
  1st sub-race – Hindu (Indus Valley)
  2nd sub-race – Arabian (Middle East)
  3rd sub-race – Iranian (Middle East)
  4th sub-race – Celtic (Europe)
  5th sub-race – Teutonic (Europe)

The Root Races and Their Cycles up to Present Day

but it's not as comprehensive as with other forms of collective karma. This places more emphasis on the actions of individuals within the race to generate its karma.

A race is under the direction of a race spirit that guides the destiny of its people. There have been cultures that worshipped these race spirits as gods in their own right in honor of their sacred duty. There are times when a human race leader emerges. Mahatma Gandhi is an extraordinary example of a race leader. We think of him as a spiritual and even political leader because of his influence in these areas, yet he held no religious post or public office. His strength came from his representation of the Indian people and their struggle for equality. Martin Luther King Jr. was a fine example of a race leader who helped the race he was a part of come out of one of its most difficult karmas.

As souls going through the human experience, you're meant to experience a variety of races. As you live in these various races, you share in their collective karma. Your racial karma can be met and finished in any race cycle, but not always. Many times, you will reincarnate in the same race until you have learned how to understand all of your brothers and sisters in that race. Other times, you will incarnate from race to race. It all depends on your karmic chart.

As with other types of collective karma, the Holy Ones use race karma to work out individual karma. Remember, race karma is not necessarily felt by the same people who started it. The fortunes or misfortunes you experience as part of a race can be connected to your own personal karma. Other times, you may have to endure hardships because of the destiny you share in a race. This becomes part of the growing process, and the divine always balances this out. If you have to go through a difficult time unrelated to a karmic condition, you earn spiritual credits that are used to balance out other unrelated karmas. Again, nothing is lost.

How do we look upon the races today? With tolerance and respect for the diversity of others. Do not try to be the same. Let each race fulfill what it is meant to be. We are all playing our part in the divine scheme. Part of your job as a member of a race is to honor your race and at the same time see beyond race and recognize that we are all part of the greater family of God. Blood ties must give way to ties of the spirit. You are a spark of God and that is greater than any human form.

RELIGIOUS KARMA

The karma of religion refers to the collective karma of a particular religious organization. Spiritual ideals are for everyone. Yet once those ideals are embraced and conscribed into a creed and become a recognized religious organization, it is imbued with its own divine power and becomes part of the divine plan. It then begins to generate its own collective karma. As with any groups, religions are karmically responsible for their conduct. One would think by their very design religious organizations would be beyond reproach, but as we too often see, they are susceptible to the same mistakes as other groups.

The purpose of religion is to inspire people as to their true purpose in life and humanity's relationship to God. It enlightens us to a healthier and more productive conduct with others, to show tolerance and patience. As part of society, religion reminds us that, ultimately, civilization itself is but a tool for spiritual advancement. In its true form, it offers us freedom and brings out our natural sense of morality and decency. The beauty of religion goes beyond our present scope of awareness and heads us into the mystery of life. It allows us to imagine a greater good, a greater life than what is now in front of us. In this way, religion serves a purpose similar to great art—to give vision and inspire humanity.

The key with religion is belief. Religion does not work if you do not believe in the spiritual ideals that brought about that religion in the first place. All genuine religions on the Earth were born as part of the spiritual plan. There are lessons for humanity in every religious practice. Through belief, your life takes direction and purpose.

It is a sad fact that often religious organizations fall short of the lofty ideals of religion's true purpose. Instead of being open-minded and tolerant, ready to receive new spiritual inspiration, they can fall into dogmas and doctrines that choke the lifeblood out of the very spiritual ideals they are entrusted to represent. This creates a karmic condition, as intolerance does not forward the spiritual advancement of the souls in their congregations.

The world religions are going through a period of change as many people are reassessing their spiritual beliefs. Many religious organizations have had to show more flexibility to reflect the changing temperament of humanity. Many are adapting Thich Nhat Hanh's philosophy: "We human beings can be nourished by the best values of many traditions."

What about the relationship between metaphysics and religion? Do they mix? Sure they do. Metaphysics is not a religion. There's no reason you cannot include metaphysics in your religious practice. At the same time, there's nothing wrong with wanting to change your religion if that is your desire, or not follow a particular religious practice at all. Religion is a choice. It represents your freedom to worship God.

If you are in a particular religious practice, it is most important to do your best to adhere to the spirit of the law than to the letter of the law. Your goal is to live the spiritual ideals that the religion represents. There are politics in every religious group, but do not confuse that with the spiritual purpose of that religion.

You don't want to become close-minded in your spiritual thinking. Religion provides a path to God, but cannot possibly provide answers to all of life's mysteries. God is unlimited, and no religion, no matter how inspired, can possibly contain the full glory of God. As H. P. Blavatsky said, "There is no religion higher than truth." We have made great progress in our understanding of the spiritual life, but there is much more to learn. The Higher calls this Earth the kindergarten planet, meaning we are still children when it comes to the full understanding of the spiritual life of God.

The job of religions today is to come together and recognize that all true religions drink from the same spiritual well. God does not favor one religion over another. Each religion was designed to suit the needs and temperament of the people its teachings were directed to and to bring out a different facet of the spiritual life. Religions were also designed as part of the overall arc of spiritual development of civilization, so by their very design they were meant to be flexible.

The rigidity and struggles we see in religion today, internally as well as between different religions, go against the very ideals those religions were founded upon. Religion is not an end unto itself, but a tool to serve God. Just as countries come and go depending on their karma and purpose, religions as we know them adapt and change depending on the purpose and service they provide to humanity.

SETTING A GOOD EXAMPLE

In dealing with collective karma, do your best to set a good example. Regardless of what the group is doing, live up to the best of your own moral integrity. Ultimately it's up to you. You're still accountable for your own actions, regardless of what others are doing.

Be active in your community, your religion, and your race. The decisions that affect cultures and nations affect us all, and we have a part to play in that process. No one is insignificant or unimportant when it comes to collective karma.

There will be times when you will see inequities and injustice. Do what you can to rectify these situations, but don't jump to conclusions. Do your best to understand the situation from different points of view. It's too easy to get caught up in the passion of the moment. Understand that sometimes there are greater forces at work. If you can change things for the better, do so. Leave the rest in the hands of God.

In terms of doing our best to contribute to positive collective karma, the Athenian oath said it best:

> We will never bring disgrace on this our City by an act of dishonesty
> or cowardice.
> We will fight for the ideals and Sacred Things of the City both alone
> and with many.

*We will revere and obey the City's laws, and will do our best to
    incite a like reverence and respect in those above us who are
    prone to annul them or set them at naught.
We will strive increasingly to quicken the public's sense of civic duty.
Thus in all these ways we will transmit this City, not only not less,
    but greater and more beautiful than it was transmitted to us.*

Chapter 12

THE COLLECTIVE KARMA
OF THE WORLD

One of the greatest blessings of the global age is the understanding that, despite our diversity, we really are one people, one planet. In earlier times, it was harder to imagine how one part of the world related to another. People then were more isolated, did not travel or communicate as much with those in other regions of the world. Now more than ever, we can see that we are all sharing the same home and are not as different as we once thought we were. We have not yet reached the brotherhood of humanity that is already within our capacity to express, yet without question we're at an unparalleled point in the development of civilization. Where is humanity heading and how does karma fit into the picture?

Yes, there is such a thing as world karma! Just as national karma relates to the activity of a country and race karma relates to the actions of a race, world karma relates to the collective activities of civilization as a whole. Ultimately, humanity is meant to work together, diverse and varied but united and cooperating with the divine plan. World karma reflects how well we have achieved that cooperation. Inevitably, world karma is one of the most encompassing of all karmas as it deals with the whole human evolution. Some of our brightest moments have occurred on a world level and some of our darkest as well.

As with other group dynamics, the events and actions of civilization are affected by its spiritual destiny, the level of consciousness of humanity, and accrued world karma. Great inventions, discoveries, and works of art that have lifted humanity to new levels of awareness are all fine examples of world destiny and good world karma. Immortal artists like Beethoven, Michelangelo, and Leonardo da Vinci may have been born and lived in a particular country, but their contribution to humanity reached far beyond their national borders. Civilization earned the karmic right to such greatness, as all benefited.

The same is true with discoveries. Great inventions and discoveries are part of the destiny of civilization. When Isaac Newton, Albert Einstein, and Thomas Edison made their breakthroughs, they were breakthroughs not only in science but also in human awareness. These events were carefully orchestrated by the divine to help humanity in its spiritual unfoldment and could have occurred only as world karma permitted it.

Unfortunately, many of our global challenges are related to world karma as well. Hunger, disease, illiteracy, poverty, illegal drugs, forced labor, and slavery are all examples of difficult world conditions in which karma plays a part.

There are many examples of events throughout history that worked on a world karma level. The conquests of Alexander the Great, Genghis Khan, the Roman Empire, the Christian Crusades, and colonialism are all examples of historical events that crossed over into world karma, for better or for worse.

To understand how it works, I would like to take three dramatic examples of world karma that represent three of the great lessons of humanity. In looking at these examples, please keep in mind that world karma does not supersede our own personal karma. Our part in world karma is dependent upon our personal karma. Also more than one type of collective karma can be going on at the same time. World, national, religious, and race karmas can be active concurrently. The divine has quite a job to lovingly orchestrate all these karmas to keep humanity moving in the right direction.

We'll call these:

WORLD KARMA RELATED TO WORLD WAR II
The lesson of choosing good over evil.
WORLD KARMA RELATED TO AFRICA
The lesson of unity and cooperation.
WORLD KARMA RELATED TO THE MIDDLE EAST
The lesson of choosing God over money.

A Spiritual History of Civilization

Before going into these examples of world karma, I must step back and offer a few insights into the history of civilization as metaphysics teaches it. The reason for doing this is that metaphysics has its own perspective on world history, and this perspective is essential to the understanding of world karma.

Just as there is a Book of Life for each of us who records the events of our experiences in our soul's spiritual development, there is a Book of Life for humanity itself. This book chronicles the events and activities of civilization from its inception. What a miraculous record this is. Here on Earth we have to work with the physical evidence at hand. The further back in time we go, the sketchier the records we have of civilization's history. Once we reach past the time of written records, history falls silent except what we can piece together from archaeological evidence. Great stretches of prehistory appear irretrievably lost.

However, in the Book of Life, humanity's history is preserved in all its details. The reflection of that Book of Life can be found in each of us—in our own soul experiences, in the DNA of the physical form we inhabit, and in the collective unconscious of civilization.

As part of my metaphysical training, I have had the privilege of being shown portions of this sacred Book of Life of Humanity. In viewing what I was permitted to see, I was amazed to discover how encompassing our spiritual history really is. I discovered that civilization goes back much further in time than we understand at present. What a surprise it was to learn that fabled civilizations such as Atlantis and Lemuria were in fact very real places with rich and varied histories.

Even more incredible to see was how these long-forgotten civilizations are connected to today—that civilization bears the mark of these ancient epochs in some of humanity's most shining moments as well as in some of our most titanic struggles.

Every civilized nation in the world today owes an incalculable debt of gratitude to the civilizations of prehistory. Although the knowledge of these ancient times is absent today, we still feel their karmic effects. We would simply not be where we are today in terms of knowledge and culture without the influence of our rich and very ancient past. While we have come to understand that humanity's origins go back much further in time than we originally thought, the time is coming when we will understand that civilization itself also stretches back much further in time than originally thought.

Although there are many questions and perplexities in the archaeological record, it is commonly agreed that the oldest civilization is the Sumerian civilization in Mesopotamia, dating back some 6,000 years. It is agreed that civilization more or less began in this part of the world.

Before that time, there are archaeological findings of primitive communities and cities dating back as far as 9,000 to 13,000 years ago, indicating that man was already living in settled groups, cultivating the land, and domesticating animals, which was an important precursor to civilization. Earlier than 13,000 years ago, the evidence points to man living more as hunters and gatherers. Yet here, too, we see signs of sophistication in the art of the Cro-Magnons, which dates as far back as 25,000 to 40,000 years ago.

Reaching back further in time, it is believed that around 50,000 years ago there was a great leap forward in which humanity evolved the necessary higher brain capacity to conceive of and develop civilization. Then going back 100,000 to 120,000 years ago, we have fossil records of the first fully anatomical modern human beings, *Homo sapiens*, which could have come into being as far back as 500,000 years ago.

Stepping back even further, we find the first evidence of early humans, called *Homo erectus*. During this period we find simple stone tools that indicate that our ancestors showed signs of a unique intelligence for millions of years. The first hominids (creatures more closely related to humans than to apes) lived about 7 million years ago and are believed to have evolved from a common Old World apelike creature as far back as 20 million years ago.

Metaphysics does not contest many of these findings or timelines. On the contrary, it has been pointing to the antiquity of man long before science made its discoveries. Where metaphysics differs is in how these findings are interpreted.

From the metaphysical perspective, the current archaeological findings do not represent a true cross section of the diversity of humanity's development and how that development came about. If we look at human life 50,000 years ago, we would find a strikingly diverse world. There would be a great number of souls living like hunters and gatherers, but we would also find human souls who lived a much more developed life. While the archaeological evidence to support such a claim has not yet been established, such civilized living did coexist with a primitive lifestyle.

So now let us roll back the film and take a panoramic view of how civilization came to be, and how the events from our ancient past have made a strong contribution to the civilization we are living in today. In presenting this, I have no way to prove what I share with you other than to appeal to your own intuition, as somewhere in the distant record of your own soul's history you played a part in the dramas of prehistory. Perhaps it is best to look at these epochs in pre–world history and the generations they represent as if you were viewing the past lives of civilization itself.

Metaphysics teaches that every phase of human development has been ushered in and guided by the divine. While humankind has had to forge the spiritual path on its own, the loving hand of God has been with us every step of the way. Little has been left to chance or happenstance. This means that every aspect of our development from our body to our soul is part of the grand design of life.

Humanity began its physical evolution on Earth approximately 18 million years ago. Science currently teaches that man evolved from a hominid or early human form into *Homo sapiens*. Metaphysics teaches that *from the beginning* there were *two* types of human species developing concurrently: the hominid *and Homo sapiens*. The *Homo sapiens* bodies were designed for human souls at a more advanced level of development. The hominid and other types of early human bodies were designed to accommodate younger souls who were not yet ready to inhabit the *Homo sapiens* forms.

These first humans were certainly primitive and apelike, but from the start they were in a separate kingdom from the animals. Humanity had an intelligence and awareness all its own. It felt a kinship to family and worked together in small groups and even had a primitive type of language.

Over the course of millions of years, the various race cycles of humanity appeared from the *Homo sapiens* line of evolution in various portions of the Earth. This was according to the divine plan to prepare humanity for civilization that was to come. At the same time, there was an evolution of the more primitive line of human development. This line would culminate millions of years later in the Neanderthal—the last line of primitive man.

Approximately 800,000 years ago, the *Homo sapiens* line of human evolution reached a level of sophistication when it was ready for the beginnings of civilization. Some metaphysical schools put the development of civilization at a time earlier than this, but in terms of the line of development of our humanity, this is the time frame I have been taught by the Higher.

The divine gathered together members of the various races in a location deep in Africa and started the first civilization. Humanity was given its first unified language, its first social order, its first sanctified marriages, and its first leadership. And most important in terms of world karma, the divine gave humanity its own collective power ray. Now humanity began to work as a whole and thus began to generate world karma.

This was a primordial civilization of one voice, one nation, and one people. It was a primitive but beautiful time. At this point, there was no domestication of animals, no agriculture, and no civilization as we think of it today. People still lived as hunters and gatherers, but they worked together and learned one of the most essential keys of any civilization—cooperation.

Slowly over the next 250,000 years, the civilization that started in Africa fanned out to other parts of the world. Spiritually speaking, Africa remained the hub of human civilization, but the understanding of how to work together was now the operating principle throughout the world. Humanity accrued good world karma.

About 500,000 years ago, the first great tragedy befell humanity. The leaders of the African nation and the races they represented became proud and aggressive. They wanted to dominate and control the other races rather than work in cooperation. On their own initiative, they began to slaughter what were the weaker races at that time. There was much bloodshed and suffering. Humanity was quickly heading into a tailspin.

The divine decided that the best thing was to divide up the races and let them form their own individual cultures and nations. In this way, the calamity that befell Africa would not spread to the rest of the world. This was a difficult time as many did not understand why divisions were being created. Now instead of one voice and one nation, there were many voices and many nations. World karma remained, but now there came the beginnings of national karma. After this division, humanity continued to thrive and slowly develop, while Africa plunged into a dark age.

Then around 200,000 years ago, the first sophisticated civilization began in a land called Lemuria in the Pacific. It was the first civilization to have a civil code, domesticated animals, and agriculture. Most important, its people had a maturing spiritual understanding of life. Once again, this next phase of civilization developed very slowly. It took over a hundred thousand years for this new form of civilization to develop and spread to other parts of the world. During this time there was a great diversity in human development. The majority of human souls still lived in very primitive conditions, but there was a portion of humanity that now lived a much more developed life.

Around 100,000 years ago, the civilization of Atlantis arose. This civilization began humbly, but quickly gained in splendor and knowledge. It was at this time that humanity was given the gift of understanding that physical life is governed by spiritual laws. This opened the door to technology, and a whole new phase of spiritual development arose in conjunction with civilization. Today we see spirituality and science as separate things, but in the days of Atlantis, scientists saw that physical life was deity externalized and formed its laws based on this principle. Over time, such knowledge allowed the Atlanteans to perform amazing technical feats, some of which are beyond our own abilities today.

Over the next tens of thousands of years, a truly sophisticated civilization arose, spiritually and technically strong. By around 50,000 years ago, Atlantis was at the zenith of its power.

It was at this glorious time that another great tragedy befell civilization. The culprit was pride. Some of the leaders of the Atlantean nations became enamored with their own spiritual powers and gifts. They began to use their great gifts for personal gain and not for the betterment of civilization. This was the beginning of evil, as some were committing terrible offenses with full awareness and knowing what they were doing. Hence, a battle between good and evil—a battle that lasts to this day—began approximately 50,000 years ago on the shores of Atlantis.

About 30,000 years ago the sophistication of Atlantis had spread to many parts of the world. But the evil elements of Atlantis were also growing, and around 25,000 years ago they had gained tremendous momentum. Many people joined their ranks, while others did not understand how serious the situation had become. Around 20,000 years ago, after a series of terrible battles, these evil souls took over Atlantis. In what turned out to be the darkest turning point in pre–world history, these corrupt souls eventually dominated most of the world over the next several thousand years. Civilization went into great decay, with arts and sciences now in the hands of very few.

Around 11,000 years ago, a natural cataclysm hit Atlantis and other parts of the world. It caused catastrophic earthquakes and floods, submerging Atlantis and devastating the world. Not being a geologist, I cannot explain the mechanics of how Atlantis sank. With the modern theory of plate tectonics, it is now commonly believed that an event such as the sinking of an entire continent in so short a time is a geological impossibility. The reasoning is, tectonic plates move from side to side very slowly and not up and down violently.

However, this is making the assumption that there are no other geological processes at work that we are not aware of. We do have evidence of sub-merged or semi-submerged continents such as Zealandia in the Pacific and the Kerguelen Plateau in the Indian Ocean. We also must make a distinction between continents and the tectonic plates they are a part of. Clearly the sinking of Atlantis was not the result of normal plate movement but was the result of other natural processes we have yet to understand.

The geological process that submerged Atlantis had more to do with the activity within the tectonic plate itself. I have been told by the Higher that these plates are not rigid. As pressure within the Earth changes, it can cause portions of a plate to rise or fall. It's an event that has not happened for 11,000 years, so it's hard to imagine today how this can happen, but it does. Atlantis was not the first land to suffer this fate and most likely will not be the last. Geologically, we are in a very quiet time, and this has contributed to helping today's civilization grow rapidly.

On a personal note, there is no question in my mind that Atlantis was real because I was there. In one of my past lives, I had an incarnation in the last days when Atlantis sank, and I shared the same fate as millions of others. In that fateful life, I was born on the eastern shores of Atlantis. On this island continent were several countries, but the most progressive was the country on the eastern side of Atlantis—Poseidon. Poseidon was where the first great advances in Atlantean civilization occurred. It became the center of world culture and knowledge. Unfortunately, it, too, decayed into the center of cor-ruption and evil.

I was born as a girl to a wonderful family. My parents were advanced spiritually and started teaching me truths at a young age. They were high initiates, and in a sense I was their daughter and also their chela. They were not part of the dominant rule of the day, and unfortunately were targets of that rule. Poseidon at that time was a strange place. As it had already fallen to corruption ages before, it had diminished in its former spiritual and mate-rial glories, but still had a level of sophistication.

The dominant rule by that time had relaxed some of its stranglehold, so people lived a fairly normal life as long as they did not challenge the authority. There were commonplace events such as human sacrifice and other atrocities, but there were also periods of relative quiet and calm. The divine still found ways to keep civilization going through these difficult times. There were pockets of resistance in the hope of overturning the corruption, but unfortunately these were not successful.

When I was around thirty years old, I was told by my parents of the cataclysm that would befall Atlantis. There were rumors that such a thing could happen but most people did not take them seriously, and I found it hard to believe at first. What's more, I was told that it was my destiny to stay in Poseidon and help other souls through the ordeal that was to come, even though it meant my own demise. I agreed to stay. It was a most difficult time for all of us as it was my parents' destiny to leave Poseidon and help civilization continue after the cataclysm.

My parents eventually left. By this time, I had my own small metaphysical school. Many of my students fled as well, but a few stayed with me. Some of the Poseidon leaders, corrupt as they were, had psychic powers and sensed that doom was coming and also fled. Many other advanced souls also left, as they would have to help pick up the pieces of civilization afterward. Yet on the eve of Atlantis's end, many millions of people had little or no idea of what was about to happen.

The fateful time began toward evening. Tremendous earthquakes began shaking the ground. They did not last long at first but kept coming back. There had been earthquakes before but not of this magnitude and repetition. The great structures and temples of Poseidon began to crumble.

By the next morning, the city I lived in was pretty much leveled to the ground. People thought the worst was over but the day brought more earthquakes, even more violent than before. The ground started to dramatically separate, creating huge gashes in the Earth. A terrible sound would accompany these quakes. And I'm not sure why but heavy rains started to fall at one point. People were completely hysterical by now, and any sense of civil order was quickly eroding. With all the trembling, the hills were now visibly crumbling, trees were falling, and rivers were disrupted and flooding. Toward the end of the second day, the land started convulsing up and down. I knew once this started happening that the end was near.

There was nowhere to hide or take cover so I took a group of people to higher ground to pray. We could see the ocean, which was violent and erratic by now. There was no point in trying to move inland. Of course, I was scared, and even though I knew what was coming, I held out hope that maybe Poseidon would be spared.

By the latter part of the third day, the end came. I could see that the land was slowly, slowly sinking. It was sinking through the rest of the day and into the night until all of us drowned in the flooding ocean waters. By the next morning, Poseidon and the entire continent of Atlantis had submerged into the Atlantic Ocean.

My life, along with so many others, was forfeited that day. Yet because I did my duty and helped to ease many souls in their last moments, I actually completed my life's purpose and reached a wonderful pinnacle in my own evolution.

Many have contended that Atlantis sank because of its sins. This is not true. The submersion of Atlantis was a natural occurrence. What made things difficult was that because civilization had decayed before the sinking, it was not able to rebound the way it could have had it been in a better place.

After this devastation, the divine went immediately to work to help rebuild civilization, but because of the poor conditions humanity had fallen into, instead of rising to its former glory, it fell into confused times. Evil had lost its dominance, but there remained a constant struggle between the light and the dark that made it very hard to rebuild civilization to where it had been. Unfortunately, humanity eventually sank lower and lower. It completely lost its former knowledge and eventually its very history. In the eyes of the world, the civilizations of Atlantis and Lemuria were now relegated to legend and myth.

Eventually, the divine helped to restart civilization. To prevent a repeat of the disasters of Atlantis, this time civilization would not have access to the spiritual wisdom of material life. That knowledge would be held back until civilization showed it was capable of using such power wisely. While certain souls would become the custodians of the ancient secrets of humanity, civilization would learn to harness the physical elements of life spiritually blind. The civilization that arose had little or no awareness of its own antiquity.

And thus we have the development of civilization as we know it. Its meteoric rise to the sophistication of today in the span of several thousand years has been possible only because humanity is retracing steps it has already taken. Today we have a society that is quickly rediscovering great truths of the past. We are at a turning point where, if we handle things well, we can reclaim the glories of our ancient past and take our civilization to greater heights than ever before.

How could so much history have happened with no record of it readily available to us today? First, let me say that eventually knowledge will resurface. Archaeology is only two hundred years old, and there is still plenty of room for new and stunning scientific discoveries.

Yet there is another reason we have no conclusive evidence of prehistoric civilizations—karma. The truth is, there is a karmic veil over this entire portion of history that prevents our awareness of these times from resurfacing. But once this collective karma is paid off, this knowledge will resurface in unmistakable ways and civilization will once again reunite with its own ancient past.

May I say here that as splendid as civilizations like Atlantis and Lemuria were, overall civilization today is more developed than it ever was at any time on Earth. There are far more people on Earth than ever before, and there is more spiritual light on the planet than ever before. Where in days past there were great gulfs between human souls in their evolution, today those gulfs are rapidly closing and we are closer to becoming unified than in ages past.

WORLD KARMA RELATED TO WORLD WAR II

World War II was without a doubt one of the most dramatic events in world history. If you include the conflicts in Europe and Asia, it is estimated that more than 60 million people were killed. World War II changed the fabric of civilization. The economic, political, and sociological climate that generated the war has been carefully studied, yet the question remains: Why? Why did this war happen? On a spiritual level, how could a loving God allow such a devastating war to occur? What purpose did it serve, if any?

First, may I say that I have the utmost respect for all who fought and died during and as a result of that conflict. My brother Philip served in General Patton's 3rd Army and was one of the first to help liberate souls from the Nazi concentration camps. My brother George was in the Navy through part of the Japanese conflict. He was among the first to go into Hiroshima after the atomic bombs were dropped.

What we call World War II was one of the most decisive moments in the spiritual development of humanity. Although free will was the deciding factor in how World War II played out, World War II was world karma. Actually, the karma connected to World War II was karma of an entire era. This karma included World War I, the Great Depression, as well as World War II and the cold war, including the spread of communism, its conflicts, and the very real threat of nuclear war. All these events are spiritually tied together. The karmic debt that permitted these events to happen did not come full circle until the fall of the Berlin Wall, and even now there are elements that are still not resolved. The focus here is on World War II because that was the defining moment in balancing out this ancient karma. Had the Allied forces lost World War II, the world would have been a very different place today.

If world karma is the actions of civilization as a whole, what past collective action in world history could have generated such a titanic effect in the twentieth century? There are many examples of conquest in history but does this account for World War II and all it encompassed?

In trying to solve this riddle, let's look at the elements of what is being presented. For one, World War II was truly a global conflict of unprecedented scale. Second, there was a clear demarcation of good and evil, a call to save humanity from tyranny. Third, there was a vision, dark and twisted as it was, that drove the Axis powers. This was not simply about conquest. There was a dark quest that inspired millions to follow, some of whom died for it. And last, World War II was a modern war fought with highly advanced weapons and technologies.

If we put these elements together, we have a global conflict, fought between good and evil in which sophisticated weapons were used by and against an organized and motivated opponent. These elements give us clues to unraveling the mystery of this world karma. But what is this karma? Nothing in known history could account for this world karma. But if we scan the chronicles of prehistory just explored, we readily see a world event that was on a scale equal to the catastrophic events of the twentieth century. I'm speaking of the fall of Atlantis.

Strange as it may sound, the world karma that permitted World War II to happen was the karmic balancing from the tragic days of Atlantis. In the fall of Atlantis, we find a developed civilization choosing evil. In that titanic battle between good and evil, evil won. Imagine for a moment that Hitler had won World War II and reordered the world to his own pleasing and you will have an idea of what civilization was like after Atlantis fell. In Atlantis, the great lesson for humanity was to choose good over evil, right over wrong. Unfortunately, civilization at that time failed that lesson.

The divine had to wait until society rebuilt itself to the point that it was heading to the same place in terms of technological advancement in order for the Atlantean karma to come full circle. The beginning of the twentieth century provided such an opportunity.

At the beginning of the twentieth century, society was on the verge of a golden age. The industrial age promised a new standard of living. The sciences and arts were flowering in new and brilliant directions. There was an explosion of inventions that brought the world together. From the spiritual realms, plans were in motion to usher in a new age of spiritual enlightenment. The world looked rosy. Unfortunately, there were those in influential places who had other plans. They saw opportunity for unprecedented global conquest, and here was the karmic trigger that unleashed the full power of the ancient Atlantean karma.

The tragic events of the twentieth century did not have to happen as they did. Even though world karma was there, had civilization better cooperated, the karma would have come around but its effects would have been far less drastic. This karma could have been greatly lessened had the world been in a more spiritual place. Once again evil was forcing itself on civilization, and once again civilization was being called upon to choose between good and evil.

Fortunately, this time humanity passed its test. It was not going to let evil win. Although civilization was to face the Cold War and the threat of nuclear exchange, by winning World War II the destructive momentum that had been brewing from the beginning of the century was broken, and by the time of the collapse of the Soviet Union and the fall of the Berlin Wall, the Atlantean karma was further diffused.

What about the millions who died? Were they all paying back karma? And if so, what karma were they paying back? After seeing the unimaginable horrors of war, many lost their faith in God. These questions open up a most intricate area regarding karma. To properly answer them is one of the reasons I have taken so much time to explore the collective karmas that are at work concurrently with our own personal karma.

First let us go back to one of the fundamental principles of collective karma: The full effects of collective karma are often felt generations later by people who had little or no connection to the people who started the karma to begin with. This means that the people who died in World War II were not the Atlanteans who generated the karma. The Atlantean souls who generated the karma have long since paid it back personally. What has taken so long to come full circle is the *collective* karma connected to the events of Atlantis. However, the lesson that the Atlantean karma presented—choosing good over evil—was an inevitable lesson that our modern civilization had to face and master.

The other fundamental principle of karma here is that the divine uses difficult experiences we are undergoing that are not old karma or our own fault, to help resolve other aspects of our karma. Please remember this. The world is a dynamic place and sometimes bad things just happen to us. Not everything is karma. Yet even in these situations, God balances things out. We are *always* taken care of by the divine.

Following these principles, once it was clear that civilization was heading toward a major conflict, the divine used the inevitable sequence of events as an act of *personal* karmic cleansing on a mass scale. In other words, those who died during World War II were not paying back personal karma related to the days of Atlantis, but the collective karma they were inescapably a part of was used by the divine to help resolve other types of personal karma. You can imagine the scale of karma that was purged and redeemed during that time.

This tells us that no soul who died during World War II died in vain. Every soul was taken care of. No one was left out, as horrific as that time was. This brings us to an even more difficult aspect of World War II to comprehend— the Holocaust.

Was the Holocaust part of the Atlantean karma? Many suffered and died, but why were the Jewish people singled out? Were they paying back karma? Some say we cannot attempt to answer such things. Better to leave them alone. Yet the Holocaust was a lesson for all humanity. It's important to understand its significance from the metaphysical perspective.

I have been taught by the Holy Ones that the Holocaust was *not* karma. It was an inconceivable act of human brutality in the modern age. It *generated* karma, a karma that has yet to be repaid. As Rabbi Yonassan Gershom states in his heart-wrenching book *Beyond the Ashes*:

> It is very dangerous to fall into a "blame the victim" mentality when dealing with karma. Nobody "deserves" to be abused and tortured, no matter what the crime in this life or another.

Sometimes suffering happens, and this is one of the most terrible and dramatic cases. I have been reassured by the Higher that every soul who died in the Holocaust had their karma for that lifetime exonerated. Whatever normal, unrelated karma they came into that life to resolve was cleared by the extreme suffering they had to endure. As horrible as the Holocaust was, God still balanced things out. In the big picture, nothing was lost.

May I also bring up the important point that the persecution of the Jewish people in general is *not* karmic. It is another example of the actions of free will *generating* world karma. As with any collective group, they've had their share of mistakes and karma throughout their spiritual development. Yet from the metaphysical perspective, the Jewish people, or Jewish spirit, if you will, play a definite and essential part in the divine plan—a part that has yet to be fulfilled.

There is a mistaken belief that the Jewish people committed the ultimate karmic offense because of the role certain Jewish leaders played in the crucifixion of Jesus. This is *not true in the least*. If any single group were to be held accountable, the collective karma would have fallen on Rome as the acting authority at the time. And this was not the case either. While it is true that there was a divine purpose in Jesus being born Jewish, it must also be remembered that He did not come for only one group of people; He came for the world. He came to uplift humanity as a whole. Unfortunately, there was a karma generated by His untimely death, but that was *world* karma. Humanity itself became responsible for His death. Had civilization accepted the role Jesus played in the evolution of humanity, the enlightened age would have already begun.

The collective karma of Atlantis is coming to an end. We are still dealing with its effects because of another world karma that is currently active, but this entire period is finally coming full circle. How long it will take to fully complete itself only God knows. But there is a New Day coming for the Earth. We will have struggles ahead of us before we get there, but it is coming. And when it does, we can finally put some of these ancient sins to rest and the world can grow in unimaginably beautiful ways.

WORLD KARMA RELATED TO AFRICA

Africa is an enigma. It is one of the oldest places on Earth, the cradle of civilization, home to some of the most diverse life forms, rich in natural resources. With so much potential, one would think that Africa would be the center of world civilization, yet today it is the most undeveloped of the inhabited continents (and here we are speaking of sub-Saharan Africa). It suffers the highest poverty rate in the world. Its resources are not fully utilized and what is utilized is often for the profits for those of other lands. There is not nearly enough growth or proper education. Through the centuries, its people have had to endure some of the most difficult hardships and atrocities committed by man. And while some people care greatly about the African plight, the majority of the world still seems to turn a cold shoulder to its troubles. Why so much potential and so little realized?

There is a great dream of Africa—to develop; to fully join the modern nations of the world and enjoy prosperity and opportunity. Why hasn't this dream been realized yet? Many recognized forces are at work, including disease, apathy, and corruption. Throughout history, colonialism, slavery, internal struggles, poor leadership, international pressures all have been conspiring to keep the people of Africa from progressing as they could.

Here again we are faced with an ancient world karma, one of the most ancient of all collective karmas. To understand the world karma connected to Africa, we have to roll back the film to the early days of civilization itself, to that time when God brought the races together to start civilization.

As we have just seen in our brief metaphysical history of humanity, the beginnings of civilization occurred much further back in time than is currently accepted by science. It started almost 800,000 years ago deep in sub-Saharan Africa. At this time, the divine gathered together select members of the various races to start the grand plan of civilization. There were eleven of these races that were assembled. The leaders of this nascent civilization were members of the third root race cycle (see chapter 11) and supported by the first sub-race of the fourth root race cycle known as the Rmoahal (pronounced *Romel*) race. What we would commonly call the black race of today is, metaphysically speaking, part of this ancient Rmoahal race. The souls of the third root race cycle were strong and proud, yet in those ancient days, overbearing pride was to become their downfall. At that time, what we would call the white or lighter-skinned races were the younger races and were not the leaders of civilization.

For hundreds of thousands of years civilization flourished. May it be said here again that what we call civilization in this time period was not what we think of as civilization today. There was no developed agriculture, architecture, or sophistication as we conceive of them. People still lived as hunters and gatherers. The keynote of civilization in those days was cooperation.

Humans were learning how to work together in larger, organized groups rather than in the smaller family units they had been operating in before.

About 500,000 years ago, it was time for some of the other races to take the lead and play their part in developing civilization. The entrenched races at the time, including the Rmoahals, refused to relinquish authority. Regrettably these ancient races took terrible advantage of the other races, particularly the ancestors of the present-day white races. The atrocities committed were extreme. Rampant killings, torture, an early form of slavery were all committed with reckless abandon. The situation became so bad that the divine had to break up the races into various nations to prevent further karma from building up. Had this tragedy in the development of civilization been averted, humanity would have developed in a much more unified manner than it did.

After the breakup of humanity into various nations, Africa plunged into a dark age. Since then it has had its ups and downs, but it has yet to regain its primal glory, which it is destined to do. Although the souls inhabiting those ancient bodies have long gone on and paid back any personal karma, the world karma has remained all this time in the collective unconscious of humanity. This is because to pay back the collective karma of Africa, humanity has to once again complete what the African plan of civilization initiated—cooperation. As it was the African tragedy that caused the breakup of civilization into various nations, humanity has to once again show it is capable of working together as one nation before the African world karma can come full circle and Africa can regain its full glory and fulfill its part in the divine plan.

As with most types of difficult karma, there is evil and there is good. There is the resolution of old debts, but there are new debts that accrue. Past karmas do not excuse present bad behavior. With the blossoming of other races, including what we would call the white races in recorded history, the last phase of that unresolved karma has finally come full swing. Yet the cruelty that the white races have shown the black races is a newly created karma that has yet to be repaid.

What is the fate of Africa? It will slowly but surely continue to strengthen and reemerge in its own right. Despite its present difficulties, Africa will rise again. The reason it has taken so long is that the divine has had to wait until humanity was once again ready to reunite in one great brotherhood as it had originally started. We cannot truly advance as a civilization when we look down on our brothers and sisters. The lack of compassion by the other nations must change as collective karma teaches us we are all part of the whole. The reemergence of Africa will be the final signal that the world truly is ready to work together again, and it will be one of the final signs that the New Day is here.

WORLD KARMA RELATED TO THE MIDDLE EAST

The Middle East is truly at the crossroads of the world. It is the cradle of modern civilization. It is home to three of the great world religions and sits on some of the richest oil reserves, giving it access to enormous wealth. Yet here, too, is a riddle. Despite its historical value and strategic location, it is full of tensions and struggles.

The world karma related to the Middle East is not of its own making. While there are collective karmas related to races, nations, and religions, the struggles in the Middle East are reflective of a karma that is affecting every nation in the world. The irony is that this world karma has not been initiated by any country, race, or religion. It's more insidious than that. The enemy is coming from within, which makes it harder to detect.

To understand this karma we have to look at the financial dynamics of the world. Civilization is richer than it has ever been in its history. Despite the uneven distribution of wealth, productivity is on the rise in almost every country. This greater prosperity is creating new dynamics and new challenges. How do we handle this prosperity? Do we recognize its place in our life and spiritual evolution, or do we become hypnotized by its allure?

The world karma related to the Middle East is the lesson of money—to choose God over money. As civilization continues to build its wealth, it is up to us to learn how to harness this greater prosperity. It is our job to learn not to become complacent and indulgent but to use this great power to serve God and take civilization to new heights. This is the collective test currently confronting humanity. If it passes this test, it will have crossed one of the last barriers to a new age of enlightenment. If it fails this test, more hardships are in store until we learn our lesson.

This world karma is not an ancient karma coming full circle. It is world karma being generated in our present era. Because of the world dynamics, civilization is not going to have to wait aeons for this karma to come full circle. It is going to happen much sooner.

Money in some form has been a part of civilization from the beginning, but never before has it taken such center stage and reached such grand proportions. And never before have so many decisions pertaining to the welfare of civilization been based on personal economic gain. As the world has been heading toward a global age, the economic sector of society has enjoyed some of its greatest fruits.

However, the tremendous wealth and influence the business and financial sectors of society are enjoying is not meant to unduly influence the decisions of nations and other areas of society, yet this is exactly what we are witnessing. Instead of economics serving people, they're manipulating people as a tool of dominance. Some say that the financial ills of today are the result of the system of economics being practiced—capitalism. Yet capitalism by itself is neutral. It's the *misuse* of capitalism that is causing so many problems. Capitalism empowers the individual. It financially rewards those who work hard and excel. It also has allowed countries to financially interact with one another in a way not possible before. This all has the potential for great good, but it can be grossly abused. The danger of a capitalistic system is that those with money and without scruples can easily use the power that money brings to dominate and control others.

The ascent of the economic sector has given rise to an unofficial economic hierarchy that goes beyond individual companies and corporations, and here is the greatest threat. Some people in this hierarchy are good people, but there are those within this hierarchy exerting tremendous influence for their own ends. These corrupt souls are not in the public eye and do not publish their full wealth. They have forced their way up the economic ladder through the most evil means. In a sense, they have pulled a silent economic coup in which they now control many of the world's financial strings.

These insiders may live in a particular country, may have been brought up in a certain culture, but they have no allegiance to any country or culture. They are clever in working around civil laws and feel they are a law unto themselves. They consider themselves the true aristocracy of the modern world—which is not true. What they have done is taken enormous wealth and leveraged their influence and power for the most perverse ambitions. They have initiated a titanic battle for control of the world's riches.

Some who have studied this topic believe that these insiders initiated the global movement to create their own world order, but this is not true. It is the divine plan for the world to come together. This is a wonderful thing. It means we can finally work together again as one great people. It means more prosperity and opportunity for everyone. Unfortunately, what these insiders are attempting to do is twist the divine plan so they can create a totalitarian world order in which they are the rulers.

The actions of these souls are not part of the divine plan. Yet they wield tremendous influence with leaders in many areas of society, and here is where the collective karma steps in. Too many nations, peoples, races, religions, corporations have succumbed to their influence. Too many have pledged allegiance with these people and willingly been a part of their activities, and this bears a heavy karma.

The reason the Middle East is in the center of all this is because of its strategic position. The tensions that exist have been *artificially* aggravated to keep that part of the world unstable. The Middle East exerts tremendous financial influence, which makes it a key source of interest. Even the terrorism we see today is artificially fueled as a tool to destabilize the region and the world.

The Middle East has some rough days ahead. It's no secret that the greatest potential threat of a world conflict comes from this part of the world. However, the Middle East plays a key role in the divine plan of civilization. The struggle for peace in the Middle East is not just a regional struggle. Peace in the Middle East will be a signal that the world itself is on the threshold of peace.

Collectively and individually, it's our duty to learn the lesson of putting God before money. Some say this is nothing more than a dream. Humanity will never outrun its own greed, but this is not true. Sure, there will be economic challenges. But what can and must become a thing of the past is money's overbearing dominance in the affairs of society. Many have stood up to this global threat and even died for it. Many are standing up today.

What can you do regarding this present world karma of rampant greed? First, know that the divine is working diligently on this. The divine has diffused many plots already and will continue to do so. Don't obsess or become disillusioned by the challenges of today. God is working with us. We are not doing this alone. Keep your sights on God and the goals of your own life destiny. Live by the highest personal moral standard.

At the same time, be aware of what is going on in the world. You are not a helpless pawn. You are playing a part in the grand plan of life. Don't despair if difficult days do come. They will pass. Do your best to be fair in matters of money, even if other people are not, and hold strong to your divinity. Ultimately there will be peace and brotherhood in the world.

THE FUTURE OF CIVILIZATION

Just as there is a destiny for every soul on Earth, there is a destiny for civilization itself. Some have tried to paint a gloomy picture of civilization's future. This is more the projection of humanity's own fears and does not reflect what the divine has in store for us. The divine has a much more optimistic picture of humanity's future. Humanity, and all life on Earth, is at the threshold of a great leap in spiritual evolution. This spiritual renaissance will affect us all and usher in a New Day for civilization. Yet this Day will not just happen by itself. In order for it to happen, it will take all our collective willpower.

It is no secret that there are great troubles in the world. But despite its problems, the world today is in a better place than it has been in in a long time. We are heading to a greater sense of unity as the world becomes a smaller place. The world economy is on the rise, offering the potential for greater prosperity for us all. Most important, we are seeing a blossoming of human consciousness. We are more aware today of what is going on in the world and ourselves than ever before.

Many challenges await us as we reach this great place. Some say an Armageddon must happen before the enlightenment can arrive. In a sense it has already begun. It is true that there will be difficult times before better times really come. We could have catastrophic events in the twenty-first century that could include economic depressions, war, or perhaps even another world war. Hopefully we can avert some or all of these things. Yet regardless of what challenges come in the next hundred years or so, a brighter future than the world has ever seen lies ahead for all of us.

Part Four

RESOLVING
YOUR KARMA

Chapter 13

FACING YOUR KARMA

In this section we focus on how you can facilitate facing and resolving your karma. The suggestions and techniques offered are the results of many years of practice and observation. They are very effective, but I should be clear: There is no clever, simple, quick-step process to resolving karma. Facing karma takes sincere effort and hard work. Yet the beauty is, God always gives you the power and tools to resolve all your karmic challenges!

The karma techniques break down into two general areas: guidelines and tools for effectively identifying and dealing with karmic challenges, and meditations and energy techniques to cleanse and uplift the consciousness and auric field of the effects of karma. We will start with identifying and dealing with karma.

We all make mistakes. It's natural and you should not be afraid to make mistakes in pursuing your life's path. The tricky part is learning from your mistakes. When you fail to learn from your mistakes, you inevitably *repeat* the same mistakes. My spiritual teachers have told me they see many people making the same mistake *ten to twenty times through various incarnations!*

Everyone comes to this Earth with unfinished business. Your soul incarnates in physical form either to learn what it has failed to learn in past lives or to learn lessons that still are a part of its framework and evolutionary climb. Your experiences in this life are but one chapter in your Book of Life. You simply cannot judge or see the whole picture of your life history from the viewpoint of a single lifetime, no matter what that life is like. There will always be good karma that you bring in and karma that you need to redeem. Whatever the karmic slate is, you cannot outrun your karma.

It takes courage to look at your faults and face your karma. There can be a natural inclination to shy away from and avoid anything that is unpleasant. One of the hardest things is to realize that as an evolving soul, you have done it all. Through your many incarnations, you have done great and noble things and you have done not so great things. It's all part of the growing process. Fortunately, God gives you the strength to face any challenge. There is no sin beyond forgiveness and no difficulty so great that you cannot surmount it.

In identifying and resolving karma, you have to distinguish between four dynamics that are working concurrently:

1. Your purpose in life
2. The expression of free will
3. The process of spiritual development
4. Karma or the effects of past actions

A big mistake is to try to fit all your experiences into one neat little package, and such a perspective skews the true picture of life. You are not a one-dimensional being, and life is not one-dimensional. There are many dynamics going on concurrently that are creating the conditions you live in. There are some who take the laws of karma to the extreme and think *everything* that happens is karma. This notion is completely *false*. Not everything in life is karma.

There are some who go to another extreme and believe that *everything* is preordained. Whatever happens in life is God's will, and we are pawns in God's hands. Whether we die of an illness or live, whether we marry this person or not, whether we succeed in life or fail is all of God's making; our free will cannot overcome this fate. This point of view is also one-sided. Not everything we see in life is an expression of the divine plan, because the divine plan is not something that happens by itself. It's something we contribute to and participate in to *make* happen. What we see in the world and in our own life is more a matter of how well we are realizing or not realizing God's plan.

Then there are those who take free will to the extreme and believe that you create *all* the elements of your destiny moment by moment, and that your free will *completely* determines your fate. Following this philosophy, you are more or less doing it yourself. This point of view is also one-sided. While it is true that free will is the agent for realizing your purpose, you are not doing it on your own. If people could see into the spiritual dimensions of life, they would immediately understand how vast this greater support is.

And finally we must keep in mind that some of the experiences in our life, good or bad, are simply part of our spiritual growth. They are not karmic conditions but learning experiences to better explore how the dynamics of life works from firsthand experience.

IDENTIFYING FREE WILL

Free will is the key to your success or failure. Through your own volition, you create many conditions in your life. These actions will bring you closer to or move you further away from your life's purpose. So the first step in facing and resolving karma is to make sure you are not creating NEW karma.

When you initiate an action based on free will, naturally there will be an effect. This effect generates karma. Generating new karma through free will is different from facing karma of past actions. You cannot undo what you have done in the past. As Omar Khayyám so poetically put it:

> *The Moving Finger writes; and, having writ,*
> *Moves on: nor all your Piety nor Wit*
> *Shall lure it back to cancel half a Line,*
> *Nor all your Tears wash out a Word of it.*

With past karma, you have to work through it to resolve it. While there are techniques to help alleviate some of the burden, in a nutshell, you have no choice but to walk through those fires of purification. If you avoid facing your karma, it only comes back, and when it does, it returns creating an even more difficult situation.

The wonderful thing with new karma is you have control over it. You have complete control over your actions right here and now. In identifying new karma, the first thing to do is:

Look at your motive.

Look very carefully at *why* you are doing something. Ask yourself what is your motive *before* putting something into action. Is it selfish or will it help others? Will it hurt someone else? Will it hurt you? Will this action contribute to your purpose in life? You are going to be held to karmic law according to the motives behind your actions. Take the example of someone who murders premeditatedly as opposed to someone who kills in self-defense. In self-defense you are protecting yourself. There's no adverse karma in that. The motive of self-defense is completely different from planning the murder of another and executing those plans.

The other thing when looking at motive is not to justify your actions. We constantly rationalize our actions to hide our true motive. When you rationalize your actions, you're only fooling yourself and creating more karma. Sure, you can come up with all sorts of rationales and make them appear logical, but you're just kidding yourself. You must go back to true motive.

Let me share with you a story my spiritual teacher, Inez, told me years ago that is a beautiful example of motive as it relates to karma.

There was a wealthy widower we will call Mitchell. Mitchell's wife died suddenly, leaving him with a son to raise on his own. Mitchell was a good man with strong character, but he was so grieved over his wife's death that he placed all his love upon his only son. He lavished all that he could in terms of worldly possessions upon his son. As you can imagine, the son grew up selfish and spoiled. He became a burden to his father and a disgrace to all who knew him.

Mitchell didn't want his son to suffer or want for anything. He didn't want his son to go through the hardships and poverty he had had to go through. He wanted things to be easier for his son. He saw his motive in raising his son as one of a desire to give.

When the son grew up, he married a woman much like him—indulgent and selfish. They had two children. One night, the son and his wife were driving home drunk and both were killed in a car accident, leaving the two children orphans. Mitchell, now a grandfather, was left with the responsibility to raise his two grandchildren, whom he loved very much and who loved him. It was ironic that his two grandchildren were about the same age as his own son was when he lost his wife.

And so Mitchell took charge of his grandchildren. As he was older now, he could see the mistakes he had made with his own son and vowed not to repeat them with his grandchildren. He saw the irony of his own situation. Here he was getting the love and respect from his grandchildren that his own son had denied him.

Mitchell could see better now through his own karmic life pattern. Although at the time he thought he was helping his son by giving him the pleasures of the world, he was really spoiling him terribly and nurturing selfishness in the young man. Mitchell's generosity had a selfish streak as he was thinking more of the pleasure it was giving *him* and not thinking what was really in the best interest of his son. This makes the giving selfish. And of course there was a price to pay.

You may ask at this point, Couldn't the father do as he wished, since he had earned that money? After all, isn't this his son we are talking about? But here again is the principle of motive. As Inez points out so beautifully in this story, clearly Mitchell loved his son, but in giving you must forget yourself and not look to the fruits of your giving. If you give in selfishness, you reap in selfishness. Give in love and place yourself within the self of the person who is receiving; then you have become one with the life flow between you and that person—and you will reap the rewards.

This is what Mitchell came to learn. He had not disciplined his son because he had not learned to discipline his own lower nature. How can you teach a loving discipline to another if you have not cultivated it in yourself?

It must be said here that although Mitchell indulged his son, the son's weakness was not the karma of the father. The son was a brilliant man in his own right and he had the right of free choice. Unfortunately, he did not exercise the will to carry out that choice or his life may have turned out very differently.

So, coming back to our story, you can imagine that by properly raising his grandchildren, Mitchell was able to clear some of his own karmic slate. He raised the children with love and discipline. They were fine children and everyone loved to be around them. They grew up to be outstanding adults. So although he had indulged his son, he raised his grandchildren with love and discipline and thereby nullified the karma created with his son.

RECOGNIZING YOUR PURPOSE

In working out karma, you must make a distinction between karma and purpose as they are not the same thing. Karma is the fruit you bear from your own actions. Purpose is the part you play in life's plan. Purpose is in play at all times, and your karma will either propel you forward to reach your purpose or delay the fulfilling of that purpose. How do you recognize destiny and distinguish between the actions (or inactions) of free will and karma?

Your purpose is the overarching theme of your life. It is the road you must travel as well as your ultimate destination. Free will is the motor that propels you on your spiritual path, and your karma creates many of the conditions you find along the path. When your path in life becomes difficult, you can too easily become discouraged and digress or give up.

Before you incarnate, you are shown your purpose. So somewhere in your consciousness you already know what you are to accomplish. The challenges of life and your own inclinations can cloud or confuse your recognition of this purpose, yet it is still there waiting to blossom.

Your purpose is specific. As you are born into a particular body, place, and time, your purpose is tied to the conditions and times of the life you are born into. Your destiny could unfold on a grand scale, such as becoming the leader of a country or making a great scientific discovery. Or it could be much more intimate, such as being a mother, a great matriarch ushering new souls to Earth and strengthening the family unit of society.

It most often takes the full breadth of your life to accomplish your purpose. When a purpose is accomplished early, more is given for you to accomplish. Really, there's no such thing as retirement when it comes to your life's purpose.

The key to understanding your purpose is *service*. Ask yourself how you can best serve life, serve humanity, and serve God. Step out of yourself for a moment and get a sense of the bigger picture. Ask not only for the things you want, but for what is best for your purpose, even if that purpose is not currently clear. The divine will guide you if you remain open.

Sometimes you may block the reception of your answer because you have already preconditioned the answer. You can let your emotional urges and tendencies get the better of you. If you are really asking for help from the divine, you have to let go and surrender the outcome. If God is life and life is good, then the forthcoming answer can be only for your highest good. You cannot get the answer if you do not let go of the results of your question. Otherwise what you are really doing is *telling* God what you want. God knows your needs before you ask. You asking is not for God's sake, it's for your sake to better connect with that miraculous purpose God already has in store for you. If you have been searching for your purpose and it seems the answer is not forthcoming, it could be you have not really put the situation on the altar of God.

Another thing that can block your connecting with purpose is impatience. There is a rhythm to life and the divine plan can unfold only in divine time. Yet too often if we don't see the results when we feel they should be there, we lose courage and hope. We must walk with complete confidence and assurance that life's plan is unfolding, regardless of whether or not the results are immediately apparent.

Some students of metaphysics confuse spiritual growth with destiny. Spiritual growth is a *tool* of purpose. Becoming spiritually awakened does not necessarily mean you walk away from the work you are doing in the world. Not only are you meant to forge your spiritual mettle while in the mix of life, many times it is through the work you are already doing that you fulfill your life's purpose.

How Do You Recognize Karma?

I had a friend, Marie, who lived in Redondo Beach, California. She was a wonderful soul, very mystical with a well-developed clairvoyance. She, too, could see the aura in great depth. Yet she had one of the most difficult personal lives. She had a mother who abused her terribly and forced her to marry very young. Her husband was just as abusive. While she was pregnant with his child, he kicked her down a flight of stairs, causing her to miscarry the baby. She hurt her back so badly she was in constant pain and had to sleep sitting up in a chair. A friend of hers urged her to run away as she feared Marie's mother or husband would sooner or later kill her. She did leave that situation and eventually built a life for herself in California. However, when I knew her she was still in pain and still slept in a chair.

How could such a wonderful soul have such a difficult life? Marie told me in confidence not to worry about her. In one of her mystical visions, she was shown why she was having so many troubles. In a past life she was a black magician in India and hurt many people. Two of the people she mistreated the most were her mother and her ex-husband in this life.

Knowing what your karma is can help you get through difficult situations without reacting to those situations or compounding them. Most of us don't have the clairvoyant advantage to recognize karma at work, so we won't always know if a situation we are facing is karmic.

This makes it especially trying when you have to face difficult hardships in a life further down the road but have no memory of what occurred to create those hardships. This is part of the suffering a soul goes through in working through karma. The soul does not remember that it murdered this man in a previous life, for example, and therefore it suffers deeply. Yet as the soul works through this suffering, it is learning invaluable lessons and, without realizing it, resolving old karmas.

The truth is, there are no simple indicators for recognizing karmic conditions. There are too many variables when it comes to karma for simple labels. It is true that if a situation repeats itself over and over again, this can be a sign of karma. If you feel checkmated in a situation, that no matter what you do you seem to end up right back where you started, this, too, can be a sign of karma. There are times when karma can come at you out of the blue. While sudden experiences or reversals of fortune are not always karma, when such things occur it's wise to step back and take inventory of the situation.

Fortunately, you don't have to worry about finding your karma; *your karma will find you.* Your karma is being administered by a Divine Intelligence greater than yourself. So the divine will set up the conditions to bring your karma into your life. The general rule of thumb is: The sooner your karma swings back, the easier the karma is, and the longer it takes for the karma to come full swing, the more challenging the karma becomes. It's far better to work out karma in the same life than to have to deal with it in a future lifetime.

Even though not everything in life is karma and even though you may not be sure that a condition you are facing is karmic, if you sense something may be karmic, the best thing you can do is *treat the situation as if it were karmic.* This way, you are playing it safe. Whether or not it's karmic, you should face any challenging situation with your entire spiritual arsenal.

The key to facing and resolving karma is to ask yourself:

What is my lesson?

All karmic conditions are teachers. When you come face-to-face with karma, you resolve it by learning the lessons you need to learn from it. You will continue to face that condition until you fully resolve it and learn what you need to learn. There is no escaping this. You must keep asking, "What do I need to see here? What action should I take?" The Higher will tell you if you are receptive enough to listen. Don't give up asking until you get your answer.

Through the challenge that a karmic condition presents, you are being given the opportunity to strengthen a character trait or to become aware of some facet of yourself you were not aware of before. For example, a wife who has a strict and stern husband has a very strong karmic testing time. This man, believe it or not, is a teacher for her. If she did not have a strong task master, she would not develop some of the qualities within her soul that she needs. If she had a very soft and easy husband, she would be lackadaisical and not learn to be strong and to stand up for herself.

Face your karma for that is the key to your salvation. Karma is a growing process. Think of it. Do you learn more from your successes or from your failures? Failures, the really painful experiences, are the biggest teachers of all. You are responsible for what you are and the conditions you find yourself in. You have made your past, you are making your present, and you are continuously making your future. As Saint Augustine said, "There is no saint without a past, no sinner without a future."

If you are unclear as to what to do, you must appeal to the highest and best in yourself and do what you feel is best in the situation you are in. Cultivate your own sense of moral rightness, but do not close yourself off to a greater understanding of the spiritual life.

Be careful not to judge or interfere with anyone else's life, lest you take their karma upon yourself. Be careful not to judge, and not to make decisions for anyone. For example, if a couple is having marital problems, and one or the other is thinking in terms of divorce and asks for your advice, do not make their decision for them. Give them comfort, perhaps enlightenment, help to uplift them and cut them loose from depression and bring them up into a position to make their own decision. If you make their decision, you have stepped into their karma and taken it upon yourself. So you have not only your own karma to contend with but theirs also.

If you are removing the chestnuts from another person's fire, you are weakening that individual and therefore are going to be held responsible for their karma. Even though that person cannot do a particular thing as well as you, give them the space to do it. By their own doing, they will learn and grow. This doesn't mean ignore them or don't give any aid. It simply means don't do it *for* them.

Some people think they can wait and finish their present karma in another life. *This is not a good idea.* While it is true that we are always given a second chance in life, there's a reason you are given the opportunity to face your karma now. If you wait for another lifetime to resolve your karma when you could have worked it out this time, your karma becomes tougher. So it's much better to get on the job and do it now. Get it behind you so you can go on.

You Are Always Given the Power to Face Your Karma

God brought you to Earth to succeed. Whatever challenges you're meant to encounter, the divine gives you the spiritual tools to accomplish them. If you have difficult family karma to work out of, you might have been given extra power to express exceptional patience or a great talent to help you rise above that difficulty. If you have financial karma, maybe you have been given a bright, keen mind to help you think of ways to bring in money. Whatever difficult karma you are faced with, you will be given the talents and abilities to work out of any difficult situation. Of course, you have to utilize those talents and abilities and not linger in the difficulty that your karma has presented to you.

You rise above every situation by your attitude. You will not always be in control of the conditions in your life, but you are always in control of how you react to and handle these conditions. Spiritually speaking, it's not what happens to you that matters as much as how you handle what happens. This is key to resolving any type of karma.

If you are facing severe karma, you must show the same inner strength and compassion that you would with any challenge in life. You need to rally all the spiritual power you have. One of my dear friends and a long-standing student of many years was faced with three crippling strokes. Somebody might ask why such a spiritual soul is going through this. It turned out to be karmic, but through her ordeal, which eventually claimed her life, she showed an amazing determination to continue in her spiritual work. Her positive attitude was heartbreaking yet inspirational. This is a fine example of using spiritual strengths to help get through difficult karma.

There will be times when the karma you face will be very trying. It will push the limits of your endurance. In these cases, you have to show extraordinary patience and persistence in resolving such conditions, but remember that no matter how difficult a challenge in your life may be, you need to show the same spiritual integrity as you would in any situation.

What happens, for example, if you are in an abusive marriage but sense there is karma? Should you stay in the relationship and take the abuse, or should you leave?

Every condition must be judged on its own merits. It's hard to make blanket statements about karma. The general rule of thumb is to first try to make things work without running away. You don't want to avoid your karma because your karma will come back and find you again if the lesson is not learned and the karma is not resolved. Having said this, being in a karmic situation doesn't mean just lying there and taking abuse. If you are in an abusive relationship and you have done everything you can to make things right but the situation has become intolerable, of course you have to take decisive action, even if the situation is karmic.

Remember, it's not the condition that counts but the lesson to be learned from the condition. If your lesson is to show kindness and patience, then that is what you must show. If your lesson is to be strong and stand up for yourself, then you must show strength. If someone is abusing you to the point of endangering your life, naturally you have to get out of that situation. You have to protect yourself. By leaving a situation like that, you're helping to lessen what could be worse karma, even if karma is not finished.

How Do You Know When Your Karma Is Finished?

You know you have resolved difficult karma when the difficult situation the karma presented is removed from your life. It simply won't be there anymore. You'll be clear of that situation and will not have to confront it again!

For example, let's say that you had chronic money problems because of money karma, and despite your best efforts, things did not seem to turn around. Through your concerted effort to do better, you are quietly resolving the old money karma, even though that resolution does not seem to be readily apparent. When you resolve the karma and learn the spiritual lessons connected to that karma, the difficult money situation will end. Maybe you get the job you've wanted or an unexpected financial windfall. Whatever it is, that good fortune will mark the end of the karmic trial. And that karma will not come back unless you start repeating old mistakes.

Of course, good karma stays with you as long as you continue to build on it. If you have earned good relationship karma, for example, you will continue to build good friendships in even greater areas of life, strengthening your love flow in even more beautiful and splendid ways. Acts of goodness encourage acts of greatness.

Karmic Guidelines

Karma is a starting point, not an end point. Whatever karmic condition you find yourself in, that is the starting point to turn things around. It is the divine tuning process to bring life back into balance.

Be careful if you find yourself saying things like, "I'm supposed to suffer like this. This is karma, and I'm supposed to go through this." Karma doesn't work like that. You can *create* karma by doing this because you are avoiding something you're supposed to be doing. Karma is not an excuse to avoid dealing with life's challenges.

You are born to succeed. It doesn't matter how dire your circumstances, the divine sees you as precious and essential. When you harmonize with your purpose, the universe brings everything together to assist in your success. When you resist, struggle and strife ensue as part of the spiritual growth to bring you back into harmony. This happens all too often. It is my understanding that only about fifty percent of the time do we actually finish all that we are meant to accomplish. This tells us that we must redouble our efforts to complete the work that God gave us to do and truly face our karma honestly and openly.

Here are some points to remember regarding karma:

LOOK TO THE LESSON.

Karmic situations are teachers. When faced with karma, ask, "What is my lesson?" Look to what you are supposed to do in this situation. How are you meant to handle what is being presented to you?

FACE YOUR KARMA.

You cannot escape your karma, no matter how hard you try. You can sometimes delay the inevitable, but it will come back to you stronger than before. It's best to work on your karma as it's presented to you.

YOU'RE ALWAYS GIVEN KARMA YOU CAN HANDLE.

Regardless of the karmic debts you have accrued, God does not give you more karma than you can handle at any one time. To do so would defeat the purpose of helping you grow spiritually. What can make your karma appear unbearable at times is if you *compound* your karma, making things worse.

YOU BRING GOOD KARMA WITH YOU AS WELL.

We all bring in good karma. We need these spiritual strengths to master our weaknesses.

KARMA IS FAIR.

Regardless of how unfair life may seem at times, the whole point of cause and effect is to balance life. If someone seems to be getting away with murder, they will meet up with their karma somewhere down the road. Or if someone seems to be living a life graced by God, it is not by some special blessing awarded to one but not another. It is because that person has learned from past mistakes and is now living the spiritual laws and reaping the benefits.

NOT EVERYTHING IS KARMA.

Some take a fatalistic point of view of karma that everything is fixed and we can't change it. Nothing could be further from the truth. While we all have to deal with the unfinished business of karma, not everything in life is karmic.

KARMA IS NOT AN ESCAPE FROM OR AN EXCUSE FOR AVOIDING LIFE CHALLENGES.

Some look at a karmic situation as an excuse not to take action, to sit back and say, "This is my karma." You must be proactive in resolving karma and take action to learn the lesson the karmic situation is presenting to you.

DO NOT JUDGE THE KARMA OF OTHERS.

It is too easy to point fingers and jump to conclusions as to a karmic condition another person may be facing. You are responsible for your own soul and no one else's. As it is not easy to understand your own karma, it is even more challenging to prejudge someone else's, even if there's a karmic exchange going on with that person. What's important is the lesson you are learning. Let others figure out their own lessons for themselves.

Chapter 14

FOUR KEYS TO EFFECTIVELY
DEAL WITH KARMA

When starting the noble task of working on your karma, it can feel bewildering. You may know you are in a tough situation, but many things can be going on at the same time and that makes it difficult to know what the first thing to do is or the right course of action to take. In this chapter, I give you four keys to help you start in the right direction. These keys do not necessarily have to be done in the order shown; regardless of the sequence, by including these keys in your work you will go far in facing and resolving your karma.

The four keys are:

1. Take inventory.
2. Meditate and pray.
3. Ask, "What Is My Lesson?"
4. Initiate right action.

Take Inventory

When faced with any challenging situation, especially karmic situations, it is always a good idea to take a moment, step back, and evaluate your present dilemma. Sometimes, there can be a knee-jerk response to a challenge without first thinking things through, and this can lead to trouble. As you have been reading these pages, I hope you have been following the guidelines at the end of each chapter and reviewing your own karmic pattern. Now it is recommended that you start a journal to keep track of your thoughts and to give yourself time to see things from a different perspective. Take your time with this inventory and do your best to enjoy the process.

Review Present Actions

Before reviewing potential karma based on actions of the past, it is a good idea to review actions you are currently taking. It is difficult to be free from old karma if you are unintentionally creating new karma. By changing present actions and the motivation behind those actions, you are clearing out any potentially new karma. In addition to the blessing this offers by itself, you can then more clearly see past karma and the lessons to be gained.

We recommend that you take the time to make your own karmic worksheet. On this worksheet, make a heading for each of the various departments of karma we have explored in this book: money, career, relationships, soul, physical, nature, and spiritual. Under each heading make an inventory of present actions you are taking. You can follow the guidelines at the end of each chapter in Part Two or your own guidelines. In this review, note what you are doing, not the actions of others. These actions can be based on activities you did or did not initiate. Do not judge, edit, or interpret these actions. Simply list them as clearly and objectively as you can.

Once this is done, review your motives. *Motive* comes from the Latin for "to move." Your motive is what calls you to action. *Why* are you doing what you are doing? Be honest with yourself. This is not about sugarcoating your actions or beating yourself up over weaknesses you are aware of; it's simply about being honest. No one is looking at this list but you. Most of us do not consciously choose to initiate actions that are detrimental, but too often selfishness and personality appetites can blind you to your true motivations. You then end up rationalizing your actions to cover the true motives behind those actions. It is very easy to rationalize, but in doing so you are only fooling yourself. The list of rationales is endless, and unless you can see through motives that are not serving the highest good, you will be caught in a seemingly endless karmic cycle.

If in doing this exercise you find it difficult to honestly evaluate your true motive, or if you recognize that some of your actions may not be the best but you are unsure what to do, then ask the question: "What is the best and most noble course of action in this situation?" When you ask this question, be prepared that the answer may not be in agreement with what you feel like doing at that moment. Too often we let our emotional moods guide our motives, and this approach can lead to so much trouble. For example, maybe someone has hurt you and you are angry and wish to hurt them back. If you initiate an action based on that anger, even if you feel justified in being angry, you will undoubtedly create new karma.

It can be difficult to come to terms with our real motives for doing things. Either we do not want to recognize that we are doing something that may not be in the best interest of ourselves and others, or we let our appetites determine our motives. A woman whom I counseled was dating two men at the same time who both wanted to marry her. She was in a dilemma. She felt like she was in love with both of them and couldn't figure out which one to marry.

She asked me point-blank who I felt was the better man for her. I told her it was not my place to tell her whom to marry; she had to determine that for herself. What I could do was give her insight to the kinds of people these men were, on the basis of their auras. It was up to her to decide which one to marry or if she was going to marry at all.

One of the men was younger than she was, passionate and sexy. His work was not so stable but he obviously gratified her on a physical level. The other man was a little older than she, not so passionate, but clearly a solid person with an excellent job who was very committed to her. Both were good-looking, and this only compounded her dilemma.

The woman was having difficulty seeing things clearly because of ulterior motives. She wasn't really asking herself what was the best course of action for her to take and who the best person for her was. She wasn't really questioning her motives at all. It turned out she was more mesmerized by the physical appeal of the younger man. She was attractive herself and on the sexy side, so she had found someone who was compatible on that level. Obviously, part of her was conflicted or she would not have been seeking help.

Once she started to see the situation more soberly, it became clear to her that the older man was the right man for her. It was not a matter of security or playing it safe, as she was making a good living herself and was plenty adventurous on her own. Rather, she saw through some of her false reasoning and realized that she had much more in common with the older man and that, in fact, she really did love him.

They ended up having a wonderful marriage. They traveled a lot together and the times I saw them they always projected a joyful exuberance. They were a lot of fun to be around. In addition, a wonderful physical relationship eventually did blossom. Most important, because she took the time to look deeper and question her motives, she passed an important spiritual test. If she had allowed herself to follow her temporary passion, she might have missed the person she was meant to marry.

If you put your personal feelings aside and ask what the best thing to do is, then the divine can work with you to produce the right outcome for all concerned. Your actions will generate good karma and strengthen your aura and consciousness. Regardless of whether or not the situation works as you hoped, you did the right thing. If you are doing your best with the knowledge and tools at hand, that is all that can be asked of you.

Karmic Worksheet

Once you have given yourself time to review your present actions and motiva-tions, you are ready to start reviewing potential karma from the past. Karma can swing back to you from this life or from previous lives. In this inventory, it is not necessary to try to understand the details of what may have hap-pened in the past. What is important is, once again, that you are honest with yourself.

It takes courage to face up to karma. Yet recognizing past mistakes does not mean owning or embracing those mistakes. Errors and weakness are not part of the immortal you. They are merely acquired traits that you are meant to work through. The idea that sins or misjudgment can condemn you to an eternal hell is completely false and goes against the very nature of life. Of course, you have to atone for mistakes, but again, there is no sin beyond redemption; you are always given another chance.

To take inventory of potential karmic situations, on a separate worksheet make similar headings as you did in reviewing your motives. You can follow the same guidelines given at the end of each chapter in Part Two if you like. In addition, it sometimes helps to look at the big picture of your life. Here are some suggestions:

1. List traumatic or dramatic moments in your life.
2. List major turning points in your life.
3. List major decisions that affected your life for better or worse.
4. List patterns in your life that seem to play over repeatedly.

Possible Signs of Karmic Conditions

Once you have taken your karmic inventory, pick a situation that stands out. You may have several areas you want to work on, but take things one at a time to understand the dynamics of this exercise and to give you greater chances of success.

The question at this point is: Is this situation karmic? In asking this question you are faced with a conundrum. If you are not clairvoyant and it is "nature's kindness" not to remember past lives, how can you begin to know what is karmic and what is not? And if you did know, how can you know what it was that you did that needs correcting?

There are no simple answers to these questions, but keep in mind several things. First, somewhere in your consciousness, you are fully aware of what your karma is. It was shown to you before you came to Earth. It is in your aura and subconscious mind. So intuitively you are quite aware of what is going on. When I conduct workshops on karma, it is amazing how well people tune in to what is really going on with them when they take the time to really put their attention on the subject. So your honesty and perseverance in this great adventure carry you far.

Second, you are not doing this spiritual work alone. God and the spiritual hierarchy are working with you every step of the way, even though you may not be aware of this divine presence. No matter how heavy the karma, the divine is working with you to bring about complete success. By your genuine effort and cooperation, you are forging a spiritual alliance with the Higher.

Third, the very knowledge you are gaining by studying reincarnation and karma is increasing your spiritual awareness, and this will automatically have a positive effect in resolving your karma. And finally, yes, sometimes you will have an unmistakable insight, revelation, or inner knowing when something is karmic. Pay attention to those signals as they can be the Higher talking to you.

What about going to a spiritual counselor for help with karmic conditions? Naturally, if you can find the right person, he or she can be of great help. However, I strongly do not recommend past life regression as a way to identify karma for reasons I outline in chapter 15.

All in all, if you sense that something might be karmic, *the best thing to do is treat it as if it were karma.* You will use many of the same spiritual tools whether a situation is karma or simply difficult. One of the hallmarks of an evolving soul is to take the magnanimous point of view in any situation. Regardless of how others are acting, if you take the high road every time, you will always be the better for it.

Having said all this, I would like to give you some possible signs—and they are only possible—of karmic conditions. These are not hard-and-fast rules but are meant to be helpful hints and guidelines.

Possible signs of karma include:

1. Being faced with something that seems to have come out of the blue and that hits you smack in the face.
2. Having something totally baffle you, something that you can't explain logically.
3. Feeling checkmated in a situation, as if no matter what you do, you find yourself in the same condition, over and over again.
4. Feeling unreasonably engaged emotionally, incensed, or obsessed with a person or situation. (Generally, when a difficult situation is not karmic, it does not bother you as much as if it is karmic, because there is no past association to compound the situation.)
5. Having repeated patterns of events or behavior in your life that seem not to be of your own making.
6. Experiencing unexplained fears and phobias.
7. Having close, intense relationships—good or bad.
8. Inborn talents and abilities.
9. Birth defects, unexplainable physical maladies.

MEDITATE AND PRAY

Once you have identified a potential karmic area you wish to work on, your most important tool is meditation and prayer. Chapter 15 outlines how karma shows up in your aura, and chapter 16 gives you twelve wonderful meditations for spiritual energy to help you work through many karmic conditions. Of course, you can meditate at any point, but it is especially important once you have identified karma. In working with your aura, you are building up tremendous spiritual power that will carry you far in resolving your karma.

ASK, "WHAT IS MY LESSON?"

Once you have started working with spiritual energy and built up more power, you will undoubtedly be seeing things from a new perspective. This is a good time to ask the all-important question: "What is my Lesson?" Karmic conditions are teachers, and it is your job to figure out what you are to learn. The condition will remain with you until the lesson is learned and the karma is resolved.

Sometimes you may find yourself skirting around the real lesson you are meant to learn in a situation. Remember, your lesson is about you, not someone else. It is about your mistakes that you are trying to correct, not the mistakes of others. There is no reason to feel squeamish in searching for your true lesson.

When you hit the right answer, you will feel a sense of inner peace. It doesn't mean everything is resolved, but there will be a calm sense of inner knowing that you are now moving in the right direction. Sometimes, you may think you have the right answer but you still feel emotionally distressed. That is most often an indication that you have not yet learned the real lesson.

Lessons come down to basic life principles: to learn kindness, to forgive, to show tolerance, to be true to yourself, to be generous, to be more loving, to see things through to their completion, to be more peaceful, to enjoy life more, to be happy with what you have learned, to be patient, to show compassion, to utilize your talents, to be more honest, to stand up for yourself, to show fortitude, to better manage your affairs, and the list goes on and on.

Lessons will be targeted to specific people and situations. While kindness is a trait to show everyone, it may be your lesson to show kindness to a particular person. In doing so, you learn some very important attributes of kindness you otherwise would not learn. Or it may be that you have to stand up for yourself at your work. At home you are fine, but at work you are too passive. So the karmic test will stay with you until you learn to assert yourself in the workplace. Karmic lessons bring out your own weaknesses, and it is these weaknesses you want to pay attention to without judgment or condemnation.

In doing this exercise in workshops, it is interesting to note that many times people have difficulty understanding the lesson a karmic condition presents, even when they know what the karma is! In one instance, a woman was having trouble with her family. She felt the members of her family, especially her mother, who was setting the tone, were being unkind to her for no reason. Even more, this unkindness directed toward her seemed to extend beyond her immediate family. She was becoming angry and feeling victimized.

During the course of her karmic work, it was revealed by the Higher that her situation with her family was most definitely karmic. In a past life in Europe, she was a he—a male in authority—so caught up in his own business affairs that he completely disregarded his family, treating them coldly and neglecting them. Her daughter in that life, whom she neglected and disregarded the most, would become her mother in this present life. Although her father was not with her in that life, she owed karma with his as well from yet another life where there was a similar scenario but different circumstances.

In this life she had come in to work out both karmas. Her parents had no idea of the karmic relationship that was going on, but unconsciously rekindled their unresolved animosity toward her even though she was their own child. Others in the family picked up on the mood the parents set and this whole "bad girl" scenario was initiated.

The truth was she was a fine woman in this life. She had clearly worked out character flaws related to those past lives, but had yet to resolve the actual karma with her parents.

If you were faced with such a situation, what would be your karmic lesson?

My student's first impulse was to stand up for herself. She thought she shouldn't take any unkindness from her family, and especially not from her parents, because she was a good person and did not deserve this. Was this her lesson, do you think?

A little more investigation revealed that she already was an outgoing person. She had no trouble standing up for herself. What was frustrating her was that her efforts seemed to have no effect when it came to her family and particularly her parents.

Clearly, this was not what her karma was trying to teach her. If she had been unkind to her parents in past lives, then her karmic lesson in this life would be to show kindness to her parents. Her real lesson was not to fight fire with fire, but to return unkindness with unconditional kindness. This was not easy for her to come to terms with. The power of forgiveness had not fully dawned on her.

For a while she could not do this, even with spiritual guidance. As a result, she continued to have problems with her family and it continued to disturb her. It took several sessions over a period of time for her to realize for herself the wisdom of her karmic lesson. Even then it took a lot of willpower to begin to apply a new attitude with her family. Slowly, she did start to show kindness regardless of her parents' attitude toward her. While this approach did not fully turn her family's attitude around, what it did do was change her attitude. The situation did not bother her nearly to the degree it used to.

This example teaches us that karmic lessons test our resolve and determination. What's more, the outcome will not always be in our hands or work out as we would like it to. But what will happen is, you will gain a stronger mastery over yourself and in the process be resolving your karma. Even though the family has not yet fully reconciled their feelings for her, she is paying off her karma, and at some point down the line the situation will resolve itself and that karma will be finished.

INITIATE RIGHT ACTION

Recognizing your lesson is a call to action. As the saying goes, "Recognition is half the battle," but the battle is not won until you complete the task. This is the true test of facing your karma. You cannot sit on the fence and think your good intentions alone will complete the job. You must follow through on your intentions. It will take your best efforts to succeed, but God has already given you the talents and abilities to do so.

Following through on your life lesson means your life will change and you want that. It means taking charge of a situation that may have been getting the better of you. Others around you may not understand what you are doing, and may want you to behave in the way they are familiar with, so you will have to be steadfast in following through.

Once you decide what action to take, you will need a great deal of willpower to carry out that action. Willpower holds your good intentions in place until you can see real results. You must show steady and consistent willpower because, by the very nature of it being a lesson, you will inevitably encounter obstacles. These obstacles are tests to see how well you are learning your lesson. It's easy to be kind to someone who is kind to you, but not so easy to be kind to someone who is belligerent to you. That's the real test of kindness. So you will have to show great resilience in mastering your karma.

There will be times when you will know your life lesson but will not exercise the necessary willpower to stay with it until the lesson is learned. As a result, you can become discouraged and disillusioned. You can start to think that maybe this was not your lesson after all, or that such things are insurmountable. All this is nonsense and is simply a sign that you need to strengthen your willpower.

Life lessons may sound simple but they are not simple to instigate. From an airplane, even the tallest mountain may not seem insurmountable, but it is a very different story if you are on the ground trying to climb it. To "be patient" sounds simple, but it can take a lifetime to learn. The wonderful thing is that when you have really learned the lesson a karmic condition presents to you, that situation will be out of your life and you will have strengthened another facet of your life and taken one step closer to enlightenment.

Chapter 15

THE AURA AND KARMA

As a clairvoyant, one of the most fascinating aspects of understanding karma has been watching how karmic energy works in the aura. In *Change Your Aura, Change Your Life* and *The Healing Power of Your Aura*, I outline the intricate world of the human aura. Everything we think, feel, and do radiates a spiritual energy that presents itself in various colors and hues: this is the aura. The aura is like the blueprint of the soul because it shows how we are using God's infinite power.

The first place you generate the spiritual power to accomplish anything is in your auric field. If it's in your aura, it will show up in your life. This principle is very true when it comes to karma. When you generate karma, you generate an energy corresponding to the karmic pattern, good or bad, and this makes a definite impact in your aura. Part of your job in learning karmic lessons is to redeem that energy in your aura. So to help face and resolve your karma, an important key is to work with the energy of your aura.

How does *karma* show up in the aura? When you are born, you bring with you the auric field you have earned through the course of your evolution. Some come in with a very bright aura, while others have an aura that is not so strong. This is all an indication of how you have developed yourself in previous lives. If you were a kind and loving person in a past life, that energy carries over into your present life, which shows itself as a deep rose-pink energy. If you were hateful and vindictive in your past life, you bring in those blemishes as well. The fortunate thing is the Higher cleanses some of the dark spots before you reincarnate, in order to give you a second chance. Yet the core of that negative energy is still there as it becomes your job to redeem these energies.

These energies start showing up in the auric field soon after you are born, and become more fully engaged by the time you reach age seven. This is one reason why children have certain tendencies from a very early age. They bring in their soul qualities and spiritual energies from their past life experience. Even though it is a child's body, there's a full adult soul in that little body. One way to look at the qualities of your own past life is to look at your natural inclinations and behavior in childhood. The aura is a wonderful example of the chronology of your karmic energetic pattern from one life to the next.

One of the clearest examples of bringing in good energy from past lives is a part of the aura called the spiritual division. The spiritual division can be seen about two feet above a person's head in seven arching bands of light. It looks like a rainbow and is most beautiful to see when developed. The spiritual division is connected to past lives you have spent developing your enlightened awareness.

When you begin your spiritual evolution, these bands of light are white. As you start awakening the mystical part of you, you earn spiritual light and some of this energy goes to the bands of the spiritual division, where they take on beautiful varied hues. In your next incarnation, you bring this spiritual division so you can tap into that spiritual power to continue in your mystical development. The brighter this division is, the more developed a soul is because he or she has been earning this mystical spiritual light through many lifetimes of effort.

We all have this spiritual division, but we don't all have it to the same degree and intensity. The irony is that many times a person has a well-developed spiritual division but is not tapping that energy. It's there, but he or she simply hasn't accessed that part of their nature yet. This indicates that in the present life, the soul has not yet fully reclaimed the spiritual powers of its own past.

SOUL IMAGES

In the aura, there is a chakra in the middle of the chest, appropriately called the heart chakra, or as it is called in the Western Mystical Tradition, the Hermetic Center. The Hermetic Center is the energetic nucleus of your human Earth affairs. All your activities make an energetic connection within this center. That means your job, your relationships, your finances all make a connection in the Hermetic Center. That's an enormous amount of activity going on in this part of your aura.

What's more, the Hermetic Center is *the seat of the soul*. Please take time to contemplate this. When you incarnate, your soul makes its connection with physical life through the heart chakra. This is so it can absorb all the experiences of life through firsthand experience. Right now, your soul is absorbing everything you're going through—good, bad, and indifferent.

If karma is related to action, then clearly there is a strong connection between the Hermetic Center and the karmic energy you initiate. This energy shows up in a couple of ways. To help work out your karma and destiny, the divine has bestowed on each of us a most unique and exquisite gift. You have been given what are known as *soul images*. These soul images are clairvoyantly seen around the heart center. They are based on the images shown in your Tapestry of Life (see chapter 2). Each image is about two inches in diameter and illuminates good and bad karmas, things you are to accomplish, important people in your life, and so on. In a sense, key elements of the story of your incarnated life are displayed in these soul images.

They are seen about a foot and a half around the heart center in a circular formation and have their own energy radiations around them. Some images have bright energies and some not so bright. The brighter images show good karma and accomplishments you are meant to reach, while the darker images show difficult and unresolved karmas you came in to resolve. You are born with these images, but they start to show up around twelve years of age. They are extraordinary but most difficult to see and require a highly developed spiritual sight.

Soul images give you power to complete your spiritual task. Your soul images are of family members, key people in your life, key events, and career. Not everything is there, but many elements of your life's path are there. As you go through the normal course of life, you will meet people or be confronted with opportunities and situations that correspond to your soul images. When this happens, these images will light up and become more intense. Although you are not aware of these images, you will feel their promptings.

For example, if you owe someone karma, there can be a soul image of the person you owe karma to. In this case, there will be a dark energy around the image, indicating this is karma that needs to be paid back. You may be having a difficult relationship with that person, but as you persist and help that person, the soul image starts to brighten. When the karma is paid back, the energy becomes bright. If this person remains part of your life, the image remains; if after the karma is resolved, the person is no longer part of your life, the image fades altogether.

If the karma with that person or condition remains unresolved, the image remains. Even if you die or the person you owe karma to dies, the image remains, to be worked out in another incarnation. In some cases, the karma can be resolved on the other side, but more likely you will come back to meet that person again and resolve the remaining karma.

What about actions taken in this life? Do they show up as soul images? Yes, they do. While soul images bring in the elements from past lives, the way you express free will most definitely affects these images. If you perform a humanitarian act that goes beyond what's in your chart, you *generate* new good karma and develop enlightened soul images. These become added blessings. Every positive thing you do adds to your aura. These images are generally seen outside the circle of core images.

The same is true if you generate negative karma. If you cheat or hurt someone, you create karma, and this can show up as a new soul image. This is your telltale heart as in Edgar Allan Poe's story of a man haunted by the beating heart of the one he killed. When you create new karma, do your best to atone for your misdeeds to erase these images from your consciousness so you don't carry them over into another life.

These soul images dramatically illustrate how close you are to your destiny. You may feel lost or confused at times, yet the pattern of your life's work is with you every day, inspiring and urging you upward.

Figure 1 on the inside front cover of this book, which is based on an actual case study, depicts a man who came in with very good karma and is meant to accomplish much in the field of biology.

There are twelve soul images shown here, indicating the various dynamics he came to this Earth to express or work out. Karma that is owed him by others is not shown in the soul images. What is shown is what he is putting out. These images are generally shown in a circle formation around the heart chakra and, in a clockwise motion, indicate the sequence of how the karmas and events will present themselves.

This depiction shows the man in the full maturity of life, but he has not yet completed his life's task. Image 1 shows that he started out with difficult karma with his father, which he brought in from a past life where he was a difficult and stern father himself. The energy started out dark, but he worked out the karma and brightened this part of himself. Now the energy is purple, indicating that he has resolved this karma. He has developed a good relationship with his father.

Image 2 shows his mother, and the energy is pink, indicating he came in with good karma with her and has maintained it to this point in his life. The silver light around image 3 of his brother is indicative of a good karma with him as well, as his brother has been a supportive friend throughout his life. The pale yellow light around the image of his sister in image 4 indicates that he had difficult karma with her from a past life where he was a cruel brother. He has worked out some of this karma, but the energy is still a little weak, indicating the karma is not fully resolved and there is more work to do. He has not shown the full kindness in this life he is meant to.

As he was starting life on his own, he encountered money karma from a past life, where he abused money, as shown in image 5. This plagued him for some time. As a result of his financial frustration, he embezzled money from a foundation he was working with. This created a new karma, as indicated in image A. Notice image A is outside the circle, which is indicative of new karma created. The original past life money karma was worked out, although he still needs to build it up more, but the new karma remains as yet unredeemed.

It was during this time that he married his first wife, shown in image 6. This was a difficult marriage and reflected an unresolved karma he brought into this life with her. They divorced without fully working out their differences. However, even though this energy started out dark, through his difficult marriage he did his part and worked through this karma, which is why this image is fading. She is leaving his aura, if you will. He still has some interactions with her and they are resolving the final pieces of their karmic entanglement. It must be remembered here that soul images show only the karma you owe or your own destiny. They do not show karma owed to you. In his first marriage, there was karma owed on both sides.

The experience of his first marriage brings strongly to the surface a character flaw of impatience, especially in personal matters, indicated in image 7. It has taken him many years, but he is finally learning to conquer this part of himself, so even though this image started out dark, it is now bright and will eventually fade out completely.

Image 8 shows a friend and colleague who was instrumental in helping him in his career. This is very good karma from a previous association that was very fruitful. In this life, this man proved to be very helpful to him and marked the end of a difficult period in his life.

Shortly after this, he met a woman whom he married and who proved to be of great help both personally and professionally. This woman is part of his destiny, shown in image 9. They are very compatible and, even though they do not have children together, they have a very happy life. This energy is a carry-over from a very happy marriage and family life they shared centuries earlier. She is also in biology and will prove to be instrumental to his success.

Some years later, he made an important discovery in the field of biology, which earned him much fame. This is part of his destiny, shown in image 10. He has had several lifetimes in the sciences and earned this right to bring this new information through. It was also at this time that his kindness came to the fore. He saved a child from a building that was collapsing, risking his own life in the process. He and the child were injured, but both pulled through. This is indicated in image B, seen to the right. Not every good deed shows up in the aura like this, but because he risked his own life and his action had such a positive effect, it generated this soul image.

It is in this part of his life that he earned other new good karma when he helped a friend and colleague who was in trouble and was being unjustly accused. This man stuck his neck out and risked his own reputation to help him. Eventually the other man was exonerated, but there were some tense moments. Again the strong positive repercussions of his actions generated this soul image, illustrated by image C.

Here is where his life is at right now. We see there are two more soul images strongly in his aura. This is not to say that these are the only things coming up for him. Other things are, too, but these are most pronounced. It is in his destiny to win a high award for his excellence in biology, indicated in image 11, and in his later years it is in his destiny to do less research, and teach more, to help others, as shown in image 12.

KARMIC SOUL ENERGY

Another area of the aura related to karma is what is known as *karmic soul energy*. Karmic soul energy is different from soul images. This soul energy is seen emanating from the nucleus of the heart chakra and directly corresponds to the karmic energy we generate over time. This soul energy is radiations of various colors of light streaming out of the heart chakra. According to your actions, you will build up this soul power corresponding to the good karma you generate, or you will dilute this energy corresponding to destructive actions you initiate, which has the effect of depleting this vital power. As with a savings account, the more good karma you create, the more spiritual power that is generated, which you can draw on later.

This karmic energy corresponds to the type of karma you have built up. If you have earned good money karma, you generate a strong soul energy related to money karma. If you have generated good relationship karma, then you generate good soul energy related to relationships, and so on. If you come into this life having earned good money karma but squander that good karma by living a frivolous life, not only do you squander money, you deplete that precious soul energy of good karma you worked so hard to achieve, and you will have to rekindle it in another life through struggle and effort.

The good news about karmic soul energy is it's something you have complete control over. Whereas with other aspects of karma there are other people and situations involved, building up your karmic soul power is something entirely in your own hands and is one of the first areas to focus on in working with spiritual energy.

For example, say you are unkind to your spouse and inevitably generate some bad karma. If this karma goes unpaid for the remainder of your life, you will need to balance it out in another incarnation. You will owe karma to your spouse for your unkindness and the lessons connected to that karma, but you will also deplete the karmic soul energy in your heart center, which you will have to rebuild in addition to paying back your spouse.

What happens if in your next life you are not able to reincarnate with the same person to work things out? Perhaps the timing is not right and you have to wait until a future incarnation further down the line. There is not much you can do regarding the unpaid debt to your spouse, but you can most definitely build up your depleted karmic soul energy by expressing kindness to others and learning the lesson of loving others, especially in the area of marriage. Through your good actions, you build up power in the soul and brighten this part of you. Eventually, when you do reincarnate to work things out with the person you originally mistreated, you will be in a much better place spiritually to handle things well.

Through your deeds in this life, you can go far in building up your soul energy. When a soul has accumulated good karma through many lives of good work, this karmic soul energy can be extraordinary to see and can radiate quite far. Developed karmic soul energy is one of the signs of a mature and enlightened soul.

In Figure 2 on the inside front cover of the book, the woman depicted has paid back her karmic debts and reached enlightenment. Through much effort, she has gotten off the wheel of necessity. The outer shell is a depiction of the causal template, which is the protective sheath for the soul. It is white in appearance with an outer glowing aura around its circumference. This causal template stays with us our whole life.

Radiating from the heart chakra is a brilliant karmic light. There are about twenty-four karmic paths depicted here in various rays that she has mastered. Each type of karma these paths represent has been built and mastered on its own terms. There are also different shadings of karma that come through in their own power. Each karmic avenue has approximately four rays that emanate from the center. Looking at all this power, we can better see why it takes 800 lives to master all the roads of life and all the karmic challenges there are to face.

The radiations extend all the way to the causal shell, indicating the high level of mastery reached. Their vibrancy and potency, which is difficult to show in an illustration, indicates the high level of development. Yet even here it can be seen that not all the rays extend to the causal shell. This is because, even at the level of a spiritual master, we have certain aspects of life inevitably more developed than others according to our own natural talents and proclivities. If you develop your skills along artistic lines, these karmic soul energies will develop a little differently than if you are a master healer or scientist. Just as no two auras are exactly alike, the way you express and mature your karmic soul light will be unique as well.

For the majority of people still building their soul karmic power, this energy will extend only a little better than half as much and the energies will not be so vibrant. If the soul is undeveloped or has depleted its power through the buildup of heavy negative karma, the energy does not go dark, but it becomes very weak and diluted, indicating there is much work ahead to rebuild that power.

In this illustration, please note the highly developed spiritual division above the head, shown as an arcing band of light, creating the appearance of a rainbow. This division also shows accumulated good energy earned over the course of many lifetimes. While this is not exactly karmic energy, it is energy earned through right action and application.

KARMA AND THE FABRIC OF LIFE

As we have been looking at throughout this book, what goes around comes around. As we put something out, it comes back to us in the same way we put it out. In the aura, this "putting out" through a karmic action takes on a spiritual energy all its own.

In initiating a karmic act, not only do we generate an energy that shows up in our aura, we also project some of that energy into what is known as the fabric of life. This fabric of life has gone by many different names—akasha, the ethers, spirit-substance. The fabric of life is the primordial material out of which everything in life is made. There are many things that can be said about this cosmic material, but in relation to our exploration of karma, the fabric of life acts as a cosmic sounding board that resonates with our every action, thought, and emotion. In a very real sense, the energy we vibrate through our aura reverberates into the fabric of life. It is through these spiritual ethers that we contribute to the greater expression of life, that we generate the power to make dreams and ideas a reality.

Once we initiate an energy corresponding to the quality of our action, that energy will go out in ethers exactly as we send it. If it is a creative and enhancing action, that harmonious act will reverberate through the ethers, adding harmony to creation, and come back to us in that same beautiful quality multiplied. If we initiate a destructive action, that energy will also go out into the vibrated ethers, but this time it creates a disharmony for which we become responsible. It's a little like polluting the atmosphere, but this is a spiritual atmosphere. This energy comes back as we put it out so harmony and balance can be restored.

Here is where we face the trickiest part of karma. Once the energy of our actions goes out into life, it is no longer in our control. We cannot say how it comes back to us. The only thing we can say is that it will come back to us.

The boomerang effect of karma is something that is strongly guided over by the divine. There is an extraordinarily intricate and beautiful process the divine orchestrates to steer and guide how this karmic energy swings back to us. Without the loving support of the divine, we would build up so much darkness so fast, we would never be able to get out of it.

The general rule of thumb is that it is better for karma to swing back sooner rather than later. The sooner it rebounds, the less severe the response, while the longer it takes to return, the stronger the reaction. Karma is a little like a pendulum. It's always better to work out karma in the same lifetime it's generated than to wait until a future life where the rebound effect will be stronger. This goes for good as well as bad karma. When we do good things but for some reason don't feel the effects of those deeds, we need not worry. When they do return to us, the effect will be all the sweeter.

Sometimes when we are learning lessons, the karmic retribution is held back to give us time to learn our lessons. If karma swung back immediately, we would not have time to grow. Some have interpreted this grace period as a sign that they can do as they wish. Perhaps they have done something they know is wrong, but because no immediate retribution came, they interpreted this as permission to continue in their missteps, not realizing they are accruing karma that will eventually swing back.

SUBCONSCIOUS IMAGES

From the metaphysical perspective, the subconscious mind is the seat of memory. Everything we have experienced in life is recorded in the subconscious. It is like a vast hard drive on a computer that records not only experiences and memories, but patterns of behavior as well. It also has recorded experiences of past lives as we carry the same subconscious mind from incarnation to incarnation.

Portions of the subconscious mind are partitioned off so that we do not bring to conscious memory past life events. This is for our own benefit. If we were to bring back awareness of the past into our present life, it would prove overbearing. Most people are simply not ready to take that journey and it would do much more harm than good.

The subconscious is a fascinating and essential study all by itself, but in connection with karma and past life memory, the subconscious works in cooperation with the soul images in helping to resolve karma. Whereas the soul images present pictures of what you are to accomplish and face in this life, the subconscious brings up what has already been. For example, if you have karma to work out with your spouse, your heart chakra will bear the image of your spouse as he or she is in this life. The energy around that image will indicate the kind of relationship you can expect from this person. Your subconscious, on the other hand, will show the image of your *past life* relationships with your spouse that have karmically brought you back together.

Most of the time, you will have no conscious awareness of this subconscious prompting, but you will feel its effect. This will cause you to have an almost instinctual reaction to the situation or condition or person being presented. If you have good karma, and a wonderful experience pops up from the subconscious, even though you have no conscious memory of those past events, you will take an automatic liking to that person. In the same way, if you are facing difficult karma, the subconscious prompting will make you feel uneasy or feel repelled by that person for no apparent reason.

In the case of subconscious patterns, you have to be very careful that the memory itself, however unconscious, does not spark a repeat of the same scenario. This happens often. You can unintentionally rekindle those old subconscious patterns and find yourself repeating past mistakes, compounding rather than resolving karma. Here again, exercise your free will and realize you are not the victim of your past as long as you choose to assert your willpower and redirect the energy along more positive lines of activity.

A Note About Past Life Regression

The subconscious mind has been a major focus when it comes to reincarnation. One of the strongest cases for proving that reincarnation exists has been the testimony of those who have undergone what is commonly called past life regression.

Past life regression comes in different forms. The idea is to find ways to tap into the subconscious mind and retrieve information about a past life. The most common way to regress is through hypnosis. Under hypnotic suggestion, people can recall experiences from a past life, often with amazing detail. The questions most often asked are whether past life regression is real or something imagined by the person being hypnotized, and if it is real, whether it is therapeutically beneficial.

The potential dangers of any type of hypnosis are obvious, but if done under the right conditions, can past life regression help, and what exactly is going on from the point of view of the aura? I am not a hypnotherapist, nor have I been hypnotized, so what I share with you comes from my clairvoyant observations of the hypnotic process, as well as from counseling people who have been hypnotized and what I have been taught by the Higher.

When someone is hypnotized, the conscious mind is temporarily bypassed and the hypnotherapist is primarily tapping into the subconscious mind. And here we are presented with a dilemma, as the very process of hypnosis challenges a basic premise we have been exploring throughout this book—free will.

The conscious mind is the place where you express free will. You are supposed to be in charge of your own thinking at all times. This is how you grow and develop an enlightened mind. Right or wrong, every conscious choice you make teaches you something. If you let someone else do the thinking for you, even if that person has the best of intentions and has your permission, you are relinquishing your free will to someone else. Under the hypnotic suggestion, you are under the will of the hypnotherapist.

Past life regression runs the risk of violating another spiritual principle of noninterference in other people's karma. If you go to a psychic or mystic for help in understanding your past lives, you are still in control of accepting or rejecting the information given. But under hypnosis, the hypnotist has actually crossed over and is now playing a part in the process you are undergoing to work out your karma. Not a good idea for you or the hypnotist, even if there is a beneficent effect through the process, as this actually creates karma rather than resolves it. You must face your karma yourself, just as you are meant to discover your destiny for yourself. No one can do it for you.

Having said this, there are times when a past life trauma is so severe that it interferes with the normal functioning of life. These situations do require special assistance. For example, if a person died horribly in a past life and in this life becomes so phobic that he or she cannot function, past life regression can be of help. In this case, it's not a matter of stepping into someone else's karma. What the hypnosis is trying to do is break the paralyzing fear that is holding the person back. There is no adverse karma here because the purpose of the regression is not to try to work out karmic lessons. Rather, it's to help alleviate a distressed mind so people can get on with their lives.

The other thing to remember regarding past life regression is not all the experiences brought up during the hypnotic sessions are real. The subconscious mind is a *subjective* storehouse of memory. It records experiences through the lens of our own personality. It is not an *objective* recording of experiences as we find with the Book of Life. So not everything that is in our subconscious mind is accurate or valid; it's simply what we have put in it. This makes past life regression an unreliable tool for research since there is often no way to determine if what is being revealed during a session is accurate or not.

All in all, past life regression can be likened to brain surgery; you choose to do it as a last resort, when everything else fails, and only under the supervision of the best trained and qualified therapist you can find.

Figure 1 on the inside back cover of this book depicts how past life memories show up in the aura.

Around the body, you have what is known as the mental template. The mental template looks like a white eggshell surrounding the body. It acts as a conduit for the receiving and transmitting of thought. As with the causal template, there is much to be said about this part of our spiritual anatomy. In this illustration, the focus is on the part it plays in understanding karmic energy in the aura.

A fascinating part of the mental template is that it acts as a type of screen on which the subconscious memories play out. It's not actually the subconscious itself but a field of mental activity for the subconscious. We can see here that the mental template is filled with images from past lives. Actually, these are not images but more like movies of past life experiences. These images mainly remain static and are inactive until something activates them or prompts them into activity. Like the soul images, they are spherical in appearance but larger. The images at the top part of the shell indicate experiences that are more pronounced and positive, while the ones in the lower part are being worked out or are difficult experiences that have been resolved. Positive experiences will retain a beautiful aura light around them. Disturbing experiences will have a dark light around them until they are resolved, at which point the image remains neutral.

When you incarnate, some of these images and movies will stand out and move to the foreground. These are the particular past life experiences that you have come into this life to work out, and they will remain a prominent part of you until you work through the karma related to these experiences and can put them behind you for good.

In this example, there are ten karmic images that are playing strongly in this person's life. (Please note: For the sake of clarity and detail, the subconscious images are larger than they actually are. In actuality the images are approximately six inches in diameter.) Image 1 at the top shows a good incarnation as an artist, which will give her strength in this life. Image 2 shows a wonderful romantic experience that she brings in from a past life that will help her in this life. Image 3 shows a lifetime where she was murdered; she is resolving that experience in this life. Image 4 shows a life where she was brutally attacked and beaten, which she has also come into this life to resolve. Image 5 shows good karma from a life where she was a religious leader and helped many people; she will use that power for humanitarian work she is meant to do in this life. Image 6 shows a lifetime where she was a chronic liar; she has come to resolve this character flaw.

Starting with image 7, we are now dealing with energies that are older and in the process of finally being resolved. Image 7 shows a life where she was abused by her father. She has worked much of this out, but there is still some karma remaining. Image 8 shows a lifetime of poverty that still haunts her to a degree. Image 9 shows an old lifetime where she was in the royal courts and used deceit to wield power. This karma is almost worked out. And image 10 shows the vestige of a lifetime of molestation, for which she is just about to resolve all associated karmic energy.

In looking at the intricacies of the subconscious, it becomes clear that one must tread very carefully when dealing with the subconscious mind.

Figure 2 on the inside back cover of the book shows how the soul images and past life memories work together in facing and resolving karma. This young woman is just starting to make her own way in life. In her soul image (image A) is a strong picture of her as a successful architect. This is her destiny in this life, which she has earned through accruing good karma. The image is very bright with a brilliant gold light around it, indicating the powerful contribution she is meant to make. In addition, she brings in very good karmic soul energy to give her power to complete her task. She also has a bright spiritual division above her head, indicating spiritual power that will help her in many facets of life, including career.

To help make this happen, she will draw on four past lives of successful work. Image 1 is a past life in France. She was male in this life and a very successful lawyer. She used her skills in the best way she knew how rather than to exploit or take advantage of people. The green glowing energy around this past life memory indicates the harmonious and balancing power this life brings and what she will unconsciously use in her present life.

Image 2 shows a past life in Italy. Again she is male and this time a creative artist. While not quite as successful as the lifetime as a lawyer, this lifetime brings out her artistic skills she will need to draw on as an architect. The pink around this image/movie indicates that in that life she put a lot of love into her work. There was great passion in what she did. And once again, this love and passion will come through in this life.

Image 3 shows a life she had in Belgium as a brilliant mathematician. The blue aura around this image/movie depicts that she was very inventive and original in her thinking, and she will need this inventiveness in solving problems in various architectural projects as well as for expressing originality in her thinking.

And finally, image 4 shows a life she lived in Spain. She was female in this life and was a fashion designer. In this life she brought together her creative and business skills. The silver aura indicates that she was a quick thinker, able to make decisions, and dealt effectively with associates and colleagues.

Of course this is what is possible for her. While all the talent and more is part of her aura, she is not consciously aware of all these past life gifts and accomplishments. Instead, she will intuitively call on all her talents in order to weave her destiny herself. And as with all of us, she will have her tests and challenges. If she passes them, which is well within her power, she will go very far in life.

Chapter 16

AURIC KARMA MEDITATIONS

A dramatic example of how working with spiritual energy is able to alleviate some very heavy karma is a case I had years ago with a woman, Sally, who killed her husband and got away with it. Fortunately, this is not a situation most of us find ourselves in, but it demonstrates just how deep the light can go to heal a situation and how no sin is past redemption.

When I first met Sally I didn't know what she had done, but I knew by her aura that something very serious was going on. There were splotches of black light in her aura, indicating hatred and murderous rage. It was pretty clear that this woman had killed someone and was having a difficult time as a result. She was not metaphysical and didn't know if she even believed in God at that time, but she was so desperate she was willing to try anything. She asked me point-blank, "Being that you can see the aura, can you see something unusual with me?" I said, "Yes, I can."

It wasn't long before she confessed everything. She was a mother of four. Her husband used to come home at night drunk and beat her and the kids. She showed me scars where he had broken her bones and such. To make matters worse, even though her husband was in business for himself and had some money, he wouldn't spend a dime on her or the kids. He literally left them to starve. She had to work cleaning houses to earn enough to buy food.

After one too many repeated episodes, she had had enough. She decided to poison him. She did it little by little so no one would notice. People just thought he was getting sick from all his drinking. He finally got so sick he died. She was not caught. No one suspected her in the least. Just the opposite, they all sympathized with her. Yet the memory of the whole experience haunted her every night to the point that she could barely sleep.

The first thing I told her was that it was not me she had to consider. I was not going to report her to the police. The deed was done. She was not dangerous or a threat to anyone at this point. This was between her, God, and her husband's soul. What she shared with me would be kept in confidence as part of therapist-patient confidentiality, although I was acting as a spiritual counselor.

As we started working, she kept defending her actions, saying she had no choice. I tried to tell her she did have a choice. She could have gone to someone for help or taken the children and left him. She again defended herself, saying she had no money and there was nowhere for her and her children to go. But then after she murdered her husband, in addition to her desperate state of mind, she had next to no money. She was spiritually and materially bankrupt. That night, we prayed together very hard for her soul. She agreed to let me work with her to try to help.

Sally began by doing some very serious prayers and meditations asking God and the soul of her husband for forgiveness for what she had done. In the beginning, she had trouble understanding that what she had done was a serious offense and that she had to atone for it. She kept trying to justify her actions but, at the same time, she was being torn apart by inner turmoil. She would lie awake at night thinking of all the things he did to her, which where considerable, and then relive the details of how she killed him. There was no question he was a cruel and abusive man and that she had to get away from him, but she had other options than what she chose to do.

Her saving grace was her children. She knew she had to do something because she and her children, who were still young, were practically destitute, and at the time she was in no mental condition to go out and work. The next step after starting her forgiveness work, and before even touching on the karmic aspect of her situation, was to get her mind off of what she had done so it would not consume her. She meditated and prayed with Divine Light, to release her hatred toward her husband and her anxiety about her life and the lives of her children. She prayed very hard for redemption and tried to turn her mind back to God. It took a lot of work to bring her into a more peaceful state of mind and release the shock of the whole experience, which was overwhelming her. Gradually she began to get a handle on herself. She calmed down and began to see things more clearly.

It was at this point that I touched on the topic of karma and reincarnation. Surprisingly, she seemed to be open and understanding. I gently shared with her that I clairvoyantly picked up that she had known her husband in a past life, but the roles were reversed. In that life, she was the husband and he was the wife. She, as the husband, was physically abusive and cruel and eventually left the wife almost penniless. The wife (her husband in her present life) carried hatred to the end of that incarnation.

In this life, she had come back to pay her karma to him. She was supposed to be loving and supportive to her husband. He was meant to be more forgiving and tolerant. Unfortunately, as sometimes happens when working out karma, he went the other way and unconsciously let loose all his pent-up rage and anger from that past life. This, of course, created new karma for him without his realizing it.

This was an unfortunate situation in which, because of his cruelty and the threat he posed to the children, her only option was to leave him, even though that meant she would leave some of the karma owed him unfinished. No matter what the karmic situation, no one has the right to be abusive. Had she found the strength to put aside her own frustration and anger, take the kids and leave him, she would have diffused the whole situation. She and her husband would have come back together in a future life and finally resolved the karma. Even if it meant a temporary hardship for her, she would have been much better off just leaving him.

Sadly, that was not what she chose to do. By killing him, she still left the old karma unresolved and now added new karma, which she will have to pay back in another life. So instead of lessening her karma, she compounded it. In her aura, I could see the soul image of her husband and how the dark energy had intensified because of her action. I could also see that some of the soul energy rays had weakened, which was going to be a source of new troubles. A person in such a spiritually weakened state is susceptible to new temptations and wrongdoings. New, unrelated karmas can easily accrue, making life even more difficult.

Fortunately, this was an area that could be helped greatly by the Divine Light. Working to build up her aura and karmic soul energy would not automatically erase what she had done, but it could give her the power to go on with her life, which would lay a much stronger foundation for facing her karma when it comes around.

It took two years of steady effort and a lot of work, but her aura began to look much better. She became truly repentant, and her aura showed it. The black spots and clouds of worry and despair were gone. In their place were now some silver and gold, showing she was in a much clearer state of mind. She knew what she had done was wrong and she was determined to do some good in her life. She was more optimistic about the road ahead and had stopped the self-punishment she had been putting herself through. She slowly started building her karmic soul energy and even the soul image of her husband brightened a little, indicating that things will be a little easier when she finally works out her karma with him.

The question now was where to go from here. As mentioned, eventually Sally will have to pay retribution for what she did in a future life. Meditation alone can't change this. It can greatly alleviate the burden, but eventually she will have to walk through the fire she created. However, this doesn't mean she has to live a desolate life in the present. She still has the opportunity to complete at least some of her purpose in life. It was now up to her to double her efforts to learn life's lessons.

So Sally began working to rebuild her life. She continued to meditate regularly and took her life more seriously. She found a job as a janitor that paid pretty well, which enabled her to care for her children better as they became the centerpiece of her life. She moved into a better place to live and even became hopeful of finding another man in her life and possibly remarrying. Best of all, she found God and lived a more spiritual life.

This story demonstrates the power of meditation and prayer in helping to work out your karma. By changing the energy within your aura, you change the energy you project into life and that positive change cannot help but have a profound impact on the situations and conditions you face. Spiritual energy gives you the needed power to face and resolve any test or challenge. It is the power behind all power, the secret to any act of manifestation. Working with your aura and spiritual energy is also something you can start doing right away. You have complete control over the process and you can start immediately. However, one note of caution: As essential as meditation is in cleansing karmic energy, it cannot bypass the part you have to play in resolving karma. You still have to stand and face your karma. Meditation and spiritual techniques give you the tools to master life, but you still have to go out in the mix of life and utilize the tools. No one can work out your karma for you. You have to do it for yourself.

12 Transformative Meditations

Meditation and prayer are two of the most important tools you have in your quest for spiritual enlightenment. Meditation is receiving—receiving from the divine. Prayer is petitioning the divine—a sending out. In working with the aura, you do a combination of prayer and meditation that is called meditative prayer. Through prayer, you petition the divine for the type of help you need, and then through meditation, you receive that help and spiritual nourishment.

Make meditation a daily practice and you will be making one of the most profound contributions to your life and spiritual development. Working with divine energy does not make karma disappear, but it gives you a tremendous booster shot to face and resolve your karma.

There are many ways to meditate. A simple way is *reflective meditation*. In this type of meditation, you focus on certain imagery and this has the effect of actually calling on the spiritual power associated with that imagery. To begin, find a comfortable, quiet place to meditate, a place where you will not be disturbed. For this meditation, you will be sitting upright in a chair, legs uncrossed. (See the appendix for a more detailed description of the auric meditation.)

Begin your meditation by envisioning a golden bubble of protection all around you. Feel very safe and supported through this process. Recognize that God loves you and is helping you. Close your eyes and envision a golden sun about two feet above your head. This golden sun is radiating a beautiful golden-white light. It is your own Higher Self that is in direct connection with the divine realms. As you put your attention in this part of you, let go of all worries or concerns. Simply feel the Divine Love and the holiness of this sacred level of consciousness.

Once you have established the golden sun above your head, you are ready to start working with spiritual energy. The following twelve exercises are suggestions for working with the Divine Light to help alleviate karmic conditions. Feel free to adapt the meditations according to your particular situation. Take your time in doing these exercises. It is not recommended that you do more than a few of them in any single sitting. And it is most likely you will have to repeat them several times to begin to feel their effect. Karmic conditions are not created overnight and you will need to show patience and persistence in turning things around.

When you finish working with spiritual energy, stay a few moments in the silence. Gently feel that you are grounding yourself and your consciousness is coming back into your body. Then give your thanks to the divine for what you have received.

Karmic Cleansing with the Orange-Red Flame

The first step in releasing karmic energy is to do a spiritual cleansing. This cleansing can be general or specific to a particular karma or condition you are working through.

Envision a radiant orange-red flaming light down-raying from the golden sun above your head. Sense this energy surrounding you and releasing any negative, disturbing energies. Feel this negative energy being released from you and taken to the mineral kingdom and dissolved in the light. You feel a sense of freedom from anything that has been weighing heavily on you.

Then see this orange-red flaming light gently enter through the top of your head to a spiritual center in the middle of your head. See this energy purifying all your thinking, releasing any disturbing, obsessive, and unhealthy thoughts. Release any thoughts that you have generated and any thoughts that others have projected onto you that are not of the divine. See that negative energy dissolved in the mineral kingdom in the light.

Then ask that this light be taken into the subconscious mind, releasing subconscious memories and patterns that are detrimental or are creating any disturbance in your life. Feel the light gently cleansing those areas, freeing you.

Then see this cleansing energy touching a spiritual center in your throat, releasing words that you have spoken that were not in the Divine Light or words spoken to you that were not in the Divine Light that you accepted or reacted to. See all negative energy being dissolved in the mineral kingdom in the light.

Then see the orange-red flame touching your heart chakra—the Great Hermetic Center. Give this energy permission to touch deep into this center, releasing burdens or pressures. Let this light out-ray into every avenue of your human Earth affairs, purifying persons, places, things, conditions, and situations and the conditions that constitute the situations. Feel any obstructions or obstacles in your life dropping away.

Then ask that this divine light of purification touch the soul images around your Hermetic Center, releasing any heavy karmic energy surrounding them. Hold in silence for a few moments while this light is doing its job. Ask that all negative energy be taken to the mineral kingdom and be dissolved in the light.

Then envision this orange-red flaming light down-raying into your abdominal/solar plexus area and into a spiritual center near the navel. Ask that this purifying light release negative emotional energies. Let the light purify confusions, irritations, frustrations, anxieties, fears, angers, and resentments. Let this light cut loose any emotional entanglements with other people. Ask those negative energies to be taken into the mineral kingdom and be dissolved in the light.

Then ask that the orange-red flaming light out-ray throughout your physical body, releasing all stresses, illness, fatigue, discomfort that you might be feeling. Ask that this light continue to out-ray through the mental template, purifying disturbing mental energies lodged in the mental template. Ask that all negative energy be taken into the mineral kingdom and dissolved in the light.

Ask that this energy continue to out-ray throughout your causal template, dissolving any negative energies connected to the soul levels. See any negative energy being dissolved in the mineral kingdom in the light.

Replenishing Your Aura with the Blue-White Fire

After any type of spiritual cleansing, it is important to replenish yourself. One of the most powerful spiritual energies to accomplish this is an energy called the blue-white fire. It looks like the sapphire blue flame on a stove top with radiant streaks of white light moving through it. In this reflective meditation, you will be asking the light to charge and recharge your aura with new life force and to heal any troubled areas.

Envision a powerful blue-white fire light down-raying from the golden sun above your head. This energy has an immediate uplifting and transforming quality. You feel strengthened and renewed in this vitalizing power. See this energy encircling your aura, charging and recharging you in a clockwise motion. Whatever was released by the orange-red flame is now being replenished by the blue-white fire.

Then see this blue-white fire gently entering the top of your head, reaching that beautiful spiritual center within your head. Ask that all your thoughts be charged and recharged in this life-giving light. You feel and sense this blue-white fire replenishing every corner of your mental self, bringing forth new, fresh ideas and inspiration, a fresh outlook on life. Any tired or stressed areas are wonderfully uplifted in this holy light. Feel this light nourishing every brain cell to respond to the impulse of mind.

Then gently ask that this light be directed to your subconscious mind to charge and recharge it in a clockwise motion. Feel a new influx of spiritual power replenishing the subconscious mind. Feel a beautiful rapport between the subconscious and conscious mind. Ask that the blue-white fire cultivate fertile soil for new divine ideas to take root.

Then ask that the blue-white fire touch any past life experiences that were positive and uplifting and are relevant in your life at this time. Ask that this subconscious pattern be quickened and exhilarated in the light so that its beneficent attribute can come more to the fore in this life to help serve the divine purpose you are here to complete. Stay in silence a moment while this light is doing its work.

Then ask that the blue-white fire down-ray to your throat area and the powerful spiritual center in the throat. Ask that the light charge and recharge every word you speak so that your words go out in spiritual tone.

Then ask that the light go to your Hermetic Center in the middle of your chest. Here let it charge and recharge every avenue of your human Earth affairs, giving new life and vigor to all that you do. See this blue-white fire release any sadness or depression; you now feel hopeful and optimistic.

Then in deepest humility and reverence, see this light touching your soul levels to strengthen and brighten your karmic soul energy to the full degree of your need. Stay in silence for a few moments for the light to do its work.

Then see the blue-white fire touching the soul images surrounding the Hermetic Center to give you more power to tune in to and better accomplish all that is in your Tapestry of Life and to give you more power and insight to fully resolve all karma you came to redeem.

Then see the blue-white fire light enveloping the beautiful center in the solar plexus near the navel. Let this light charge and recharge all of your emotional nature, replenishing tired areas and healing any emotional distresses. Feel that your emotions are coming back into a strong centering and equilibrium and coordinating with all other levels of your consciousness.

Then see this light out-raying through your physical body, through every cell, charging and recharging this body in a clockwise motion. See this light healing any ill or disturbed areas, bringing forth perfect health and well-being.

Then see this light continuing to out-ray through your mental template to charge and recharge all of the mental activities going on and to accentuate all the positive, enlightened thought patterns. See this light out-ray through the causal template to uplift the soul and refresh it with the Holy Breath of God.

Redeeming Soul Karma with the Pure White Light

The pure white light serves many spiritual functions. It brings in the purity and holiness of God. This energy is excellent to work with to help strengthen and redeem soul karma character blemishes that are carryovers from past lives. It is also an excellent energy to work with when you know you have done something wrong and are trying to correct it.

Envision a radiant beam of the pure white light of God down-raying from the golden sun above your head. You immediately feel uplifted by this light as it encircles your aura. Feel its purity and power of redemption. You feel strengthened by this light and more in tune with the divine. You feel that with God all is possible.

Then see this light gently entering through the top of your head, touching the mental center. Here the white light uplifts all your thought, illuminating you with the mind of God. Let it touch any dark corners of the mind so that the light can redeem you and bring this part of you back into the light. Let go of any unhealthy or unproductive habits or character traits into the light. Feel yourself surrendering any bad habits into God's loving hands.

Then see this light illuminating your subconscious mind, again shedding light into any dark corner and releasing any subconscious patterns that are adversely affecting you. Feel it all going into the light.

Then feel this light touching the spiritual center in your throat to redeem any words that you have spoken that were hurtful to another whether intentionally or unintentionally. Ask that the white light go into your speech pattern to release harsh sound and to bring forth the uplifting sonorities of spiritual tone. Ask that the light help you to use words that are constructive and filled with Divine Light.

Then see the pure white light touching your Hermetic Center to equalize, center, and attune all aspects of your personal affairs and action in the Divine Light of God. Ask that every step you take be in rhythm with your divine purpose. See that white light going into your soul levels to strengthen the soul images and karmic soul energy, uplifting everything in the purity of God and redeeming any dark corners by bringing them into the light.

Here take a few deep breaths and stay in the silence for a few moments while the light is doing its work.

Then ask that the light touch any weaknesses in the soul, to first bring them to your attention so you can work on them and to bring more spiritual power to strengthen them in the Divine Light.

If you know you have done something wrong, ask the white light to diffuse any negative karmic energy created and give you more spiritual power to redeem yourself and take actions needed to set things right. Ask that this white light be projected into the vibrated ethers to derail any negative energy that you have set in motion and to bring everything back into balance. Ask for illumination for the right course of action. Stay in the silence for a few moments while the light does its work.

Then see this energy going to the spiritual center in the solar plexus near the navel. Ask that it uplift all of your emotional nature, releasing any regrets, remorse, guilt, or frustrations. Also ask that the light release any resistance to the light touching the emotions. Feel your emotional nature coming into alignment and feel yourself coming into the knowing that there is no sin past redemption and that you are always given a second chance to set things right. Feel a strengthening of your emotional power and an even stronger desire to pursue your goals in life.

Then see this light out-raying through the physical body, working into every atom to rarefy the physical framework. Then see this energy out-raying through the mental and causal templates, uplifting them in the light.

Healing Karmic Relationships with
the Deep Rose-Pink Ray of Spiritual Love

The deep rose-pink ray is one of the most potent spiritual powers there is. It is the very embodiment of Divine Love. This energy is indispensable in any relationship and is especially important when working through any karmic entanglements with others. This energy works very well with the forgiveness work covered in chapter 17.

Envision a luminous deep rose-pink light down-raying from the golden sun above your head. You feel its warmth and tenderness as it encircles your aura, embracing you in the glow of its light. You feel at one with God. You sense that this light is saying that you are never alone; God is always with you.

Then see this light gently down-raying through the top of your head and enveloping the mental center in the middle of your head. You feel soothed by the healing balm of this light. This deep rose-pink light infuses all your thoughts with love, releasing any unkind thoughts you have directed to others or any unkind thoughts directed at you.

Then see this light touching your subconscious mind to release and heal any old hurts or wounds of the past, whether in this or a past life, connected with any person or situation. You feel yourself letting go of any old animosities into this loving light.

Then see this Divine Light touching the spiritual center in the middle of your throat, healing any unkind verbal exchange with others whether initiated by you or someone else. Let the deep rose-pink light fill every word you speak with love.

Then see the deep rose-pink light down-raying into your Hermetic Center in the middle of your chest. Feel your heart warming and softening with this light. If you have been holding back your love flow for whatever reason, feel all of that dropping away. Let every exchange with others come from a place of love—the unconditional love of God. Surrender any sense of judgment or condemnation. Let your heart beat with the very heart of spiritual love. Hold in the silence for a few moments to let the light of love do its work.

Then ask that deep rose-pink light to go to any person you owe karma to or to any person who owes karma to you to redeem your actions and bring everything into the light and love of God so that this karma can be resolved to the benefit of all concerned. Ask for strength, guidance, and courage in any karmic relationship that feels difficult to bear. Once again hold in the silence for a few moments while the light is doing its work.

Then see this loving ray down-raying into the spiritual center in the solar plexus area near the navel. Ask that every emotion be bathed in the light of love, healing any emotional hurts or resentments. Ask to be released from any false sympathies, energetic tie-ins or hook-ins so that you are in your own emotional center. Let your emotions feel the joy of this love, how it nurtures you and makes you feel one with God.

Then see this light out-raying through the physical body, letting every aspect of the body drink in this love. Then see this energy out-raying through the mental template to fill it with spiritual love. And then see this light out-raying through the causal template, uplifting it in the light of love.

Strengthening Good Money Karma with the Turquoise Ray of Abundance

The turquoise ray is the spiritual energy of prosperity. This power brings you into the consciousness of wealth. It helps you to release limited thinking and to think in unlimited terms. As a child of God, you are part of God's kingdom and are meant to partake of infinite abundance that is part of the Kingdom of God. This energy is very helpful in working through money karma, as it helps you to learn the spiritual lessons that money presents.

Envision a brilliant turquoise light down-raying from the golden sun above your head. Feel it uplifting you as it encircles your aura and consciousness. Whatever financial troubles you may be having seem to vanish in the presence of this light. This spiritual energy surrounds you in a good luck halo of wealth and well-being.

Then see this energy gently entering through the top of your head and quickening the spiritual centering in the middle of your head. You feel this turquoise light filling your mind with thoughts of wealth and prosperity. Thoughts of poverty or lack disappear and you feel as one with God's infinite supply.

You feel that this light is giving you the right pictures of how to use money for God's divine purpose. If you feel you have misused money, ask this light to redeem you and teach you the right use of abundance. If you are enjoying good money karma, ask this light to expand your wealth consciousness and show you the right channels of expression your wealth is meant to take.

Then feel this energy touching your subconscious mind, filling the subconscious with thoughts of prosperity. It touches into past life memories where you were wealthy and used that wealth for the greater good of humanity. It also touches difficult lives where you mishandled money or suffered poverty, releasing negative energy connected to those experiences. Stay in silence for a few moments while the light is doing its work.

Then see this energy down-raying to the spiritual center in the middle of your throat. See this light activating every word you speak in the Divine Light of prosperity, releasing any words of lack or limitation, purifying any speech patterns of worry, fear, distrust, deceit regarding money matters. Ask that your words become the spiritual tone of prosperity.

Then see this energy down-raying to the spiritual center in the middle of your chest—your Hermetic Center. See this center filling up with the turquoise ray of abundance and supply. Let it out-ray into every avenue of your life, increasing present avenues of abundance and generating new avenues of prosperity. Ask that you become a living witness to God's great riches.

Feel this energy healing any areas of your life that are hurting financially. Ask that this energy release areas where you are holding back your prosperity flow out of fear, worry, greed, possessiveness. As this energy quickens your heart center, let your kindness and generosity flow freely. Be generous and giving with others as God is generous with you.

Then feel this energy touch deep into your soul levels and your karmic soul energy, redeeming money karma you may have accrued and building good money karma to greater heights. Ask this light to quicken soul images connected to abundance, brightening them in the Divine Light. Feel your prosperity is boundless. Your cup is truly running over with God's great riches. Stay for a moment in the silence as the light is doing its work.

Then see this energy down-raying to the spiritual center in the solar plexus area near the navel. Let this light touch deep into your emotional nature so that you are emotionally in agreement with this divine power. *Feel* wealthy. Feel like you are a mighty monarch. Let this light dissolve frustrations, fears, anxieties related to money matters. If you know you have done something wrong when it comes to money, ask for God's forgiveness. If you have cheated, stolen, or lied for monetary gain, ask for God's forgiveness. If you are stingy or possessive with your money, ask for God's forgiveness. If you have been reckless or careless or mismanaged money, ask for God's forgiveness. Feel that through this light, God is giving you a fresh opportunity to build and freely express your divine prosperity. Stay in the silence for a moment while the light is doing its work.

Then feel this light out-raying through your physical body so that you feel rich and abundantly healthy in body as well as mind and soul. See this energy out-raying through your mental and causal templates, filling them with the turquoise ray.

Harmonizing Physical Karma with the Emerald-Green Ray

Physical karma can be tricky. Illnesses and physical distress can be caused by physiological problems, by wrong thinking and feeling, and can be the result of physical karma. Regardless of the cause of your physical distress, it is strongly recommended that you use all means of healing at your disposal: medical, holistic, and spiritual. Working with the orange-red flame, the blue-white fire, and the white light is essential in helping to heal the body. In addition, a powerful energy that helps with physical karma is the emerald-green ray of balance and harmony.

Envision a glowing emerald-green light down-raying from the golden sun above your head. As this light surrounds your aura, you immediately feel that all parts of your consciousness and being are coming into balance—mind, body, soul harmony. You feel that you are tuning into God's divine rhythm.

Then see this energy gently entering through the top of your head and entering the spiritual center in the middle of your head, filling your mind with thoughts of balance and harmony. Ask that this light dissolve discordant thoughts, especially disturbing thoughts regarding your health. Feel that your mind is harmonizing with the mind of God and giving you the pictures of perfect health.

Then let this light reach into your subconscious mind to harmonize all of the subconscious patterns. Ask that this light release memories of past lives of physical abuse to you or to others, to cut loose memories of illness and physical distress. Ask that the emerald-green light harmonize good physical karma from past lives of physical accomplishments to help give you strength in this life. Stay in the silence for a moment while this light is doing its work.

Then see the emerald-green ray touching the center in the middle of your throat, harmonizing every word you speak so that you speak words of health and well-being. Ask that this light release disharmonious and disturbing words spoken to you that reinforced any false images of ill health.

Then ask that the Divine Light of balance and harmony down-ray to the Hermetic Center in the middle of your chest, filling it with the emerald-green ray. Let this light out-ray into every avenue of your life, bringing your personal activities into divine rhythm and serving God's plan for you. If you are facing physical distress that is affecting your life, feel this light balancing those conditions.

Then see this energy touching your soul levels and helping to build up more spiritual power in your karmic soul energy connected to physical well-being. If you know you have abused your body or the bodies of others, ask for God's forgiveness. Through this light, ask that God give you the power to take better care of your body and to use it for the purpose it was intended for—to act as a vehicle of physical expression for your soul. If you are enjoying good physical karma, ask that this light rarefy the physical form to become a more eloquent expression of your soul. Stay for a moment in the silence while this light is doing its work.

Then see this energy down-raying to the center in the solar plexus near your navel. Feel the emerald-green ray balancing your emotional nature. If you have been feeding life to your ills through your emotions, feel this light derailing those negative emotions and redirecting your emotional nature so that the emotions are now reinforcing and nourishing the body with healthy vibrations.

Then see the emerald-green energy out-ray throughout the physical body to heal and restore perfect harmony to every aspect of the material form. Ask that this light touch any area of the body that is affected by physical karma. Feel this light releasing dark areas and bringing in more spiritual power to distressed areas. Ask that this emerald-green ray strongly go into the spine, releasing stresses and impingements, opening up the spiritual currents that flow up and down the spine. Stay in the silence for a few moments while the light is doing its work.

Then ask that the emerald-green ray out-ray through the mental and causal templates and also what is called the astral body to bring perfect equilibrium to all levels of consciousness.

Balancing Nature Karma with the Emerald-Green Ray

The emerald-green ray is excellent for helping to balance karmic condition with nature. Karma with nature works a little differently from other types of karma (see chapter 9), but you can most definitely create karma with nature when you misuse it. This meditation is designed to help redeem negative energy created from misusing nature.

Envision an emerald-green light down-raying from the golden sun above your head. See this energy encircling you, uplifting all levels of your consciousness. Ask that this vital energy balance your relationship with nature and all the kingdoms of nature. Feel that you are a part of nature—its crowning glory.

As this emerald-green light enters gently through the top of your head, it activates the center in the middle of your head, filling your thoughts with this radiant energy. You feel at one with nature, in rhythm with the divine pulse beat that flows through every kingdom of nature. Any misconceived thoughts regarding the relationship between nature and yourself are released.

Then see the emerald-green light flow into the center in the middle of your throat, activating your speech pattern with balance and harmony, releasing any discordant or abusive words related to nature.

Then see this energy entering into the Hermetic Center in the middle of your chest. Let it fill all areas of your personal affairs with this divine power. If you have initiated any action that was harmful to nature, ask that this emerald-green light harmonize the discordant energy and bring your relationship with nature back into balance. Then see this light touching your soul levels, building up the karmic soul energy and increasing your appreciation of nature. Stay in the silence for a moment as the light is doing its job.

Then see this emerald-green light down-raying into the center in the solar plexus near the navel to harmonize your emotions. Ask to redeem any carelessness or insensitively when it comes to nature. Feel the unconditional love between nature and yourself.

Building Good Career Karma with the Golden Ray of Wisdom Light

There are many dynamics to consider when it comes to career. One of the most important is the recognition that, through your chosen pursuit, you are contributing to the divine plan and fulfilling your life's purpose. Dynamic power is essential to help you work through obstacles and make a career flourish. In the same way, if you have been ruthless in your career pursuits, it is essential to redeem and temper that aggressive attitude while at the same time continuing to put your best foot forward.

The golden ray of wisdom light is the strongest dynamic spiritual power there is. By working with this energy, you can strengthen and fortify your aura and consciousness. This power has a strong connection to the divine mind. When this energy is seen in the aura, it indicates that one has earned that wisdom through experience and application.

Envision the dynamic golden ray down-raying from the golden sun above your head. This power surrounds you in its dynamic power. All irritations and fears melt away in the presence of this holy light. You feel courageous and strong.

Then see this power gently entering through the top of your head, blessing the spiritual center in the middle of your head. Feel your thoughts illuminated with wisdom and understanding. You feel decisive and confident, full of faith in God. All confusion drops away and you feel this golden light bringing forth clarity and insight. If you have been careless or ruthless in your career path, let this light redirect your thoughts along more compassionate and constructive lines.

Then let this golden light flow into the subconscious mind to strengthen past lives where you excelled in your career. Ask the power of this light to rekindle some of the knowledge and power to help you complete your life's task in this life. See this energy touching memories of a past life where you created career karma and released negative karmic energy.

Then see the golden light down-raying into the spiritual center in the middle of your throat. Ask that this light strengthen your spiritual tone so that you speak in the voice of spirit. Ask that through the words you speak, you accentuate your career potential and your spiritual purpose.

Then see this golden ray entering your Hermetic Center in the middle of your chest, filling it with this dynamic power. Feel yourself full of confidence and self-assurance in your career. If your purpose in life is not yet clear, feel the inner recognition that you do have a definite part to play in the divine plan. If your purpose is already clear, ask that this golden light give you more power to complete the full breadth of your life's task.

Then see this energy entering your soul levels, redeeming weak areas in your karmic soul energy and building up good career karma to even greater heights. Ask that this light touch your soul images to strengthen the images of your career destiny and to brighten any difficult career karma that you need to resolve. Stay in the silence for a few moments while this work is being done.

Then see the golden light entering into the center in the solar plexus near the navel. Feel your emotions strengthened in this light and giving you all the willpower you need to complete your career potential. If you feel discouraged or disillusioned, this power brings you hope and encouragement. If you feel lost or misdirected, this power gives you purpose and conviction. Ask that this vital power give you the strength to refuse the emotional energy of others who might be directing discouraging feelings toward you.

Quieting the Consciousness with the Purple Ray of Peace

With the purple ray, you want to bring in peace to quiet your soul and consciousness. When in the midst of a karmic trial, your consciousness is going to be buzzing. Your head will be filled with all sorts of ideas about what is going on, and many of those ideas will be wrong. Quiet your mind and heart so you can hear what God is trying to say to you. When going through a trying time, you won't always know if it's karma, but you know it's a difficult time. In your prayers say, "Whatever it is, God, here I am. I am ready to listen. I need the peace and need it strong."

Envision the deep purple ray of peace down-raying from the golden sun above your head. As it comes down, feel it enveloping like a blanket of peace and tranquillity. Feel yourself letting go of all worries or concerns and relaxing in the still waters of peace. You are putting your life in God's loving hands. There is only peace—the peace of spirit. Take a few deep breaths to draw in this peace.

Then see this purple light of peace entering through the top of your head to the spiritual center in the middle of your head. Your mind is filled with the purple ray of peace. You are letting go of your worries and letting God guide your life. Let your mind rest on the still waters of peace. Let this peace ray quiet mental chatter and tense and disturbing thoughts. Turn off the intellect and let your mind become a beautiful receiving station for the thoughts of God. Know that in the silence the soul is most ready to hear. Still your mind.

Ask that the purple ray touch your subconscious mind, quieting any disturbing memories from this or any other life that are causing distress. Let your subconscious mind come into harmony with your conscious mind and both come into harmony with the higher mind.

Then let this light down-ray into the center in the middle of your throat to bring peace to the words you speak and that are spoken to you. Release words that have caused distress or harm either to you or to others.

Then envision this peaceful light entering your Hermetic Center in the middle of your chest. Let it radiate throughout your personal affairs—your job, your relationship, your finances—bringing peace, peace, peace. Let your actions come from a place of peace and poise. Then let this light touch your soul levels to quiet the soul, releasing anxieties and restlessness. Let your soul rest on the still waters of peace so it can better tune in to the divine presence. Let this purple ray bring peace to your soul. May you feel at peace with your life and at peace with God. Stay in the silence while this light is doing its work.

Then see this energy down-raying to the spiritual center in the solar plexus near the navel. Give permission for this purple ray to touch deeply your emotions, bringing you "The Silence of Peace and the Peace of Silence." Feel hyperactivity dropping away and your emotions resting on the still waters of peace.

Then envision this light out-raying through your physical body, relieving you of physical pressures and stresses, especially those related to karmic situations that you may be facing. Let this light bless the nervous system to relax it in the Divine Light.

Then let this light out-ray through the mental and causal templates to establish divine peace throughout all levels of your consciousness so you are more receptive to what the divine has to say to you.

Exercise to Illuminate a Karmic Situation

When in the midst of a karmic situation, naturally you may not see all facets of what is going on. The white light is excellent to work with in this situation as it brings in the high spiritual illumination and revelation. Working with this ray helps you to gain more self-knowledge and keeps you from getting caught in personality entanglements that can complicate working through karmic situations.

Sometimes, karma can be like a mirror. The things you are seeing in other people are really things in yourself. If you notice you are doing this, then what you are facing could very well be karmic. If it's the other person's traits that you're always seeing and not your own, then you are not seeing yourself at all. You notice it out there because it is reflecting to you. So stop looking out there and start looking inside yourself.

Ask that a beautiful ray of the pure white light descend directly to the golden sun above your head—your Higher Self. As this light blesses your Higher Self, feel God's very essence, the divine purity.

Let the condition you are praying about rest with God. Relinquish the situation out of your hands and put it completely in God's hands. Ask that this white light lift whatever is blocked and not getting through so you can see for yourself the true nature of the situation you have placed on God's altar. Say, "I think I am facing a karmic test. I request angels of illumination and enlightenment to work with me to reveal if I am facing a karmic test. Reveal unto me that which I'm not seeing about this situation. Whatever it is, reveal unto me what I need to know."

Then hold your attention in your Higher Self and do your best to stay open and receptive. If you are inspired with something that seems appropriate and constructive, act on it even if it appears simple at first. The divine usually does not reveal everything at once. The divine gives you the next step, which leads to the step after that, and so on. Remember, calling on the divine is not shortcutting the natural spiritual growth process; it's not asking the divine to do the work for you. It's asking for the power to do it for yourself. If nothing comes through during the meditation, give your thanks and hold to the spiritual knowing that your answer is forthcoming.

Sending Divine Light to Others

There will be times when you want to send light to others to help heal karmic conditions for things that you may have done to them or for things they may have done to you. We cover forgiveness in chapter 17, but you can request any of the spiritual energies we have been working with in this chapter to help other people.

Ask that the energy you are requesting be sent from the golden sun above your head—your Higher Self—directly to the Higher Self of the person in need of this energy. Ask permission of the other person's Higher Self and always ask "according to divine law and love for the good of all concerned."

Hold for a few minutes while this is being done. Do not try to direct the light to the other person's Higher Self; the divine will send it where it needs to go. When you feel the connection has been made, your meditation is done. Don't do more than one or two energies in one sitting. When you are finished, give thanks to the divine for the blessings sent.

Here is a list of spiritual energies that we have used in this book:

Orange-red flame—purification
Blue-white fire—new life force, healing power
Pure white light—purity, redemption, and upliftment
Emerald-green—balance and harmony
Deep rose-pink—love and compassion
Purple—peace, tranquillity
Turquoise ray—prosperity, abundance
Gold—wisdom, confidence, dynamic power

Sending the White Light to the Fabric of Life

In this exercise, you are asking the light to redeem negative energy that you may have projected into the fabric of life. Remember, when you initiate an action, that action reverberates through the creative fabric of life, and this energy sooner or later will come back to you as you have put it out. Unfortunately, you cannot do much to affect the fabric of life energy that is already in action from previous lives, but you can help to redeem any negative energy that you initiated in this life. In doing this exercise, be sincere and contrite. Follow up this light work with redemptive actions.

Ask that the pure white light energy out-ray from the golden sun above your head—your Higher Self—directly into the fabric of life to derail and redeem any negative karmic energy that you have projected into the vibrated ethers. Ask for forgiveness for anything you have done wrong and ask for guidance to set things right. Hold for a moment while the light is doing its work.

In another flow of energy, ask the pure white light once again to out-ray from your Higher Self and into the fabric of life to redeem any negative energy initiated by others that was directed at you to release any ill effects you may be feeling from this adverse action.

Stay for a few moments in the silence while this light is finishing its work. Then give your thanks to the divine. Gently feel that you are grounding yourself and your consciousness is coming back into your body.

Chapter 17

The Healing Power

of Forgiveness,

Compassion, and Grace

I once attended a spiritualistic service with my good friend Donna. Donna worked in public relations and was an excellent psychic. When I first met her, she psychically saw my father, who had crossed over to the other side some years earlier, and described him in great detail. We became instant friends. She recognized my spiritual gifts and became a big supporter of my work. She eventually became president of the Society for Psychical Research in Southern California.

At this service, there was a medium answering questions from the audience. I'm cautious about attending meetings of this kind as sometimes the psychic or medium leading the group is not always what he or she presents themselves to be. I was studying the aura of the medium and saw he was sincere and effective at his craft.

During the course of his answering questions and giving messages, he turned to a lady in the front row and told her that her husband was communicating from the other side and was begging her forgiveness. The woman's face turned red and she screamed, "Never! I'll never forgive him!"

The medium was persistent in saying that the husband was pleading with the wife to forgive him. Evidently, the husband had not been good to her and cheated on her with another woman, which hurt her deeply. He died of an illness before they could reconcile. Now on the other side, he saw things from a very different perspective and understood how cruel he had been and was doing what he could to make things right. Unfortunately, the wife adamantly refused to forgive him.

This story demonstrates very clearly how hard it can be to forgive and resolve personal issues even when people pass on from this life. One might have thought that once her husband had died, she would have found it in her heart to let this go. Instead her anger continued to burn, and there was a very good chance she would take that resentment to her grave.

The power of forgiveness is undeniable. No matter how serious an offense, we always have the power to forgive if we choose to exercise that power. There are many examples of the power of forgiveness in the worst of situations.

Forgiveness is the great healer of love. Through the act of forgiving you free yourself of the destructive effects of wrongs that have been done to you. When someone hurts you, naturally you have a reaction to that experience. You may become angry, hateful, resentful, and so on. This creates a negative energy in your aura that remains as long as you hold on to that negative experience. Through the act of genuine forgiveness, you purify that negative energy from your consciousness. This has the healing effect of freeing you from the haunting effects of wrongs that have been done.

Holding on to grudges and resentments has a crippling effect on your life. It's as if a part of you has stopped growing. I know the more serious the offense, the more difficult it is to forgive, but also the greater the sense of freedom when you finally let it go.

Many people say it's natural to be angry when we are wronged. On one level, this makes perfect sense. Yet I have learned from my many years of working with the aura that a negative energy is a negative energy. Right or wrong, anger is anger, and, regardless of the cause it will have a destructive effect on us if we permit that energy to linger. Of course, we will have a natural initial reaction when someone hurts us, but I am speaking of weeks, months, or even years later when that same reaction still remains.

When it comes to karma, forgiveness is one of your most important tools. Forgiveness has tremendous power in balancing the karmic slate. The surest sign you will be back to work out karma with others is when there is no forgiveness.

Normally if someone has created karma with someone else, the two must reincarnate together in a future life to work things out. This means that the person who was wronged has to meet up again with the person who wronged them to resolve that karma. It's not always easy to synchronize the timing to reincarnate two people at the same time, and sometimes when they do, instead of working things out, the karma still is not resolved or the conflict continues and karma compounds.

This is why it's so important to do your best to work out your problems with others *now*. It's a more complicated affair to work it out in a future life. If you are mistreated and you do not forgive that individual, you *tie* yourself to that person *and* to the mistakes they made. This only serves to hold you back and slow down your spiritual progress. If you truly forgive the person who mistreated you, you *free* yourself of the negative attachment to that individual, *and you do not have to face each other again in a future life to resolve that karma.*

I can't emphasize this enough. Forgive people who have injured you and you absolve yourself from having to face that issue in a future life. But you really have to forgive; it can't be lip service. If you say you forgive but a situation still haunts you, you haven't really forgiven.

Some people think, "I don't want to forgive that individual. They did a terrible thing and I don't want them to get away with it." Forgiveness doesn't mean someone is getting away with something. The offending person is not off the hook. Forgiveness means the two of you are released from each other. The person who did the wrong will still have karmic lessons to face, but it won't involve you. This is why it doesn't matter if the person you are forgiving is asking for forgiveness or not, or if they are contrite or not. Forgiveness releases *you* from the karmic bond created by the offense.

There is a story from the other side of a woman who died in the Nazi concentration camps. She died with a consuming hatred for a jailer who was particularly abusive to her. He died soon after her. What do you think happened when the two found themselves on the other side?

Because of his heinous deeds, the jailer found himself in the lower regions, known as the netherworlds. This is a place where souls go who have sunk so low, they cannot yet reincarnate to work out their karma until they can work their way out of this terrible place. I have seen these regions and, while they are not quite the fire and brimstone of traditional theology, they are dark, miserable places where souls feel the extreme anguish of their own misdeeds.

Where do you think the woman found herself? She was a good woman, but her extreme hatred of this man bound her to him and she found herself in the netherworlds with him! How could it be otherwise? All her attention and emotional energy were directed at him and what he did to her, so she found herself right there with him. Of course, the divine was able to lift her out of there, but it took effort as her hatred was so intense.

What happens if you don't forgive and end up on the other side with an unresolved issue? Is there still time to forgive? The answer is yes. If you cross over to the other side and you haven't forgiven, you can forgive those people who hurt you once you are on the other side.

However, as strange as this may sound, many people who cross over take their anger and resentments with them and refuse to forgive even on the other side! They can be in the presence of magnificent celestial beings and still refuse to forgive! One would think that once you are in the exhilarated environment of the spirit world, you would drop old animosities. Yet all too often this is not the case. This tells us again that our crossing over to the other side does not make you a better person than you are right now. This is why it's so important to work on your faults now. And this is why it is so important not to go to your grave with a grudge. No matter what has happened, forgive those who have offended you. The sooner you forgive, the better!

What about the mistakes of past lives? Can you forgive others for *past* life mistakes in the same way you can be released from present life mistakes? The answer is yes. You can forgive others for past life offenses against you. Forgiveness is essential at any point in the process of working out karma. If you are in a challenging relationship with someone and recognize a karmic condition, you can still forgive that person for a past life mistake. And you will still experience the same spiritual release through that forgiveness. There is no such thing as someone being past forgiveness. There's always time to forgive.

What about when you are in the wrong? The same laws of forgiveness apply. If you mistreat someone and they truly forgive you, *you are absolved.* You will still have to atone for the wrongs you have done, but it will not have to be with that person. If they do not forgive you, you have no choice. You must work it out with that person. Either way, the karmic slate has to be balanced, but through forgiveness, the job is a lot easier. Do you see the incredible power forgiveness has?

It is fascinating to see the act of forgiveness in the aura. It comes through as a pink light above the person's head. Forgiveness has the effect of releasing negative energy and brightening the aura, which uplifts and enlightens the soul. With true forgiveness, there is a particularly uplifting effect in the heart chakra.

Forgiveness Prayer

Here is a very effective prayer for resolving karma with others. In doing this prayer, see yourself in a bubble of deep rose-pink light of spiritual love and separately see the other person in a bubble of deep rose-pink light. Feel that God is working with you. You can do this prayer as often as you need to in order to feel that you have truly forgiven.

FORGIVENESS PRAYER
I forgive you for everything you have done to me in this or any other life that injured me knowingly or unknowingly in word, thought, act, or deed.

I ask your forgiveness for everything I have done to you in this
or any other life that injured you in word, thought, act, or deed.
May you walk in the light of love and may I walk in the light of love.

COMPASSION AS A CALL TO ACTION

There is a wonderful story about compassion attributed to Arya Asanga, the founder of the Buddhistic study known as Yogacara.

Asanga was a Buddhist monk studying meditation. After several years of study, his understanding equaled that of his teacher. He then received an initiation and withdrew to a cave, where he sought communion with a heavenly being known as Lord Maitreya. Lord Maitreya, which means "loving kindness," is considered a bodhisattva, a Buddha in the making. He is said to reside in the heaven worlds and will one day incarnate on Earth to revive Buddhism after it falls into a period of decline.

For twelve years, Asanga meditated but could not make contact with this heavenly being. He started to give up several times, but every time he was about to give up, something urged him to continue his efforts. Once he saw a vision of a huge rock being slowly split open by a small tree root, which he interpreted as a sign to persevere, so he returned to his cave and again continued in his meditations. Another time when he decided to give up, he saw a vision that the wings of birds had gradually worn down the rocks around their nests, and interpreted this as yet another sign to continue to make contact with Lord Maitreya. He was to have several more encouraging signs, but after twelve years of persistent effort and with no vision of Maitreya, he finally decided to quit and leave his mountain retreat.

With a heavy heart, he slowly started making his way back toward the city. Alongside the road, he saw a half-dead dog, infested with maggots and whimpering in pain. Great compassion arose in Asanga. He realized that the dog would die of the infestation, but his Buddhist vows forbade him to kill the maggots. So he determined to give them flesh cut from his own body. No sooner had he made the sacrifice of his physical form than the dog vanished and in its place stood the blessed Lord Maitreya. Asanga burst into tears of joy. But then he began to wonder why Maitreya had not come sooner but only after many years and much anguish.

Maitreya read his thoughts and said, "Although rainfall and sunshine may be plentiful, impotent seeds will never sprout. Similarly, wherever Buddhas appear, they will never be seen by those people with karmic veils. Your karmic obstructions were much reduced by your invocations, but until now, the most important factor, Great Compassion, had not fully arisen within you."

After this experience, it is said that Asanga was taught by Maitreya and was given The Five Books of Maitreya, which he wrote down and gave to the world, rejuvenating Buddhist thought and practice in India.

In this story, we clearly see the power of compassion. Compassion is an essential part of karma. Just as there is the karma of taking wrong actions, there is the karma of not taking action when we are called upon to do so. There are sins of omission as well as sins of commission. If we see a person drowning and are capable of helping that person but do not do so, then we *generate* negative karma by our inaction when life called us to act. It doesn't matter if this event was destined or karmic. By its very presence in our life, it becomes our destiny and karmic duty.

Compassion is not an idle thought or a kind wish. It is a call to action. Compassion is holding to the divine image of love. It is the ability to recognize the divine spark in yourself and in those around you. Through compassion, you learn to see others as your loving spiritual brothers and sisters. Who does not help a brother or sister when they are hurting?

As part of your destiny, you are meant to seek out and help others—truly help others as the divine being you are. When people who need help cross your path, they become part of your life. It becomes your duty to offer a helping hand. It matters not if you are asked, if the need to help is presented to you; it's like the whimpering dog in the story of Asanga. It becomes your karma at that moment to be of service. To not help in such a circumstance would cause you to generate negative karma.

If you find yourself in a privileged position in life, it is your duty to find ways to be of real service. We have seen those with great wealth give large portions of their wealth in service to others through various philanthropic enterprises, and this is as it should be. Great humanitarian acts not only offer service to others, but also can help absolve unrelated karma we may have in other parts of our life. Our blessings multiply when we learn to make giving a part of our life.

One of the greatest mistakes people who embrace the tenets of reincarnation and karma make is thinking that people deserve hard times because of their karma. The untouchables in India are too often ignored because of the mistaken belief that they should stay in their deplorable situation to pay back karma. Nothing could be further from the truth. Karma may have put them in that place (and this is not always the truth), but any karmic situation is a starting point, not an end point. It is the karma of those more fortunate to help those less fortunate.

Refuse to judge. You can't know all the reasons people are where they are. You also can't anticipate what people will do. People will surprise you. Even if people have done terrible things, if the need is genuine, it is still your duty to help. If you are having trouble doing that, ask God to love them for you until you can learn to love them compassionately.

Helping others is too often looked upon as a burden. Yet the truth is, it's a privilege to be in a position to help. Through your compassionate actions, you are becoming more intimately involved in life's creative process. Help in the way it's needed—emotionally, mentally, physically, financially, or spiritually. People too often take care of every little need for themselves but will not help those in front of them who need help. And perhaps most important, make sure when you help, you put your heart into it.

GOD'S GRACE IS WITH YOU THROUGH EVERY KARMIC TRIAL

One of the most reassuring aspects of karma is that we are always given the power to succeed in facing and resolving our karma. This is accomplished by bringing to the fore our inherent strengths and also through what is commonly called God's grace.

Grace translates from the Greek word *charis*, which means an undeserved act of kindness. However, it is not altogether accurate to call God's grace undeserved. As God's children, we are all deserving of God's love and support. What is really meant here is that many times we are given support by the divine that we have not earned by our own actions.

You are constantly being given God's grace. Don't think for one minute that you can climb the spiritual ladder without God's unfailing support. You do not walk the path alone. Certainly, you must do your own growing and express free will, but it is the support of the divine that keeps you on the path and growing. Without the help of the divine, you would be utterly lost. As it says in Philippians: "The success of our life is entirely related to how much grace God gives us."

God's grace is like the sun that shines on us regardless of our actions. It is like the rain that falls on the Earth to nourish the plants, flowers, and trees. The tree or plant has done nothing to "earn" that rain other than to be a tree and fulfill its place in the divine plan. In the same way, there is not a day that goes by where we are not personally blessed by the divine, even if we are the worst of people. God's grace is the source of our spiritual nourishment.

God's grace is essential in working out karma. We could not arise out of our own spiritual muck without God's help. When we are born, as a gift from the divine, we are given extra spiritual power to succeed in life. This power is with us when we face our karmic trials and challenges. Sometimes we do not feel this help because instead of working out our karma, we are compounding our karma, complicating matters. Yet even then, God's grace is patiently with us.

The divine helps work out collective karma as well. For example, there is a spiritual healing rain that falls on the Earth to cleanse some of the karmic burdens we have accrued.

One of the greatest acts of divine grace was the mission of Jesus. We speak of Jesus coming to Earth to take away the sins of the world. What sins are we speaking of? The sins referred to here are *collective* karma that had accrued.

As we have seen, race, national, and world karma are part of a collective experience. We inherit the collective karma—the merits and demerits—from generations before us. Part of the Jesus mission was to alleviate some of this world karma, as it was building up too much and humanity would have gotten lost without help. In this way, all great sages and world teachers are part of this redemption process.

God's love and grace can intercede in human affairs if the need arises. Generally, the divine lets us go through the normal expression of free will and the balancing of the karmic slate so we can learn our spiritual lessons. However, there are times when the divine has to intercede directly in the affairs of humanity, but only if the actions of humanity take it too far off course. It is my understanding that during the days of the Cold War, the divine had to intercede three times to prevent a nuclear exchange between the Soviet Union and the United States. This is God's grace at work.

Some say that it is completely by God's grace that we evolve. This is not quite true. While it is true that without God's grace we cannot evolve, our own efforts count. Grace helps us to grow but we still have to make the effort and earn our way up the spiritual ladder. We may water a plant to give it nourishment to grow, but the plant still has to do its own growing.

Grace is an act of Divine Love. The divine can bestow grace at any time and in any place regardless of the karmic condition. As we have learned by studying the laws of karma, God permits bad things to happen as part of the learning experience. However, if the lesson is not yours to learn or already has been learned, God may block certain experiences from happening in your life because they are not necessary to your spiritual development.

Chapter 18

The Road Ahead

The person you are today is the result of a long, fascinating journey. Yet the story of your life is only half told. There is the journey that lies ahead, the road you have yet to travel. The choices you made yesterday brought you to the place where you are today, and the choices you are making today are setting up the conditions of your future.

How you express free will—your coin of wisdom—determines what that road ahead will look like. If you have been building up good karma, you will inevitably reap those rewards down the road. And if you have misused the gift of free will, you will feel those effects further down the line.

Ultimately, regardless of present conditions, we are all marked for greatness. We all have a glorious destiny. There is an overall plan for each of us that was set in motion before even beginning our pilgrimage on Earth, before even our very first incarnation in physical form.

As your future lives have not yet been lived, they have not been recorded in the Book of Life. They exist in the mind and imagination of God as a continuing story and master plan. In preparations to incarnate on Earth, you are shown glimpses of the master plan, which helps enormously in encouraging you to move in the right direction.

The future is not set in stone. It must be molded by you. The future does not become real until it becomes the present, as life exists only here and now. Bless the past for it brought you to where you are now. Plan for the future as this is your destiny, but live in the present for here is where life is.

The stage is set by God, yet you must actually weave your Tapestry of Life through your free will. Life is precious and so are you. Although you may not fully see the great plan of life, nevertheless you are part of that plan. Regardless of how those around you are behaving, live up to your highest ideal, your highest moral right and goodness. Let hope live in your heart no matter how challenging the road may be. Tough times may come but they will pass, and your true destiny will come shining through.

Show patience as life unfolds gradually in God's time. You cannot change that, so live in God's flow and enjoy the road you are embarked upon. Yet be persistent. Your every effort counts. Brick by brick, you are building your house of glory.

Your coin of wisdom is yours for the spending. Through free choice and willpower, you decide if you complete the task you came to Earth to fulfill. You have all the qualities and tools to succeed brilliantly. Stay on the path and your life will truly be a blessing to you and to everyone around you.

God bless you.

Appendix

Auric Karma Meditations

The Higher Self Point

The Higher Self Point is twenty-four inches above the physical head and is the emissary for all the light and inspiration flowing from the divine source. It can be thought of as an eighth spiritual center and appears like a golden sun. All spiritual energy passes through the Higher Self to reach you.

The Four Key Spiritual Centers

There are seven spiritual centers, or chakras, within that are part of our spiritual anatomy. However, in working with spiritual energy, there are four key spiritual centers within the body that you will use a great deal in your spiritual light work. They look like golden spheres of light with beautiful light rays moving out of them.

1. *The mental center:* Located in the middle of the forehead, this is the nucleus of your conscious thinking self.

2. *The throat center:* Located in the middle of the throat, this center is the nucleus of your creative tone.

3. *The Hermetic Center:* Located in the middle of the chest, this center is the nucleus of your personal affairs.

4. *The emotional center:* Located in the solar plexus area, where the navel is, this is the energetic nucleus of your emotional nature.

Meditating with Divine Light

The meditations offered in this book are part of a practice called the Higher Self meditation. The Higher Self meditation is one of the greatest tools for accessing spiritual light.

For a complete description of the process, please refer to my book *Change Your Aura, Change Your Life.* The six steps of the Higher Self meditation are provided here.

The six steps to down-ray light are:

1. *Relax:* Do not begin meditation in a highly agitated state. Do your best to let go of your worries.

2. *Establish protection:* Place a golden bubble of protection around yourself before beginning your meditation.

3. *Check your spiritual centers:* Make sure that your spiritual centers are moving clockwise, as if you are the clock.

4. *Connect with your Higher Self:* Put your attention on the golden sun above your head and feel that you are in the divine presence.

5. *Down-ray the Divine Light.*

6. *Ground yourself:* After receiving Divine Light, give your thanks and let the light equalize throughout your body and consciousness before you end your meditation.

Acknowledgments

We are grateful to the many people who contributed to the making of this book. This work is the result of many years of experience and practice. It follows a long, rich spiritual tradition. The Holy Ones who work under God have been the guiding force of this work all along; it is their teachings and ideas that we hope are well represented in these pages.

We wish to thank students and supporters of Spiritual Arts Institute who helped create the environment in which this work could grow. Special thanks to George and Christine Moraitis, Melinda Noble, A. J. Le Shay, John Harrison, Juliana Nahas, Jim Dydo and Terri Quinlin, Daryl Harris, Oresa Nour, Cathy Dowdell, Caridad Acosta, Joel Morris, Tanis Lee, Mark Hafeman, Anne Slater, Phil and Ann Marie Moraitis, Patricia Schembari and Allan Brown, and Patricia Bowman.

Thanks to Simon Warwick-Smith for his skill and diligence in getting this book to the right publisher. Our thanks to Joel Fotinos at Penguin/Tarcher for taking on this project and believing in the importance of its message. Thanks to Michael Solana for his excellent editorial work as well as helping to shepherd the book's publication. Our thanks go to the marketing and production staff at Penguin. We also wish to say thanks to Nita Ybarra for her excellent cover design and Michael Garland for his wonderful illustrations.

Index

Page numbers in italics refer to charts.

Abuse
  animal, 128–29
  career, 92–95
  child, 71
  nature, 128
  physical body, 110
Actions
  review of present, 215–17
  right, 223–24
Addictions, 105
Adversarial karma, 79–80
Africa, 178, 179, 189–92
Afterlife. *See* Hereafter; Other side
AIDS epidemic, 115
Akasha. *See* Fabric of life
Alexander the Great, 174
Analogies
  mirror, 262–63
  seed, 39
  stone, 7
Androcles, story of, 127
Angels. *See* Higher
Anger, 267–68

Animals
  abuse of, 128–29
  domestication and, 126–27
  eating of, 130–31
  mass killing of, 131
  soul evolution and, 41
Apes, 165
Appearance, physical, 109–10, 114
Appetite, *5*
Arc of development, 138–39
Archaeology, 184
Arya Asanga, 271–73
Aryans, 165–66
Astral body, 19
Astral planes, 18, 24
Athenian oath, 171–72
Atlantis, *167*, 176, 179–84, 189
  World War II karma connection to,
    186–87
Augustine, Saint, 208
Aura, xviii
  age of fully developed, 72
  auric karma meditations, 279–80

Aura (cont.)
  children's, 71–72, 226
  cleansing of, 226, 249–51
  karma and, xvi, 225–41
  marriage and, 75
  murder and, 242
  sexual intimacy and, 121–22
  spiritual division of, 226, 234
  spiritual evolution and, 226–27
  See also Color, aura; Ray

Beethoven, Ludwig van, 24, 174
Berlin Wall, 185, 187
Beyond the Ashes (Gershom), 188
Bible, 50
Birth defects, 114
Black magician, 139, 141
Blake, William, 124
Blood ties, spiritual versus, 66
Blue
  dirty dark, 62
  light around heart, 133
  -white fire, 249–51
Body, 178, 190–91
  abuse of, 110
  appearance of, 109–10, 114
  astral, 19
  deformities of, 114
  evolution of, 165–66, 167, 177
  first human forms on Earth, 165
  karma of, 109–23, 256–58
  purpose of, 109–10
  soul and, 111
Book of Life, 22–23. See also
    Reincarnation stories
Boomerang, karma as, 235
Bubonic plague, 115
Buddha, 12, 49, 110
  story of Buddhist monk, 271–72
Burgess, Frank Gillette, 109
Burial, cremation versus, 19

Call, spiritual, 134–38
Capital punishment, 118

Capitalism, 193
Career, 51–52, 76–78
  abuse of, 92–95
  accumulating good karma in, 88–92
  building good karma in, 259–61
  change in, 82–83
  confusion, 85–87
  karma, 84–85, 92–95, 259–61
  karmic review of, 97–98
  love of, 95–97
  past-life, variety in, 83
  path, 85–88
  potential, 96
  spiritual purpose of, 84–85
Causal template, 233, 249
Caveman existence, 31
Cayce, Edgar, xviii
Cayce, Hugh Lynn, xviii
Celestial beings. See Higher
Chakras, 61, 133, 227, 231, 236, 270,
    279–80
Character, 101–4, 105
Children
  abuse of, 71
  auras of, 71–72, 226
  independence of, 73
  karma created by, 73
  karma between parents and, 70–74
China, 9–10, 111–13
Christ. See Jesus
Christian Crusades, 174
Church-state relationship, 162–63
Civil laws and Divine laws, 153–54
Civilization
  Africa as cradle of, 190
  cooperation and, 191
  Divine impulse and, 152
  first, 178
  future of, 195–96
  prehistoric, 176, 184
  spiritual history of, 175–84
  tragedy befalling, 179, 180
  wars, Divine plan in, 164
Clairvoyance, xix

Cleansing
  aura, 226, 249–51
  karmic, meditation for, 247–49
Coin of wisdom, 32
Cold War, 187
Collective karma, 90, 114, 147–72
  definition, 148
  evil dictators and, 155
  government and, 149
  individuals/groups and, 150
  marriage and, 149
  personal integrity and, 157
  race versus, 166, 168
  race karma, 164–69
  in relationships, 161–63
  of world, 173–96
Color
  emerald-green ray, 256–59
  forgiveness, 270
  good money karma and, 254–56
  orange-red flame, 247–49
  primary ray, 102
  purple ray of peace, 261–62
  rose-pink ray, 253–54, 270–71
  silver, 241
  soul images and, 229
  spiritual energies, list of, 264
Color, aura
  gray, 62
  love, 60, 61, 240
  money, 46, 58
  primary ray, 60, 61
  silver, 241
  spiritual awakening, 133
  spiritual energies, 264
Compassion, 271–73
Con man, spiritual, 139–40
Confucius, 88
Conquest, karma of war and,
    163–64
Consciousness, quieting, 261–62
Cooperation, 191
Countries
  evolution of, 152

nations versus, 151
  war karma for, 156
Creation, evolution versus, 37
Credits, karma, 168
Cremation, burial versus, 19
Crucifixion, of Jesus, 189
Cycles, race, 165–66, *167*, 178, 190–91

Daughter, parents unkind to, 222–23
Death
  as birth, 16
  first seven days after, 20
  forty-four-day period after, 21–22
  karma and, 115–17
  life review after, 22–23
  moment of, 19
  returning to Earth after, 25–27
  time of, 115
  what happens during/after, 18–25
Deformities, physical, 114
Déjà vu, 14
Desire, Metaphysics definition of, 4–5
Devachan (rose room), 21
Devas, 125
Dharma, 36
Dictators, evil, 155
Divine impulse, 152
Divine laws and civil laws, 153–54
Divine Light, 22, 133, 245, 252
  in food, 132
  in leaders, 155
  meditations on aspects of, 246–65, 280
  of prosperity, 255
  sending, 263–64
Divine love, 79, 253–54, 275
Divine plan, 35–36, 97, 199–201,
    276–77
  career and, 84–85
  change in career and, 82–83
  civilization/war and, 164
  Earth's species and, 125–26
  leaders as part of, 154–55
  Middle East and, 194–95
  national karma and, 152–53, 179

Divine plan (*cont.*)
  religious organizations and, 169
  time of death and, 115
  unexpected pregnancies and, 73–74
Divine source, vision after death, 24
Divine Spirit, 101
Divine will, 6
Divorce, 76
Djedkare Isesi (pharaoh), 158–61
Doctors, 116
Dostoevsky, Fyodor, 90–92
Dynamic/magnetic polarity, 102

Earth, 124–25
  first humans on, 165, 177
  geological processes of, 37
  hierarchy of kingdoms on, 125–26
  life on, geology and, 37–38
  memories of life on, 20
  number of lives on, 30–31, 32, 33, 34
  returning to, 25–27
  as schoolhouse, 53
  visiting during death transition,
    21–22
Earthbound souls, 20
Edison, Thomas, 174
Ego, Individuality, 107–8
Egypt, reincarnation story, 158–61
Einstein, Albert, 90, 174
Emerald-green ray, 256–59
Emerson, Ralph Waldo, 79
Emotional center, 280
Employees, 78
Endangered species, 129
Enemies, 79–80
Energy, karmic soul, 231–34
Enlightenment, 31, 33, 233
  arc of development toward, 138–39
  reincarnation scenario and, 135–38
  soul images and, 228
Environment, soul/character influenced
    by, 103
Epochs, *167*
  fifth epoch of evolution, 166

Lemurian, 165, *167*, 176, 179
  See also Atlantis; *specific epochs*
Eternal life, drinking from the well of, 24
Evil, 155, 180
Evolution
  arc of development, 138–39
  beginning of physical, 165, 177–78
  caveman and, 31
  of countries, 152
  creation versus, 37
  definition of, 36
  fifth epoch of, 166
  geological processes of Earth and, 37
  God and, 151–52, 177
  God's guidance in human, 177
  Homo sapiens line of human, 176,
    177–78
  human, as separate cycle of, 165, 178
  human kingdom stage of, 41
  kingdom of Earth and, 125–26
  of nations/humanity, 151–52
  reincarnation and, 11
  root races/human body, 165–66, *167*,
    178, 190–91
  slow pace of, 34–35
  soul's stages of, 38–42
  spiritual, 36–38
  Spiritual Etheria plateau of, 34
Exercise, to illuminate karma, 262–63

Fabric of life, 234–35
  sending white light to, 264–65
Fairies, 125
Family
  example of karma with, 222–23
  independence and, 66
  karma of, 65–75
  reunion in hereafter with, 24
Father, selfish son raised by, 202–4
Females, primary ray of, 102
Food prayer, 132
Ford, Henry, 10
Forgiveness
  karma resolved through, 268–70

prayer, 270–71
refusal/difficulty of, 266–67
Forty-four-day period, 21–22
Franklin, Benjamin, 96
Free will, 3–4, 133–34, 141, 236
    career and, 84
    character and, 105
    dynamics of karma and, 199–201
    future incarnations and, 26–27
    identifying, 201–4
    intellectual phase as beginning of, 32
    past life regression and, 237–41
    soul and, 99
    tapestry of life and, 26–27
    willpower and, 4–7
Friends
    karma between, 78–79
    reunion in hereafter with, 24

Gandhi, Mohandas, 13, 155, 168
Gems, life force in, 125
Gender, 102
Genetics, 103, 113–14
Genghis Khan, 174
Genius, 12, 88–89
Genocide, 163
Gershom, Yonassan, 188
God
    abundance/generosity of, 45–46
    attention of, 133–34
    divine source experience after death, 24
    evolution as guided by, 177
    evolution of humanity initiated by,
        151–52
    as harmony, 7
    human body design and, 165
    karma balanced by, 187, 188
    karmic trials/grace of, 273–75
    leadership power from, 155
    over money, choosing, 192–93, 195
    other side and, 28
    poverty and, 53
    religion and, 170
    search for, 32–33
    soul as spark of, 39
    See also Divine Light
Golden age, 152, 186
Golden ray, building good career karma
    with, 259–61
Golden Rule, 162
Good versus evil, 180
Government, 161–62
    church-state relationship, 162–63
    collective karma and, 149
    forms of, 153–54
    responsibility of, 153–54
Grace, 273–75
Grandparents, 74
Graph of relationship karma
    scenarios, 64
Gray, 62
Greed, 46, 93
Groups
    collective karma for, 150
    karma between, 161–63
    races as distinct, 166
    terrorist, 149
Guardian angel, xvii

Hall, Manly P., 11
Harmony, God as, 7
Healing
    karmic relationship, 253–54
    temple, 22
Heart chakra, 61, 133, 227, 270
    nucleus of, 231
    subconscious images in, 236
Hereafter, 15–17
    death and, 18–25
    experience of visiting, 16–17
    first experience of, 16–17
    reunion with family/friends in, 24
    See also Other side
Hermetic Center, 227, 248, 252,
    253, 280
Higher (celestial beings/holy ones), xvi
    alliance with, 219
    aura cleansed by, 226

Higher (*cont.*)
  early experiences with, xvi–xvii
  guardian angel, xvii
  healing temple and, 22
  Lords of Karma as, 22–23
  organization of, 148
  romantic love and, 81
  specialized skills of, 84
  unexpected pregnancies handled
    by, 74
  See also Reincarnation stories
Higher Self
  meditation, 280
  point, 279
History
  civilization's spiritual, 175–84
  karmic veil over, 184
Hitler, Adolf, 155
Holocaust, 188
Holy Ones. *See* Higher
Hominid, 178
Homo erectus, 176–77
Homo sapiens, 176, 177–78
Humans
  apes and, 165
  as Aryans, 166
  first, 165, 177
  God's guidance in evolution of, 177
  human kingdom, stage of evolution, 41
  karma of animals versus, 129
  relationship with Nature, 130–31
  separate evolution of, 165, 178
Hurd, Inez, xviii, 61, 66, 151, 202
Husband
  communication from other side by,
    266–67
  -wife karma, 75–76, 242–46
Hyperborean Epoch, *167*
Hypnosis, free will and, 237–41

Illness, 22, 114–15
Images
  soul, 227–31
  subconscious, 235–41

Incarnations
  enlightened phase, 31, 33
  intellectual phase number of, 32
  life waves, 33
  number of, 30–31, 32, 33, 34
  role exchange in, 71
  training for next, 25
  vision of upcoming, 26
  See also Past lives
India, untouchables in, 273
Individual karma, credits and, 168
Individuality Ego, soul's, 107–8
Instinctual phase, 31
Intellectual phase, 31, 32
Inventory, 215–20
Involution, 31

Jealousy, 67–70, 84
Jesus, 17, 61–62, 154–55, 189, 274–75
Jews, 188–89
Justice, 8

Kabala, 40
Karma, 7–8
  accumulating good career, 88–92
  adversarial, 79–80
  aura and, xvi, 225–41
  backlog of, 123
  boomerang effect of, 235
  career, 84–85, 259–61
  career abuse, 92–95
  cleansing, meditation for, 247–49
  credits for individual, 168
  death and, 115–17
  dynamics of free will and, 199–201
  earning good nature, 126–27
  earning good physical, 110–13
  as escape, 213
  exercise, to illuminate situations with,
    262–63
  fabric of life and, 234–35
  facing, 200, 211–13
  family, 65–75
  finished/resolved, 211

forgiveness and, 268–70
four keys to resolving, 214–24
between friends, 78–79
generating new, 201, 202, 228, 272
genetics and, 103, 113–14
God's balancing of, 187, 188
God's grace in trials of, 273–75
between groups, 161–63
guidelines for relationship, 63–65
history veiled by, 184
human versus animal, 129
husband-wife, 75–76
illness, 114–15
incarnations based on, 27
judging others', 213
karmic worksheet, 228
leaders', 154–61
lessons versus, 105
life review and, 23
life's purpose versus, 204–6
Lords of Karma, 22–23
meditations, auric karma, 279–80
money, 55–59, 192–95, 254–56
motive and, 156, 162, 202–4,
      215–16
of murder, 117–21
national, 151–54, 179
of Nature, 124–32, 258–59
other side and, 228
parent-child, 70–74
physical body, 109–23, 256–58
poverty, 52–58
power to face, 209–10
professional, 76–78
race, 164–69, *167*
recognizing, 206–9
relationship, 60–81, *64*, 253–54
religious, 169–71
of romance, 80–81
between siblings, 74
signs of possible, 218–20
sins of omission as, 272
soul, 99–108, 160, 231–34, 251–52
of spiritual offenses, 139–41

things outside, 213
war/conquest, 163–64
wealth, 47–52
of world population, 122–23
See also Collective karma
Karmic conditions, as lessons, 46–47,
      221–23
Karmic review
   career, 97–98
   life, 22–23
   money karma, 59
   nature, 132
   physical karma, 123
   present actions, 215–17
   relationship, 81
   soul, 108
   spiritual karma, 142
Kepler, Johannes, 37
Khayyám, Omar, 201
King, Martin Luther, Jr., 168
Kingdoms
   Earth's hierarchy of, 125–26
   evolution of human, 41
   mineral, 127

Laboratory experiments, on animals,
      128–29
Laziness, 55, 84
Leaders
   ancient civilization, 190
   choice of, 159
   karma of, 154–61
   race/spirit, 168
   religious, 162–63
Lemuria, *165, 167*, 176, 179
Leonardo da Vinci, 174
Lessons, 46–47, 207–9, 221–23, 235
   karma versus, 105
Life
   on Earth, 37–38
   fabric of, 234–35
   long view of, 10, 34
   purpose of, *35–36*
   review of, 22–23

Life (*cont.*)
  tapestry of, 25–27, 106, 227
  waves of, souls born in, 33
  well of eternal, 24
Life force, devas and, 125
Light. *See* Divine Light
Lincoln, Abraham, 155
Lion, Androcles and, 127
*Lipika*s (Lords of Karma), 22–23
Literature, Dostoevsky's contribution to,
      91–92
Lives, number of, 30–31, 32, 33, 34.
      See also Past lives
Lords of Karma, 22–23
Love
  aura color of, 60, 61, 240
  of career, 95–97
  Divine, 79, 253–54, 275
  lack of, aura color and, 62
  romantic, 75, 80–81
  universal, 61

Magician, black, 139, 141
Maitreya, Lord, 271–72
Males, primary ray of, 102
"Many mansions," 17–18
Marriage, 66, 75–76, 88–89
  collective karma and, 149
  Dostoevsky's, 91
  sexual intimacy and, 121–22
  spiritual benefits of, 149
Meditations, 220
  auric karma, 279–80
  karmic cleansing, 247–49
  murder karma example and, 242–46
  reflective, 247
  techniques for transformative,
      246–65
Melancholy mood, reincarnation story,
      106–7
Memories
  of life on Earth, 20
  other side and, 20
  past life, 13–14, 206–7

seat of, 235
subconscious, 235, 238–39
Mental center, 279
Mental template, 238–39
Metaphysics
  desire defined by, 4–5
  religion and, 170
  See also Spiritual evolution
Michelangelo, 174
Middle East, 192–95
  in Divine plan, 194–95
Mind, gift of, 32
Mineral kingdom, 127
Mirror analogy, 262–63
Money, 53–59, 138–39
  aura color and, 46, 58
  choosing God over, 192–93, 195
  good karma in, 254–56
  karmic review for, 59
  loss of, 50–51, 54
  wise use of, 49
  world *karma* and, 192–95
  See also Wealth
Motives, 156, 162, 202–4, 215–16
Mozart, Wolfgang Amadeus, 88–89
Murder
  aura and, 242
  karma, 117–21
  poisoned husband/karma and,
      242–46
  reincarnation story, 119–21

National karma, 151–54
  beginning of, 179
  choice of leader and, 159
  definition of nation versus country, 151
  dynamics of nations and, 152–53
  leaders and, 154–61
  soldiers and, 154
Nature
  abuse of, 128
  balancing karma with, 256–58
  disasters in, 129
  honoring, 131

humans in relationship with, 130–31
 karma of, 124–32, 258–59
Neanderthal man, 178
Newton, Isaac, 7, 174
Nhat Hanh, Thich, 170

Oath, Athenian, 171–72
Offenses, spiritual, 139–41
Orange-red flame, 247–49
Organization, 148
Other side, 17–18, 136
 acclimation to, 20–24
 duration of stay on, 25
 forgiveness and, 269
 husband's communication from,
  266–67
 karma resolution on, 228
 knowledge of God on, 28
 support from, 18–19
 travels to, 16–17, 25
Overpopulation, 122–23
Overy, Richard, 151

Parents
 daughter treated unkindly by, 222–23
 karma between children and, 70–74
 meeting with next incarnation's, 27
 purpose of, 71
 spiritual journey and, 137
 unexpected children and, 74
Past lives
 Dostoevsky's, 92
 friends in, 79
 number of incarnations and, 30–31,
  32, 33, 34
 past life regression, 237–41
 physical appearance and, 114
 present influenced by, 11
 remembering, 13–14, 206–7
 subconscious images of, 236
 talents drawing on, 240
 visions of, xvii–xviii, 9–10, 206
Peace, purple ray of, 261–62
Phases, human soul, 31

Physical body
 appearance of, 109–10, 114
 beginning of evolution, 165, 177–78
 deformed, 114
 evolution, 165–66, *167*, 177
 harmonizing karma of, 256–58
 karma of, 109–23, 256–58
 karma review for, 123
 soul and, 111
Pink, 60, 240
Plague, bubonic, 115
Planetary influences, on soul/character,
  103–4
Plants, 127, 128
 souls of, 41
Poe, Edgar Allan, 229
Polar Epoch, *167*
Polarity, dynamic/magnetic, 102
Police, 154
Pontius Pilate, 154–55
Poor Folk (Dostoevsky), 90
Population, karma of world, 122–23
Poseidon, 181, 182–84
Poverty, 48, 52–58
Prayer, 220
 food, 132
 forgiveness, 270–71
Pregnancies, unexpected, 73–74
Present actions, review of, 215–17
Pride, 179, 180
Primary ray, 102
Professional karma, 76–78
Prosperity prayer, 58–59
Purple ray of peace, 261–62
Purpose
 karma versus, 204–6
 See also specific topics
Pythagoras, 104

Race
 cycles, 165–66, *167*, 178,
  190–91
 karma, 164–69, *167*
Rags-to-riches scenario, 48–49

Ray
  power, 178
  primary, 102
Reflective meditation, 247
Reincarnation, 9–12
  goal of, 11
  origin of word, 10
  other terms for, 10
  process of, 15–42
  suffering explained by, 12
  training for next life, 25
Reincarnation stories
  Chinese woman's, 111–13
  Dostoevsky's, 90–92
  enlightenment, 135–38
  family karma, 66–70
  melancholy mood, 106–7
  money karma, 55–58
  murder, 119–21
  singer in, 87–88
  tyrant, 158–61
  unfulfilled career potential,
    93–95
  unfulfilled medical career, 51–52
Relationships
  church-state, 162–63
  collective karma in, 161–63
  guidelines for karmic, 63–65
  healing karmic, 253–54
  human-nature, 130–31
  karma of, 60–81, 64, 253–54
  review of karma in, 81
Religion
  karma of, 169–71
  metaphysics/God and, 170
  purpose of, 169, 170–71
  religious leaders, 162–63
Remorse, 63
Responsibility
  government's, 153–54
  spiritual path, 142
Right action, 223–24
Rmoahal race, 167, 190–91
Role exchange, parents/children, 71

Roman Empire, 174
Romantic love, 75, 80–81
Root races, 165–66, 167, 178,
    190–91
Rose
  -pink ray, 253–54, 270–71
  room, 21
Rumi, Jalaluddin, 40

Samsara, 10
Schoolhouse, Earth as, 53
Seed analogy, 39
Self-awareness, 32
Service, 205
Sex (gender), dynamic/magnetic polarity
    and, 102
Sexual intimacy, 121–22
Shakespeare, William, 99
Sheath, soul's protective, 233
Siblings, karma between, 74
Siddhartha, 49, 135
Silver (color), 241
Singer, reincarnation story, 87–88
Sins of omission, 272
Smith, Huston, 37
Society for Psychical Research, 266
Solar plexus, 250
Soldiers, 154
Son, father raising selfish, 202–4
"Song of the Butcher, The," 96
Soul
  as androgynous, 102
  auric power and, 71–72
  awakened, 134
  body and, 111
  Divine Spirit as help to, 101
  dynamic/magnetic polarity of, 102
  earthbound, 20
  energy, 231–34
  environment and, 103
  family circle of, 65
  free will and, 99
  hominid and, 178
  images, 227–31

Soul (*cont.*)
  Individuality Ego of, 107–8
  influences on character of, 101–4
  karma, 99–108, 160, 251–52
  karma review, 108
  life waves of, 33
  number of human souls, 31
  phases of, 31
  planetary influences on, 103–4
  plant, 41
  protective sheath for, 233
  qualities of, 100–104
  race experiences of, 168
  as spark of God, 39
  stages of development, 38–42
Species
  Divine plan for, 125–26
  endangerment of, 129
Spirit leaders, race karma and, 168
Spirit qualities, 101
Spiritual awakening, 133
Spiritual call, 134–38
Spiritual division, aura's, 226, 234
Spiritual energies, colors of, 264
Spiritual Etheria, 34
Spiritual evolution, 36–38
  aura and, 226–27
  civilization's spiritual history,
    175–84
Spiritual offenses, 139–41
Spiritual ties, blood ties versus, 66
Spiritual training, author Martin's,
    xvii–xviii
Standing Bear, 131
Star formation, heart chakra, 61
Stone analogy, 7
Stories
  Androcles, 127
  compassion, 271–73
  See also Reincarnation stories
Subconscious
  connecting conscious mind to, 250
  images, 235–41
Suffering, 12

Suicide, 116, 118–19
Sumerian civilization, 176

Talent
  accumulating good career karma, 88–92
  Dostoevsky's, 90–92
  genius and, 12, 88–89
  past lives and, 240
  unused, 93
Tapestry of life, 25–27, 106, 227
Teachers, spiritual, misguided, 139,
    140–41
Tectonic plates, 180–81
Temperament, seven varieties of, 101–2
Temple of Instruction, 25
Temptations, 6
Terrorism, 149, 194
Thought
  stabilizer of, 5
  will versus, 5–6
Throat center, 280
Time, beginning of, 37
*Times Complete History of the World,
    The* (Overy), 151
Tower of Babel, 152
Training
  author Martin's spiritual, xvii–xviii
  before reincarnating, 25
Trees, chopping down, 130, 131
Turquoise (color), 46, 58, 254–56
Tyrant, reincarnation story, 158–61

Universal love, 61
Untouchables, 273
Upbringing, 103
Ussher, James, 37

Vipaka, 7
Visions
  divine source, 24
  past life, xvii–xviii, 9–10, 206
  upcoming incarnation, 26
Vyadha-Gita ("The Song of the
    Butcher"), 96

War, 156, 163–64, 184–89
Wealth, 88–90, 138–39
    aura color of, 46, 58
    karma of, 47–52
    Prosperity Prayer, 58–59
    rags-to-riches scenario, 48–49
Wheel of necessity, 30, 34–35, 138
White light, 264–65
    redeeming soul karma with, 251–52
Wife, karma between husband and,
       75–76, 242–46
Will, thought versus, 5–6

Willpower, free will and, 4–7
Worksheet, karmic, 228
World karma, 173–96
    Africa-related, 189–92
    Atlantis and, 186–87, 189
    Middle East and, 192–95
    money and, 192–95
    World War II as, 184–89
World population, 122–23
World War II, 184–89

Zealandia, 181

About the Authors

Internationally recognized author and aura specialist Barbara Y. Martin is one of the leading clairvoyants and spiritual teachers of our time, with a career spanning more than forty years. Affectionately known as "the Mozart of Metaphysics," she was born with the gift of seeing the aura and other spiritual phenomena in great detail. She has taught thousands of people how to better their lives by developing their spiritual nature. Martin is the coauthor of the award-winning book *Change Your Aura, Change Your Life*, which is now being published in thirty countries, and *The Healing Power of Your Aura*, a Benjamin Franklin Book Award winner, which has been endorsed by medical luminaries Dr. C. Norman Shealy and Dr. Richard Gerber.

Dimitri Moraitis is cofounder and executive director of Spiritual Arts Institute, an educational and publishing organization dedicated to helping people understand and develop the spiritual side of their nature through books, CDs, classes, workshops, and seminars. He facilitates the workshops and classes taught at the institute. He holds a BFA from New York University. Moraitis is an accomplished spiritual teacher and healer, and has lectured with Barbara Martin across the country. He is coauthor of *The Healing Power of Your Aura* and *Change Your Aura, Change Your Life*.

About Spiritual Arts Institute

To contact Barbara Y. Martin and Dimitri Moraitis, and to learn more about private aura consultations, healing sessions, classes, workshops, books, and CDs, please write, phone, or fax:

Spiritual Arts Institute
P.O. Box 4315
Sunland, CA 91041-4315
Phone: (818) 353-1716
Toll-free: (800) 650-AURA (2872)
Fax: (818) 353-0506

Or visit the institute's website: www.SpiritualArts.org.